University of Cambridge
Department of Applied Economics
OCCASIONAL PAPER 17

PRODUCTIVITY IN TRANSPORT

A Study of Employment, Capital, Output,
Productivity and Technical Change

University of Cambridge

Department of Applied Economics

Occasional Papers

Productivity in Transport

A Study of Employment, Capital, Output, Productivity

and Technical Change

by B. M. DEAKIN

and T. SEWARD

CAMBRIDGE

AT THE UNIVERSITY PRESS

1969

PUBLISHED BY

THE SYNDICS OF THE CAMBRIDGE UNIVERSITY PRESS

Bentley House, 200 Euston Road, London N.W.1

American Branch: 32 East 57th Street, New York, N.Y. 10022

© Department of Applied Economics University of Cambridge 1969

Library of Congress Catalogue Card Number 74-85716

Standard Book Numbers 521 07433 9 cloth
521 09605 7 paper

ω+α Set by E.W.C. Wilkins & Associates Ltd., London, and printed in
Great Britain, by Lowe & Brydone (Printers) Ltd., London, N.W.10

Contents

LIST OF TABLES

Tables   *Page*

LIST OF FIGURES

Preface

This study was developed from a research project on productivity in the service industries of the United Kingdom, which was started at the Department of Applied Economics at Cambridge in 1964. In 1965 a Paper on 'Productivity in the Service Industries, 1948–1963' by B.M. Deakin and K.D. George was published in the London and Cambridge Economic Bulletin (No. 53). The project then progressed along the lines of studies of particular service industries. In 1966 K.D. George published 'Productivity in Distribution', and in 1968, in collaboration with P.V. Hills, 'Productivity and Capital Expenditure in Retailing'. Both are in the Occasional Paper series of the Department of Applied Economics (numbers 8 and 16 respectively). The present Paper sets out the results of research into productivity in seven sectors of public transport and communication in the United Kingdom in the period 1952–1965.

Most of the work was carried out while we were in receipt of a grant from the Social Science Research Council which we gratefully acknowledge.

In the early stages of this project we received much help and advice from people engaged in different sectors of the transport industry. The official and other organisations we approached gave us most willing co-operation, and we wish to record our thanks to the staff of the Central Statistical Office, of the Statistics Division of the Ministry of Transport at St. Christopher House and at Hemel Hempstead, of the Ministry of Labour and the Commercial Manager's Department of the British Railways Board. Our special thanks are due to the road haulage operators who took trouble to complete our questionnaire and to the Road Haulage Association, particularly the Secretary of the Cambridge branch, Mr. K.E. Williams, who gave a great deal of help with the pilot survey.

We are indebted to Mr. C.D. Foster who in the early stages of our work made useful comments and suggestions on one chapter. We also received much benefit from the discussions which we had at various times with Dr. C.H. Feinstein, Mr. Z.A. Silberston, Professor W.D. Shipman, Mr. D.W. Glassborow, Mr. R.W.S. Pryke and Mr. H.T. Burley.

Our thanks are due to the assistant staff of the Department of Applied Economics: to Miss Marion Clarke and her assistants for carrying out much of the computing work and to Mrs. Lilian Silk and her staff for typing the manuscript.

We owe a special debt of gratitude to four people whose advice and assistance was invaluable to us. Mr. M.F. Fuller undertook a great deal of our statistical work and in the course of this he made many useful suggestions for dealing with some of the more complex problems encountered. Mr. E. Bougourd gave us a very large amount of patient and competent assistance in dealing with a great variety of statistical and collating work; without his help the completion of the Paper would have taken much longer. Mr. K.D. George read the manuscript in its entirety and his comments and suggestions were invaluable. Professor W.B. Reddaway, Director of the Department of Applied Economics, made penetrating comments on our first draft, and these enabled us to remove some flaws in our argument and helped us to improve our presentation.

Any errors and shortcomings which remain in the Paper are entirely our responsibility.

University of Cambridge   T.S.
Department of Applied Economics   B.M.D.
May 1969

1 Introduction. The Approach to Productivity Measurement, Interpretation and Explanation

The general problems associated with productivity measurement, interpretation and explanation are the subject of an extensive literature, and no attempt is made here to go over this ground except in so far as it aids the description which it is proposed to give of the methods which have been used in this present study.

Two economists who have made particular studies of productivity change, W.E.G. Salter and J.W. Kendrick,[1] have both started their analyses by drawing attention to the very limited usefulness of the time-honoured but 'partial' (Kendrick's term) productivity ratio of output per unit of labour input (in terms of either manyears or manhours). The superficial implication that such productivity ratios measure the personal efficiency of labour is disposed of at an early stage in the work of both these economists,[2] and at a later stage of analysis Kendrick uses the more general ratio of output per unit of total factor input, that is, per unit of combined labour and capital input. The partial, labour (or other factor) productivity ratio can be useful in measuring the saving in that input which is achieved over time, due to *all* causes,[3] but it cannot measure, in any sense, total changes in productive efficiency since such changes are affected by changes in the composition of total factor input due to factor substitution as relative factor prices, and the techniques of production, change through time.

---

[1] W.E.G Salter. *Productivity and Technical Change*. Second Edition, with an Addendum by W.B. Reddaway. Cambridge University Press, 1966. J.W. Kendrick. *Productivity Trends in the United States*. National Bureau of Economic Research. Princeton University Press, 1961.

[2] Briefly by Kendrick op. cit. p. 6, more fully by Salter op. cit. Ch. IX, who shows that there is no association between movements in labour productivity (output per operative) and earnings (per operative). The product moment coefficients of correlation with respect to changes in these two variables are + 0.10 for 28 selected British industries in the periods 1954–63 and – 0.09 in 1924–50 (Addendum p. 202). He concludes that 'the hypothesis that the increases in labour productivity originate in greater personal efficiency of labour is rejected because of the lack of any association between movements of labour productivity and earnings, the extreme unevenness of productivity movements and the behaviour of labour and non-labour costs'. p. 145.

[3] If the partial productivity ratio is inverted to read 'factor input per unit of output', the meaning of this passage may be clearer. A decline in this inverted ratio over time indicates a saving in the use of the factor input concerned.

These considerations appear to lead naturally to the perception that the production function underlies all really meaningful analyses of productivity change. It is necessary to understand that the volume of net output (gross value added) — and it is this measure rather than the volume of gross output which must be the numerator of the productivity ratio — is dependent upon the quantities of factor inputs of labour and capital employed, the state of technical and organisational knowledge and its availability, the scale of operations, the manner in which the factors are utilised, the degree of capacity utilisation and, more generally, the efficiency with which the entire production process is organised over time in relation to changes in total demand, competition, relative factor prices, technical knowledge, organisational practices and external factors of various kinds.

Despite formidable difficulties which are at once conceptual, theoretical and practical, and which stem from the currently incomplete state of both the theory of production and of knowledge of input and output movements, it is thought essential for the reasons given to attempt to apply an interpretative treatment of productivity movement in transport which includes the fitting of a production function to the data. The way in which this is done is explained a little later (Section B), and is accompanied by definitions of the assumptions and limitations involved, which are made as rigorous as possible; but first it seems logical to explain the treatment of the measurement problems.

It should be noticed that an interpretative treatment of movements in productive efficiency is not fully *explanatory* of such movements. It is a first stage analytical process which provides estimates in quantitative terms of the breakdown of the several sources of a given amount of movement in productive efficiency. Behind these sources of change lie more fundamental causes which are later subject to explanatory analyses and to attempts to test explanatory hypotheses.

A.   Measurement

1.   Output

It has already been noticed that the numerator of all productivity ratios must be net output, or at least a proxy variable for net output. The reason for this is clear enough, it is the results achieved by the factors employed within the industry or sector concerned which it is necessary to relate to the quantity of such factors employed. Non-factor inputs such as bought-in materials, fuels, component parts and services are the product of other factors of production located outside the industry or sector concerned. The net output of a particular industry or sector is therefore defined as the difference between the selling value of its gross output and the value of its non-factor inputs. In theory the latter should include stock appreciation and 'true' depreciation, but in practice true depreciation is very hard to measure, and rather than introduce the errors which would be involved in estimating it, the best practical course is to assume that it moves with output over a short period of years.[1]

Given the availability of sufficient information, the compilation of a time series of net output movements for an industry would ideally comprise two series, both at constant prices, one of gross output and one of non-factor inputs (including true depreciation and stock appreciation). In practice, net output can be measured only for some years (the census years) for some industries (the ones which participate in the Census of Industrial Production). For service industries and trades there is no census of production and net output is commonly measured by adding together total factor rewards. Even if it were possible in the practical sense to have a Census of (Industrial) Production every year and to measure total factor rewards in all other industries, the movement of real net output could not be reached because it is not possible to distinguish quantity changes from price changes. The practical method used, generally and in this study, to measure net output movements is to estimate real net output in a base year and then to estimate the movement of real net output in other years from movements in a proxy variable or indicator. The more accurate indicators are measures of gross output in either physical or deflated value terms. Estimates of changes in real net output over the period since the base year derived in this way, involve the assumption that the ratio of gross to net output in each sector of industry concerned remains unchanged over time. Events which alter this ratio, such as changes in the quantity of real non-factor inputs per unit of net output due to technical progress, or changes in the amount of processing done or services used in the sector, will not by this method be reflected in the estimated movements in real net output. Where many sectors are separately distinguished, and separate net output weights and corresponding indicators are calculated, such errors in the aggregate result are likely to be less than those in the results for undifferentiated sectors. Moreover, reweighting and rebasing at short time intervals tend to minimise errors and to prevent a continuing bias in the results.

In a study of productivity in services industries[2] in the United Kingdom, one of the chief problems encountered (in addition to the usual difficulties inherent in all productivity measurement) was the lack of definition and measurement (or even measurability) of gross output movement, as an indicator of net output movement, in either physical or financial terms. In such industries as education

---

1 For a full discussion of the theoretical aspects see W.B. Reddaway, 'Movements in the Real Product of the United Kingdom, 1946–1949'. *J.R.S.S. Series A.* Vol. CXIII, Part IV, 1950, pp. 435–463. The principles and practice (in the United Kingdom) of output measurement are described in detail by C.F. Carter, W.B. Reddaway and Richard Stone in '*The Measurement of Production Movements*'. Monograph I of the Department of Applied Economics, University of Cambridge. Cambridge University Press, 1948 (reprinted 1965).

2 'Productivity Trends in the Service Industries, 1948–63'. B.M. Deakin and K.D. George. *London and Cambridge Economic Bulletin No. 53.* March, 1965. pp. xvi–xx. Also appears in Department of Applied Economics Reprint Series No. 237.

and public administration, the service produced is only exceptionally valued by market forces and is not easily identifiable in physical terms; the gross output of the civil service cannot be measured in such terms as memoranda completed or even decisions taken.

The difficulties tend to be rather fewer in the measurement of net output values (gross value added at factor cost and current prices) in single base years. Although these service industries, and they include the transport industry, are not included in the periodic Census of Production, net output can be measured by aggregating gross factor rewards (wages, salaries and non-wage income), and deducting stock appreciation where applicable. But for any service industry where output is not identifiable in either physical or financial terms, it is virtually impossible to find a series to serve as an output indicator which would be of any validity in productivity measurement. Wage and salary bills deflated by an index of wage rates is a method which takes some account of changes in the composition, and therefore in the quality, over time, of labour input and therefore, in rather tenuous and indirect terms, of contemporaneous changes in net output. The least satisfactory expedient used officially[1] is changes in numbers employed. In industries where this type of proxy variable is employed no meaningful or valid measurement of productivity can be made, and account must be taken of this limitation at the start when deciding which sectors of the transport industry are 'measurable' in productivity terms and which are not.

The sectors in Transport where the output measures available meet the criteria of measurability which have now been established are designated collectively 'Measured Transport' and are as follows[2]

> Railways
>
> Road Passenger Transport
>
> Road Haulage Contracting
>
> Sea Transport
>
> Port and Inland Water Transport
>
> Air Transport

For the purpose of studying trends and sector shares in employment the sector, Miscellaneous Transport Services and Storage is included in the analysis. In addition the sector Postal Services and Telecommunications, which is 'measurable', is included for comparison of trends in employment, capital, output, productivity and technical change with those in the Measured Transport industry.

The examination of any aspect of employment, capital, output, productivity and technical change is quite exceptionally difficult in the sector Non-contractual Road Freight Transport, which has been separately distinguished in this paper.

---

[1] By the Central Statistical Office.

[2] Full details of the coverage of each sector and of the output indicators used are given in the appendix note to this Chapter.

20

The problems involved in measuring labour input are examined in the next section of this chapter. Capital measures do not exist. An output measure in physical terms of ton mileage performed is available. The special limitations of this measure in general terms are discussed below, but it is judged a sufficiently accurate measure to warrant the inclusion of Non-contractual Road Freight Transport in the analysis of output movements at the first stage only. The sector is excluded from the employment, capital and productivity analyses but is included for comparative purposes in a separate analysis of capacity utilisation in freight transport by road and rail.

The provision of road space and traffic regulation facilities is a service which is bought in by road users. It constitutes a non-factor input to the sectors in road transport which are 'organised', in the sense that they comprise business units and establishments concerned solely with transport activities. In addition, the service is supplied to 'unorganised' owners of private cars and commercial vehicles and to pedestrians. The net output of roads and the associated lighting and traffic regulation facilities finds a place in the national income in Order XXIV, Public Administration and Defence (partly under Minimum List Heading 901, National Government Service, and partly under MLH 902, Local Government Service). From the point of view of a study of output and productivity in the transport sector of the economy, this treatment of roads is unsatisfactory, and particularly so when the output of track services is included in Railways (although unfortunately not separately organised as such); but an examination of output and productivity in a road service industry is not included here for reasons of time and space.

The services provided by private passenger cars to their owners[1] and passengers accounted in physical gross output terms for 80.0 per cent of the passenger mileage by road in 1966 and for 71.5 per cent of total passenger miles by all motorized forms of inland transport, including air transport.[2] Yet no measure is available of net output, and no satisfactory method has yet been devised to measure labour input. With the only other major and widely owned consumer durable good, dwellings, national income statisticians have developed the measure 'imputed rent' to assess the net output of the service of house accommodation provided to owner occupiers. No similar exercise has yet been undertaken to impute the value of services provided by motor cars to their owners. There is no doubt that such a task would be more difficult than has been the case with imputed house rents, as the data on market rents, on which the imputed rents are based, are much more extensive in the case of houses than their equivalents are in the case of motor cars. Any attempt at estimating the 'imputed rent' of services provided to owners of motor cars is regarded as outside the scope of this paper.

---

1 Taxis and cars let out for hire, with and without drivers, are included under Road Passenger Transport. See appendix note to this Chapter. Section (a).

2 Derived from statistics of total passenger mileage in Great Britain 'Passenger Transport in Great Britain, 1966'. Table 1, p. 2. Ministry of Transport, H.M.S.O. 1968.

The gross output measures currently available for the transport sectors in the British economy clearly differ considerably in their accuracy as indicators of changes in net output value, and this obviously true of other sectors of the economy. One general reason for this is that in any sector the output which is produced and sold is heterogeneous. Where a physical measure of gross output is used as an indicator, and this is common in transport, an aggregation of output in terms of ton miles or passenger miles, as the case may be, will overlook differences in the economic qualities and values of the individual ton miles which make up the total, and the changing proportions over time which ton miles (or passenger miles) of particular types bear to the total.

The first distinction between, say, ton miles of output of different types may be made in terms of the differences which exist in the physical characteristics of the goods carried, and therefore in their loading and stowage characteristics. These in turn will be likely to affect the amount of work involved, and therefore the net output (value added), in the processes of loading and transporting goods of different characteristics of these kinds. A ton mile of relatively easily loaded and compactly stowed cement will entail less work, and therefore less value added, than a ton mile of furniture, which has very different loading and stowage characteristics; other factors, such as the distance each ton travels, being assumed equal in the two cases.

The second distinction follows from the assumption that other factors are equal which was made in the first distinction. A ton mile of transport service for cement will entail less value added if the haul, or distance over which the cement is carried, is 100 miles than if the haul is only 50 miles. The reasons for this are clear enough. The terminal costs (at both ends of each haul), which include the costs of work done by the labour associated with the transport service and of waiting time for the vehicle are fixed regardless of the length of the haul; but in the case of the shorter haul they constitute a larger proportion of total cost than they do in the case of the longer haul. Operating costs per ton mile may be assumed constant where the same vehicle is used for both hauls, and therefore in the case of the shorter haul the same terminal costs are incurred as in the case of the longer haul but they are spread over a relatively smaller total of ton miles, making each ton mile representative of more work done and value added than is so when the haul is longer. Changes in the size, speed and efficiency of vehicles are factors which are constituents of productivity change and so they are not relevant to a consideration of the degree of accuracy of the output measure.

The conclusion which may be reached from a consideration of these distinctions in transport output measurement is that where the measure is in heterogeneous, physical terms of ton mileage or passenger mileage, the accuracy may be improved if the total output can be differentiated; and the greater the differentiation the greater the accuracy. At one extreme there is the case of Road Haulage Contracting where net output movements are represented by changes in a single indicator of undifferentiated ton miles. At the other end of the scale, the most differentiated sector in Measured Transport is the Railways where total net output is divided into eleven separate sub-sections each represented by a separate indicator. The degree of differentiation, however, is not so great as might appear at first, as some of it is due to the multiplicity of activities. Nevertheless, rail freight transport output, measured in ton miles, is sub-divided into three separate types of traffic, and three separate types of passenger transport output are distinguished in a similar way.[1] In each case separate net output measures and indicators are applied.

The opposite extreme to the completely undifferentiated is of course the completely differentiated measure, which in the case of, for example, Road Haulage Contracting, would involve the measurement of net output (value added) produced by every individual haul. Such a process of measurement is clearly not practical, but accuracy may be improved by moving from the completely undifferentiated measure to one which incorporates a greater degree of differentiation, and this is what has been done in this study.

In Road Haulage Contracting and Road Passenger Transport systems of price-relative weights have been constructed from data which have been assembled from field studies and from various other sources on the cost to user of transport services differentiated, in the case of goods transport, by type of commodity transported and, in the case of road passenger transport, by type of service (stage, express, excursion etc.). The same technique has been applied in rail freight transport where data on cost to user of freight transport services distinguished by commodity class have been used to weight the corresponding time series of ton mileages of the commodities carried.

The choice of periods for our analysis is circumscribed chiefly by the availability of data on the output of Road Haulage Contracting. Data from surveys are available only in the years 1952, 1958, and 1962. For intermediate years, interpolations checked against the results of road traffic counts give a lower grade of estimate which is usable for some purposes; although the traffic counts do not distinguish between contractual and non-contractual road goods transport vehicles. For subsequent years, extrapolations and rather more comprehensive traffic counts provide estimates of physical output which provide a basis which we use for strictly provisional estimates of output and productivity in Measured Transport up to and including the year 1965.

2. Labour Input

The measurement concepts involved here are concerned with standardisation and 'quality' shifts of two distinct types. Much productivity measurement has been based on a labour denominator of the productivity ratio which is 'crude' in the sense that no distinction is made between male and female labour, and therefore no account is taken of any changes in the proportions of male and female labour to total work force over time. In an attempt to improve, from the labour input side,

---

[1] See appendix note to this Chapter, Section (b) for a detailed description of net output weights and indicators.

the accuracy of the productivity measure output per man per year, labour input is here standardised into 'standard male equivalent labour units' or, more shortly, 'standard labour units' (SLU). The first step in the process of standardisation is to convert part-time labour, which is frequently female labour, to 'full time equivalent' labour. In some service industries, such as Distribution, part-time working is common, but in Measured Transport it is such a tiny fraction of total labour input that it has not been thought worthwhile to convert the figures to 'full time equivalents'.

The process of standardisation involves the economic theory of marginal productivity which states that factors are paid according to their marginal contributions to net output. Under freely competitive conditions in the product and factor markets wages are equal to the net product of labour. Market imperfections and institutional factors hinder the precise, practical applicability of the theory, but nevertheless it tends to be true that of two units of the factor labour A and B, A will be paid more than B if A's contribution to net output is deemed to exceed B's contribution. We have therefore adopted the assumption that in the sectors of the transport industry which are distinguished for the purposes of this study, the establishment of annual coefficients from the ratios of the average hourly earnings of female labour to the average hourly earnings of male labour, and similarly for the earnings of youths and boys, is an acceptable method of converting 'crude' labour input (i.e. simply counting heads) into 'standardised male equivalent labour units'.[1]

It may be noticed that, with the exception of road passenger transport, the female labour in each sector is concerned largely with clerical and similar work which is very different in type from the work of the majority of male labour in the sector. In road passenger transport the work of women as bus conductors is much closer in type to that of men in this sector and this is reflected in a coefficient which is as high as 0.9 in some years. The influence of residuary institutional factors no doubt finds some reflection in this ratio and, less evidently, in those relating to the other sectors.

The process of standardisation is extended to both female labour and to the labour of youths and boys. In both cases the proportion of each to the total sectoral crude labour input has, in some sectors, changed significantly over the time period under study.

The difference in the rate of change of 'crude' labour input and of standardised labour input yields a measure of the *intra*-sectoral shift in labour input, which is due to the changes in the composition of labour input which have been described.

The next step in the measurement and adjustment of labour input is the identification and calculation of the *inter*-sectoral labour 'quality' shift. This is done by weighting the rate of change of the standardised labour force in each sector by the ratio of their remuneration per standardised manhour to the

---

[1] A full explanation of the method of standardising labour input is given in the Statistical Appendix, Section B.

remuneration of the standardised labour force in the industry in a base year. The resultant sectoral rates of change are then weighted by the number of standardised labour units (in manhours per annum) in each sector in the base year. This approach, without the incorporation of the intra-sectoral shift, was developed by B.F. Massel. [1]

The further adjustments to labour input which are needed are those relating to hours of work and holidays. Both public and annual holidays allowed and the changes in both over time are brought into the calculation.

The finally adjusted measure of the input of the factor labour brings into account both the inter- and intra-sectoral shifts in standardised labour input, changes in hours of work and changes in the length of public and annual holidays allowed. A productivity measure of output per unit of 'labour input adjusted for changes in hours, holidays and intra- and inter-sectoral shifts' is more reflective of reality than a measure of output per employed person per annum.

Changes in labour skills over time, as distinct from the shift components, are not measured, and should not be measured by the process of adjustment and standardisation which has been outlined. Such changes in the application of labour skills to the production process are reflected in productivity change. Under the interpretative system applied in this Paper, and described in section B of this chapter, such changes will be attributed to the residual factor which is named 'applied technical and organisation knowledge and external factors' (ATOKE). The interpretative treatment of productivity change will be based, as has been indicated, on a production function. The aim is to show separately the contributions to output movement of movements in the input of labour and capital *as such*. It is, therefore, not desirable to pre-adjust labour input to take into account changes in applied labour skills over time within each sector. Although it would be of interest to have a separate measure of this factor, it is also necessary to be able to distinguish the effect on output and productivity change of changes in *all* 'applied technical and organisational knowledge and external factors', including that which is applied in the form of changes in labour skills. It is therefore important to make clear that the 'qualitative' aspects of labour input, for which allowance is made before the productivity ratios and trends are calculated, relate to the sex composition of the labour force and to certain defined aspects of its age structure; this is the intra-sectoral shift. The other

---

[1] 'A Disaggregated View of Technical Change'. B.F. Massel. *Journal of Political Economy*. December 1961. The formal relationship used in our calculations is:

$$\frac{\Delta LI_i}{LI_i} = \sum \frac{\Delta LI_s}{LI_s} \cdot \frac{W_s}{W_i} \cdot \frac{LI_s}{LI_i}$$

Where LI_i and LI_s are labour inputs, in terms of standardised manhours, into the industry and sector respectively; W_i and W_s are the average hourly earnings per standardised manhour in the industry and sector; both measures relate to a common base year.

qualitative aspect of labour input for which allowance is also made relates to changes in the relative importance of individual sectors of the Measured Transport industry, in terms of both the 'quality' of labour (as measured by its remuneration) and of the proportion which each sector's labour force bears to the total industry labour force in a base year; this is the inter-sectoral shift element. Both types of allowance and shift are later referred to collectively, for the sake of convenience, as the aggregation bias for which allowance has to be made before productivity ratios and trends are calculated.

3. Capital Input

The approach to the measurement of the input of the factor capital is based on capital stock measurement rather than upon any measure of fixed asset formation. The concept of capital is gross, valued as new at constant prices. The available capital stock figures are in this form, as produced officially, and are based upon the work of Philip Redfern[1] and Geoffrey Dean.[2] The thinking behind this concept of capital stock is briefly as follows.[3] Capital stock comprises assets completed and installed over a fairly long period of years, at least this is so for the more durable types of physical asset such as buildings. Consequently the stock of capital at any one time comprises assets which vary in age, in the intensity with which they have been used and in the extent to which they have become obsolete. These disparities ought to be allowed for, but in practice no means has yet been devised of doing so. The deduction of estimates of accrued capital consumption from gross capital stock would yield net estimates which would be of use for some purposes, but such figures would not be relevant to the measurement of capital as a factor in current production which is the use to which Dean's estimates are put in this study and which corresponds with the primary aim of the estimates. It is clearly true that assets become less valuable as the stock of unexpired services which they represent diminishes, but any decline in productivity with age would not necessarily correspond to this decline in value. There is however clearly some decline in the productivity of assets with age. This leads to some over valuation of assets under the present method when the use to which the estimates are put is the provision of a base for measuring through time the contribution to output of the factor capital.

In a little more detail, the process of estimation is that the capital goods are valued at what they would cost 'if they were to be replaced by new but otherwise similar assets'. They are therefore, described as being at '1958 prices new'.

---

1 Net Investment in Fixed Assets in the United Kingdom, 1938–53'. *J.R.S.S. Series A*. Volume 118. Part 2, 1955.

2 'The Stock of Fixed Capital in the United Kingdom in 1961'. *J.R.S.S. Series A*. Volume 127. Part 3, 1964.

3 The remainder of this paragraph and the next one following is based upon the notes on capital stock measurement given in the National Income and Expenditure Blue Book, 1967, p. 125.

This is the same price basis as is used for constant price estimates of capital formation, but whereas the latter generally relate to new assets, the capital stock consists mainly of used assets and the word 'new' is added to the description 'at 1958 prices' to emphasise that used assets are being valued 'as if they were new'.[1]

Many and great difficulties arise in any measure of capital over time. R.M. Solow[2] has said 'the capital time series is the one that will really drive a purist mad'. The problems are somewhat reduced by the method described, and the estimates are the best available. They are consistent and enable inter-sectoral relative comparisons of capital intensity by sector to be made. The measure is of course of capital in place and not capital in use. Not only is some reserve capacity usually necessary in transport operations, and so the 'in use' description should be widened beyond a narrow interpretation, but also a separate investigation is made in this study of capacity utilisation, which is expected to be a particularly important factor in productivity change in transport and involves both capital and labour utilisation in terms of the combined production units which commonly occur in marketed transport services.

In the case of labour input, adjustments are made for both the intra- and inter-sectoral 'quality' shifts which occur in this factor over time. For capital, no practical method is available for estimating any intra-sectoral quality shifts which may occur over time due to changes in the proportionate share in the sectoral total of different types of capital input. The inter-sectoral 'quality' shift, however, may be estimated for the Measured Transport industry. The method used is to weight the rate of capital input in each sector by the ratio of the sector's gross rate of return to capital to the gross rate of return to capital for the industry as a whole; both the reward to capital and the capital stock itself being calculated gross of depreciation. The resultant is then weighted by the percentage share of the sector's gross capital stock of the total gross capital stock of the industry. The measures of return and of capital stock are for a common base year.[3] The grounds for this process are that higher percentage

---

1 *National Income and Expenditure, 1967*, p. 125. Central Statistical Office. H.M.S.O. London, where a fuller description of the methods of estimation may be found. See also our Statistical Appendix, Section C.

2 'Technical Change and the Aggregate Production Function'. *Review of Economics and Statistics*. Volume 39, August, 1957.

3 The algebraic relation is:

$$\frac{\Delta K_i}{K_i} = \frac{\Delta K_s}{K_s} \cdot \frac{r_s}{r_i} \cdot \frac{K_s}{K_i}$$

where K_i and K_s represent the gross capital stock in the industry and sector respectively, and r_i and r_s the gross rate of return to capital in the industry and sector; both measures are gross of depreciation and relate to a common base year.

rates of return to capital reflect higher productivity of capital.

As in the case of labour input, the adjustment of capital input change for change in a 'quality' shift factor does not remove from the scene any growth element which should rightly appear in the production function, either as part of the contribution of change in capital intensity to change in output per manhour, or as part of the change in output per manhour which is attributable to change in applied technical and organisational knowledge and external factors.

B.   Interpretation

The interpretation of productivity change in transport in this study is founded on a production function. A distinction is made between interpretation and explanation. By interpretation is meant the decomposition of output movements into the concurrent and contributory movements in labour input and in capital intensity (the K/L ratio),[1] and the net movement in residual factors which in this study are termed 'applied technical and organisational knowledge and external factors.' (ATOKE).

R.M. Solow[2] has developed a relatively simple method of applying a production function to the task of segregating variations in output per manyear (or per manhour) which are due to the net effect of changes in the residual factors from those which are due to changes in the availability of capital per head. Three assumptions are needed. The first is that labour and capital are paid their marginal products, an assumption already made in the process of standardising labour input. The second assumption is that technical change is 'neutral' in the sense of Hicks[3] and therefore a shift in the production function will leave the marginal rate of substitution unchanged. The third assumption is implied in the second, and is that the marginal productivities of the factors will change as the ratio of capital to labour changes. There is no need to assume a constant capital/output ratio. In support of the use of this type of production function, there is an observed constancy in the relative shares of labour and capital in total factor rewards in Measured Transport. (See Statistical Appendix, Section D, Table D. 2.).

---

1 Gross capital stock 'in place' at constant replacement prices divided by the total number of persons in employment and self-employment.

2 Op. cit.

3 The neutrality of technical innovation has two senses. First, in the sense of Harrod an innovation is neutral if it leaves the capital/output ratio unchanged when interest rates are also unchanged. Second, Hicks neutrality involves the condition that where certain quantities of two factors of production are being used to provide a given output, the effect of a neutral innovation is to increase the marginal productivity of each in exactly the same proportion. In the assumption made here it is neutrality in the sense of Hicks which is involved.

On these conditions a simple production function of this type may take the form

$$\Delta Y = (1 - a)\,\Delta L_{mh} + a\,\Delta K_g + t$$

where Δ signifies exponential rate of growth per annum, Y is net output, L_{mh} labour in standardised male equivalent manhours per year, K_g is capital gross, in place at replacement values and constant prices, a, a constant, is the average share of capital in total factor rewards over the period concerned, and t is time incorporating net residual factors in which are included technical change which in turn includes net improvements to capital, labour and 'organisation'.

This function measures the approximate contributions to output of labour, capital and 'technical change'. Where the need is to study separately the contributions of change in capital intensity $(\Delta(K/L))$ and of change in applied technical and organisational knowledge and external factors $(\Delta\,\text{ATOKE})$ to labour productivity change, as is the present purpose, then it is permitted to write

$$\frac{dy \cdot L_{mh}}{dl_{mh} \cdot Y} = a\left(\frac{dk}{K} - \frac{dl}{L}\right) + \frac{d\,\text{atoke}}{\text{ATOKE}}$$

or, in terms of annual exponential rates of change,

$$\Delta\left(\frac{Y}{L_{mh}}\right) = a\,(\Delta K - \Delta L) + \Delta\,\text{ATOKE}$$

and
$$\Delta\,\text{ATOKE} = \Delta\left(\frac{Y}{L_{mh}}\right) - a\,(\Delta K - \Delta L)$$

where L is manpower in work.[1]

The contribution of movements in capital input to movements in productivity must involve the distinction between that part of the change in capital input which is capital 'widening' and that part which is 'deepening'. It is the latter which brings about changes in 'capital intensity'. Hence that portion of capital growth which is required to provide capital for any new workers entering the labour force (capital 'widening') is allowed for before the percentage contribution of gross capital formation by capital 'deepening' is estimated and subtracted from productivity change to reach the estimate of the contribution to productivity movements which is due to movements in 'applied technical and organisational knowledge and external factors'.

So the end product of this whole process is the interpretation of output movements in terms of the contributions to it attributable to movements in labour input adjusted for hours, annual and public holidays allowed and the intra-sectoral shift described earlier. This leads on to a sectoral measure of productivity levels and productivity movements over time in terms of output per unit of adjusted labour input. On an industry basis, and for trends only, further adjustments must be made to allow for the inter-sectoral shifts over time in both labour and capital.[2]

---

1 See Chapter 4, Section B, for a further discussion of this function.

2 See p. 24 (labour), and p. 27 (capital).

The production function can then be applied to the data which have been adjusted and prepared in the way described. This process yields the contribution of weighted[1] movements in capital per head[2] to movements in adjusted productivity. This is done by sector for the short periods 1952 to 1958 and 1958 to 1962, for the longer run 1952 to 1962 and for each year 1952 to 1965.

When the exponential rate of change of capital intensity is subtracted from the exponential rate of change of adjusted productivity, the positive or negative remainder, which is designated Δ ATOKE above, represents the exponential change in applied technical and organisational knowledge and external factors.[3] Where it is positive it has been regarded as 'progress',[4] and it does approximately measure the *net* effects on productivity movements of movements in the 'residual' factors.

The ATOKE, 'progress' factor, is shown as a derived exponential rate of change and also as an index over the period 1952 to 1965.[5]

Further differentiation of the residual factor ATOKE involves attempts at explanatory analysis, the approach to which is set out in the next section.

The interpretation of productivity movements needs to be joined, in order to give a more complete view, to the results of an interpretative treatment of productivity *levels*. In Measured Transport there exist wide inter-sectoral variations between the levels of labour productivity and between the levels of capital intensity. In the analysis which is set out in Chapter 4 the measures of comparative productivity, in the absolute sense, are given in terms of output per unit of combined factor input. It would be virtually meaningless, where substantial inter-sectoral differences in the K/L ratio occur, to make any comparative interpretation of productivity level on the basis of labour productivity alone.

The approach to the estimation of output per unit of combined factor input is similar to that adopted by R.C.O. Matthews.[6] The value of net output in a sector

---

1 By non-wage income as a decimalised fraction of total factor rewards; the term α in the function written above.

2 Not per standardised manhour or otherwise adjusted labour unit, because of the character of the association between labour and capital in transport which has already been described. See pp. 26 and 27.

3 R.M. Solow, op. cit. regards the residual term as representing any kind of shift in the production function, presumably however caused. 'Thus', he goes on, 'slowdowns, speedups, improvements in the education of the labour force and all sorts of things will appear as technical change.'

4 By W.B. Reddaway and A.R. Smith, *Economic Journal*, March, 1960.

5 See Statistical Appendix Section D, Table D.1 and related methodological note.

6 'Some Aspects of Post-War Growth in the British Economy in Relation to Historical Experience'. Paper read to the Manchester Statistical Society on November 11th 1964. Cambridge University, Department of Applied Economics. Reprint Series No. 240.

in any given year is divided by a factor which comprises the sum of total labour input (as defined below) and the product of the value of the sectoral capital stock, gross, at current replacement cost, multiplied by the average percentage gross rate of return to capital in the industry divided by the wage rate in the industry. The resultant is the value of sectoral output per unit of combined factor input. The latter is in terms of equivalent manhours. The formal expression is

$$TFI_s = LI_s + \frac{r_i}{w_i} . K_s$$

where TFI_s is total factor input in a sector, LI_s and K_s are sectoral inputs of labour and capital measured in standardised manhours and gross value respectively, and r_i and w_i are the industry average rate of profit (including depreciation) on capital and wages per standardised manhour respectively.

Since, in the industry as a whole, w_i/r_i units of K earn the same amount as one standardised manhour, the above expression gives a measure of total input in equivalent manhours. A conceptual difficulty is that this method makes no allowance for the fact that differences in the gross rates of return to capital may be due partly to differences in the durability of capital; such differences in durability would be found, for example, between the capital stock in the railways and that in the road passenger transport sector. What the productivity figures measure is essentially a weighted average of the extent to which the wage and the profit rate in any sector depart from the industry average.

These estimates of comparative productivity levels are made for the years 1954, 1958 and 1963.

Different levels of wage rates between sectors may be the result of differences in the quality of the labour used. If all differences in wage rates were due to this cause, an adjustment to the previously described formula could be made.[1] The result of this modification is to provide a measure of differences in the rate of return on capital between sectors, weighted by the importance of capital in the sector.

C.   Explanation

There would seem to be a need in any productivity study involving transport to look carefully at capacity utilisation levels and trends and to consider any explanatory value these measures may have in relation to total factor productivity.

---

[1] The adjusted expression is

$$TFI_s = \frac{w_s}{w_i} . LI_s + \frac{r_i}{w_i} . K_s$$

where, in addition to terms already explained, w_s/w_i is the ratio of the average wage in the sector to the average wage in the industry.

All measures of aggregate capital stock in money terms have limitations which are well covered in economic literature. Physical capacity, as a major factor input in transport, has certain advantages in measurement terms over a monetary measure of capital, although the two are not equivalent. This point and the limitations of physical capacity as a measure of input is investigated further in Chapter 6.

Capital utilisation is employed in this paper in a sense which is wider than the load factor ratio, its sense is that of output per unit of physical capacity available for service (e.g. passenger miles per rail passenger seat maintained and available for service, including an allowance for normal out of service maintenance time). A further development of this measure is one of total, combined input productivity. This is named the productivity of total capacity (PTC) and is found from the expression

$$\Delta PTC = \Delta\left(\frac{Y}{C}\right) - (1 - \alpha)(\Delta LI - \Delta C)$$

where, in addition to PTC, Y is output as measured; C is physical capacity as measured; $(1 - \alpha)$ is the share of labour in total factor rewards; LI is labour input in terms of standardised labour unit hours; and Δ is exponential rate of change per annum in the variable concerned.

This is a measure of output per unit of capacity with an allowance for movement in the 'labour intensity' of the capacity concerned. A comparison of the results of applying this alternative, physical productivity measure with total factor productivity has confirmatory value. The physical measure also enables some light to be shed on the effects on productivity movement of change in average speed in rail transport, and it gives an opportunity for making some separate estimates of productivity in rail freight and passenger transport, which is not possible in terms of the total (labour and capital) productivity measure. The alternative measure, therefore, has explanatory uses.

Another approach to explanatory analysis is to seek to test a number of hypotheses about the behaviour of certain variables in relation to each other. Coefficients of correlation between variables may (subject to the usual limitations) provide *some* aid in confirming or refuting explanatory hypotheses.

Of established doctrine perhaps the best known is the positive relationship between exponential rates of change of output and of productivity in a number of industries. Both Salter[1] and Kendrick[1] have confirmed the positive nature of this relationship which yields a coefficient of undoubted significance. This can be attributed partly to economies of scale which make possible increases in productivity as output rises, and partly to the lower relative prices at which output can be sold as productivity increases. Given an elastic demand, such

---

[1] op. cit. It has recently been recognised that this relationship, which was explored and applied by both Salter and Kendrick was first formulated by P.J. Verdoorn in 'Fattori che regolano lo sviluppo della producttività del lavoro'. *L'Industria*, 1947, and has now become known as 'Verdoorn's Law'.

relative price reductions tend to stimulate demand and therefore output at a second round. If, therefore, a significant positive correlation is found to exist between output movements and productivity movements in transport, we should expect to find a significant negative correlation between movements in net price and in both output and productivity.

The initial pair of explanatory hypotheses set up for testing on the results obtained from our exercise in measuring productivity and related variables in the Measured Transport industry are as follows.

A.   That movements in output (ΔY) and labour productivity (ΔP_{LI}) correlate significantly[1] (across sectors of the Measured Transport industry) in a *positive* sense.

B.   That movements in labour productivity (ΔP_{LI}) and in net price (ΔNP) correlate significantly in a *negative* sense.

A fairly natural development of the Verdoorn, Salter, Kendrick thesis on the significant correlation between movements in output and in labour productivity, would be to explore the relationship between movements in output and in technical change, as measured by our residual term, $\Delta ATOKE$, which stands for a group of factors: applied technical and organisational knowledge and external factors.

The hypotheses tested in this case is:

C.   That movements in output (ΔY) and in technical change ($\Delta ATOKE$) correlate significantly in a *positive* sense.

If hypothesis A (ΔY and ΔP_{LI}) and hypothesis C (ΔY and $\Delta ATOKE$) are both validated then, by deduction, movements in ATOKE and in labour productivity (P_{LI}) will be found to yield a significant positive correlation, and this may be checked by a direct test.

In the interpretative analysis (outlined in section B above) a Cobb–Douglas type of production function is fitted to labour productivity and capital intensity data; the object being to segregate labour productivity movement into that part which is due to movement in capital intensity and that due to technical change. The extent to which capital is a vehicle for technical change (as represented by $\Delta ATOKE$) is a matter of some interest, suggesting the final hypothesis which is:

D.   That movement in capital stock input (ΔK) and technical change ($\Delta ATOKE$) correlate significantly in a *positive* sense.

If this hypothesis is validated it would suggest that the influence of technical change ($\Delta ATOKE$) is exerted upon labour productivity movement through the application of technical knowledge which is embodied in additional capital goods, and through such economies of scale as require increased capital in their realisation. If, on the other hand hypothesis D is not validated, but hypotheses

---

[1]   The minimum values above which coefficients of correlation are 'significant' (at the 5 and 10 per cent levels) in the relatively small field of the Measured Transport Industry are given in Chapter 6.

A and C are, then the influence of ΔATOKE must be exerted upon labour productivity movement by other means. These other means will not require significantly large amounts of additional capital for their application and they could include: changes in labour skills; economies of scale not requiring significant amounts of additional capital in their realisation; organisational and managerial skills of all kinds, including that of managing labour relations; and finally external factors such as road congestion, licencing constraints and legal obligations to the public to provide services in relatively underpopulated regions.

These four hypotheses are set up as a framework and general guide for explanatory analysis, in the course of which it will be of interest to discover whether or not such relationships between output and productivity which have been found to correlate closely across goods industries[1] will apply equally to the service industry of transport as measured sectorally in this Paper.

Summary of Objectives and Scope

The general object of this paper is to measure employment, capital, output, labour productivity and technical change (total factor productivity); to interpret the results of measurement by fitting a production function to the data; to probe for more fundamental explanations and to test four hypotheses which are here set up as a guide to the explanatory analysis.

The scope of the work is to some extent limited by the available quantity and quality of data. Not all sectors of the transport industry in the United Kingdom are 'measureable' in the sense of there being available adequate and usable measures of output, factor inputs and productivity. Those which are judged measureable are included separately and collectively, under the title 'Measured Transport' in the full analysis which follows in the main body of the Paper. The fully measurable sectors are as follows:

> Railways
>
> Public Road Passenger Transport
>
> Road Haulage Contracting
>
> Sea Transport
>
> Port and Inland Water Transport
>
> Air Transport

Nearly all public, marketed freight and passenger transport services are included in this list. Excluded are the transport services provided by private passenger cars (including business cars but excluding hire cars and taxis which are included with public road passenger transport) and by privately-owned 'C' licenced road haulage vehicles. These sectors are included only in the analysis of output and prices (Chapter 2). Miscellaneous Transport Services and Storage is included only

---

1 W.E.G. Salter, op. cit., with particular reference to W.B. Reddaway's Addendum, pp. 195–203.

in the analysis of labour input.

Postal Services and Telecommunications are measurable in the sense described and are included in the full analyses except for the tests of hypotheses where the exploration of relationships and the conclusions are confined specifically to the public transport services.

The scope of the Paper may be seen at a glance in Table 1.

Table 1.1.   The Scope of the Analysis by Variable and by Industry and Sector

M.L.H.	Employment	Capital	Output Level and Trend	Productivity	Capacity Utilisation	Technical Change
701 Railways	*	*	*	*	*	*
702 Road Passenger Transport	*	*	*	*	*	*
703 Road Haulage Contracting	*	*	*	*	*	*
704 Sea Transport	*	*	*	*	...	*
705 Port and Inland Water Transport	*	*	*	*	...	*
706 Air Transport	*	*	*	*	...	*
MEASURED TRANSPORT	*	*	*	*	...	*
709 Miscellaneous Transport Services and Storage	*	...	...	...	...	...
707 Postal Services and Telecommunications	*	*	*	*	—	*
TOTAL TRANSPORT AND COMMUNICATION (Order XIX)	*	...	...	...	...	...
Non-Contractual Road Haulage	...	...	φ	...	...	...
Private Road Passenger Travel	...	...	φ	...	...	...

*   Included in the analysis.

...   Not available, or not available in usable form and excluded from the analysis.

φ   Trend only included in the analysis.

Appendix to Chapter 1

(a)   Sectoral Definitions and Coverage

(i)   *Measured Transport*

Minimum List
Headings
SIC 1958

701   *Railways* both underground and surface railways including those operated by the London Transport Executive. Excluded are ancillary undertakings, such as locomotive, carriage and wagon workshops, catering services, air, omnibus and steamer services, docks and canals.

702   *Road Passenger Transport*
Includes the operations of omnibus, motor coach, trolleybus and tramway services. Also included are the operation of taxi-cabs and private-hire cars (in both cases owner-drivers are included), and car hire (where vehicle is driven by the hirer).

703[1]   *Road Haulage Contracting*
Includes cartage and haulage contractors (whether using motor or horse-drawn vehicles) of all types, including furniture removers. Transport departments of establishments carrying goods in connection with their own businesses are excluded.

704   *Sea Transport*
Includes the shore establishments of companies (including railways) operating sea-going ships for the conveyance of either passengers or cargo or both; the crews of sea-going merchant ships; the provision of pilots for sea-going ships. The operation and the crews of fishing vessels are excluded.

705   *Port and Inland Water Transport*
Includes harbour, dock, canal, lighthouse, lightship etc., authorities, and establishments conducting marine salvage operations; the loading and unloading of vessels and the operation of tugs, lighters, barges, ferries, etc., in ports and inland waterways. Excludes the hiring of pleasure boats, punts, etc.

706   *Air Transport*
Includes airline companies operating on regular schedules or on charter (including establishments of Commonwealth and Foreign airlines in the United Kingdom), and aerodromes, including

---

[1] Non-Contractual Road Haulage is excluded from this sector and included under 'Other Transport'. See paragraph (ii) below.

airports, air traffic control centres and communication centres operated by the Ministry of Transport and Civil Aviation. Excludes flying schools, and flying and glider clubs.

(ii)   *Other Transport*

Minimum List
Headings
SIC 1958

709   *Miscellaneous Transport Services and Storage*
Includes services incidental to transport, viz : ship brokers, freight brokers, shipping agents, forwarding agents, travel ticket agents, tourist and excursion agents and similar establishments which facilitate the transport of passengers or goods but are not transport operators; flying schools, motoring schools, car parks, the road patrols and other motoring services of the motorists' organisations; the operation of toll roads and toll bridges.

Includes warehouses (including bonded warehouses), cold storage, furniture repositories, safe deposits, etc.

Includes messenger services, porterage; hiring of hand trucks, barrows, tradesmen's cycles, bath-chairs, etc.

Non-Contractual Road Freight Transport [1]
Includes the operation of all road freight transport vehicles carrying goods in connection with the business of their owners. Also included are the operations of vehicles exempt from licence duty and owned and operated by central and local government authorities (including vehicles operated under the Crown vehicles scheme). Vehicles operated under defence permits are excluded.

Private Road Passenger Travel [1]
Includes travel by motor cars (including by three-wheeled vehicles), motor cycles, taxis and private hire cars. Travel by vans and pedal cycles is excluded.

(iii)   *Communication*

Minimum List
Headings
SIC 1958

707   *Postal Services and Telecommunications*
All Post Office establishments, except the factories manufacturing telephone and telegraph apparatus and except the Post Office

---

1 These sectors have been established for the purposes of this research.

Savings Department; cable and radio services (excluding broadcasting and relay services) and other telephone and telegraph services.

Note applicable to all the above sectors
Separate establishments engaged in the repair of vehicles or aircraft are excluded from the above sectors, but ordinary maintenance and running repairs are included.

(b)   Output Weights and Indicators

(i)   *Measured Transport*

Weights, per thousand, 1958

MLH

701	Railways	236
702	Road Passenger Transport	208
703	Road Haulage Contracting	184
704	Sea Transport	211
705	Port and Inland Water Transport	114
706	Air Transport	47
	Measured Transport	**1,000**

Source : Supplied direct by the Central Statistical Office in value terms (1958 prices) and converted here into weights per thousand.

Weights and Indicators by Sector, 1958

		Weight	Indicator
701 Railways	British Railways		
	Passenger Traffic		
	Ordinary	54	Number of passenger miles
	Early morning	3	Number of passenger miles
	Season	9	Number of passenger miles
	Freight Traffic		
	Merchandise and Livestock	45	Number of ton miles
	Minerals	23	Number of ton miles
	Coal and coke	58	Number of ton miles
	Parcels	16	Receipts deflated
	Mail (letters and parcels)	9	Number posted

	Weight	Indicator
London Transport Railways	12	Number of passenger miles
British Railways collection and delivery services		
Parcels	2	Number of parcels handled
Freight	5	Quantity of freight handled
	236	

702 Road Passenger Transport

	Weight	Indicator
British Transport Commission:		
London Transport Road Services	30	Number of passenger miles
Road Passenger Services	34	Number of passenger miles
Other Operators	144	Number of passenger journeys
	208	

703 Road Haulage Contracting — 184 — Number of ton miles

704 Sea Transport

	Weight	Indicator
Vessels in foreign trade:[1]		
Tankers	54	Active tonnage adjusted for increase in average speed of fleet
Dry cargo:		
Liners	105	Freight receipts less charter hire paid deflated
Tramps	18	by indices of freight rates
Passenger:		
British Railways	3	Passenger movement by sea between U.K. and
Other	21	Continent and non-European countries
Vessels in coastal trade	10	Arrivals and departures with cargo
	211	

---

[1] The weights allocated to the separate indicators are based on the results of the 1958 Chamber of Shipping enquiry.

	Weight	Indicator
705 Port and Inland Water Transport		
Port Services	106	Total entrances and clearances of shipping in foreign trade and coastal trade
Inland waterways	8	Number of ton miles
	114	
706 Air Transport		
Corporation and associate airlines:		
Passenger Traffic	26	Number of passenger miles
Freight Traffic	5	Number of short ton miles
Mail Traffic	3	Number of short ton miles
Independent airlines:		
Passenger Traffic	11	Number of passenger miles
Freight Traffic	1	Number of freight ton miles
Airport services	1	Total flights between the U.K. and abroad plus twice internal flights
	47	

(ii) *Postal Services and Telecommunications*
Net output and indicators by type of activity

	Net Output (£m. in 1958)	Indicator
General Post Office		
Postal services	145	Number of letters and parcels posted
Remittance services	2	Number of money orders issued
	9	Number of postal orders issued
Counter services	27	Number of pensions and allowance forms paid
	2	Number of broadcast licences issued
Telegraph and Telex services	6	Number of overseas telegrams
	4	Number of inland telegrams
	4	Private telex rentals
	2	Number of telex calls

	Net Output (£m. in 1958)	Indicator
Telephone services	65	Number of exchange connections
	48	Number of trunk calls
	44	Number of local calls
	4	Number of international calls
	9	Private wire rentals
Cable companies	6	Number of telegrams handled by cable companies
	377	

iii)   *Other Transport: Indicators of Output*

Non-Contractual Road Freight Transport	Number of ton miles
Private Road Passenger Travel	Number of passenger miles

2 Output and Prices

In this chapter we look first at the problem of output measurement in greater detail and in particular examine the extent to which it is possible to make more accurate measurements. Secondly, we examine the trends in output and output shares in the Measured Transport industry and thirdly, we look in detail at one of the factors influencing these trends, namely, the relative prices charged by different transport modes.

A.　　　　　Method of Output Measurement

In the introductory chapter the principles underlying the measurement of output in the national economy were outlined. The value of net output (gross value added) is obtained for a base year and the movement of output in subsequent years is estimated by the use of gross output indicators. In transport it is possible to use a physical measure of gross output in the majority of cases, the most common indicators being number of ton miles or passenger miles.

The aggregation of ton miles, or passenger miles, implicitly assumes that each ton mile or passenger mile involves an equal amount of value added. What may be overlooked in making this assumption is the heterogeneous nature of the goods transported, the differences in the quality of various types of passenger transport services, and the differences in the average distance which goods and passengers are carried. The distance (or haul) differential is shown in the following example two journeys of 50 miles with loads of 20 tons of bricks, would give the same aggregate number of ton miles as one journey of 100 miles with the same load of 20 tons of bricks; the amount of value added in the first instance will, however, be larger because of the terminal costs and waiting time which are fixed regardless of length of haul. Abstracting from differences in length of haul, differences between ton miles which arise from differences in commodity type may be illustrated by an example as follows: 20 tons of meat carried for 50 miles in one haul is equal in terms of ton miles to 20 tons of cement carried for the same distance in one haul, but the net output created is likely to be much higher in the case of meat when the amount of work and value added involved in handling and refrigeration is taken into account, than in the case of cement. Passenger miles can also be differentiated in this way; that is, express services can be distinguished from urban stage services as requiring a different amount of net output per passenger mile and, similarly, London stage services from rural stage services. Differences of this nature may be important when comparing output over time if different types of ton miles (or passenger miles) account for changing

42

proportions of the total output; the use of a simple aggregation as an indicator of net output (gross value added) may well then involve error.

As can be seen from appendix to Chapter I, Section (b), the gross output indicators in rail and road passenger transport and in rail freight transport are not so crude as a completely undifferentiated aggregation of ton miles or passenger miles, although in rail freight transport the disaggregation of ton miles is more apparent than real. Until 1962 rail freight was separated into three groups, coal and coke, minerals traffic and general merchandise traffic, and the three groups are given weights in proportion to the gross receipts in each group in the base year, 1958. Within the two broad groupings minerals and general merchandise, however, a wide variety of commodities are carried and one of the purposes of this study is to obtain a more accurate estimate of output by using a finer breakdown by type of commodity carried and type of passenger mile.

Unfortunately, because of the paucity of data, any attempts to improve the gross output indicator had to be confined to rail freight, road haulage contracting, and road passenger transport. No attempt was made to differentiate to a greater extent than is already done in national income statistics the ton miles or passenger miles or the other indicators used in sea transport, port and inland water transport, or air transport, even though there is a need for greater accuracy in these sectors also. However, neither the time nor the resources were available in this study to cover all sectors of the transport industry in this respect. Even so, the more differentiated net output measures devised for this paper cover over fifty per cent of the net output of the Measured Transport industry in the base year, 1958.

Various methods could be used to measure more accurately the output of a transport sector. At one extreme could measure the value added by each individual haul or journey; alternatively, factor rewards could be aggregated in a base year for each type of commodity transported or type of passenger journey and such output indicators as commodity ton miles or specific types of passenger miles could be applied to reflect the movement of net output in other years. Both of these methods are conceptually feasible but somewhat impracticable. The simple method used in this study was to take price as a proxy for net output. That is, the assumption was made that the prices charged by individual operators would reflect not only the total cost incurred in carrying commodities of different types (including the cost of bought in materials and services, and a share of terminal costs) and the customary average length of haul or journey, but would also reflect relative differences in value added in the transport of different commodities or types of commodities. This simple method does of course break down in some instances. For example, the high proportion of fixed costs which are joint costs to passenger and freight in rail services makes the allocation of costs in rail freight hazardous. The British Transport Commission, following nationalisation, did attempt to make this allocation and to introduce a freight rate structure which would reflect more accurately than in the past the relative costs

of carrying different commodities – introducing the concept of loadability.[1]
In both road and rail passenger and freight transport, some distortion of relative
prices may however occur if freight is transported for a price which is less than
average total cost in order to maintain or increase traffic of a more remunerative
kind. This cross subsidisation has not been uncommon in rail freight traffic in
the past; the extent to which it occurs in road passenger transport and in road
haulage contracting will depend, in part, on the strength of competition between
firms in a particular area for the total business which is available. It may be
expected, however, that relative prices for transporting various commodities would
show the same *pattern* both within the road haulage contracting and between road
haulage and rail freight, except where the provider of the service has a spatial
monopoly or where the user of the service can exercise monopsony power.
Examples of these may be (i) in a policy of charging 'what the traffic will bear'
and (ii) the case of a single producer of a particular commodity who may be able
to play off several transport providers against each other.

These qualifications to the use of price relatives to weight ton miles or passenger
miles of different types in order to obtain a more accurate aggregate figure of
output were not considered to be so great as to make the exercise worthless.
Two constraints to the extent of the study were set, however, by the availability
of data and the years for which data could be obtained. In the event, information
on ton miles by commodity or commodity group was obtained for road haulage
contracting for two years, 1958 and 1962. The railway authorities were able to
supply us with detailed information for the same years and estimates were made
for the various types of public road passenger transport in 1958 and 1962.

The methods used to obtain a weighted output index in each of the sectors
concerned are outlined briefly below and fuller details are given in the appendix
note to this chapter.

B.   **Application of Methods**

1.   Road haulage contracting

Commodity coverage

The starting point was the information published by the Ministry of Transport on
the results of the enquiry into road goods traffic held in 1962.[2]

---

1 The revised rates came into effect in 1957, but it has been estimated that
charges for approximately 10 per cent of freight were still below cost when the
revised rate structure was introduced. See K.M. Gwilliam, *Transport and
Public Policy*, Allen and Unwin, 1964, p. 172.

2 Ministry of Transport Statistical Paper No. 4. 'Survey of Road Goods Transport
1962. Final Results. Commodity Analysis'. Published 1964.

The final results, which were based on sample surveys conducted during one week in each of the last three quarters of 1962 and in the first quarter of 1963, included an analysis of the main types of commodities which move by road and, in all, 34 commodities or commodity groups were identified. Figures were published of tonnage moved and ton mileage performed in each of these commodity groups for holders of carriers' licences in categories 'A', Contract 'A', 'B' and 'C'. (Holders of 'C' licences are not part of the sector, road haulage contracting as defined for the purposes of this study, and therefore tonnage moved and ton miles performed by this category of licence holder were ignored). Similar information was obtained by the Ministry of Transport in 1958; the figures published, however, were for tonnage and ton miles by licence category but not by commodity group although these data were obtained. The 1958 results[1] were based on a survey carried out during one week in April, and although the commodity results were not published, the Ministry of Transport made the data available for the purposes of this study. The commodity analysis in 1958 was less comprehensive than in 1962 — 20 commodities or commodity groups were distinguished but, unfortunately, these groups were not exactly comparable with the commodities or commodity groups used in 1962. In order to compare tonnage and ton mileage by commodities, it was necessary to combine the commodity groupings so that the composition of each group in 1958 and 1962 was comparable. This meant that the extent to which a finer breakdown of output could be made was limited to seven broad commodity groups. Of these, the final group under the label 'Other goods' includes such heterogeneous items as machinery and transport equipment, wood, timber and cork, furniture removals and a residual grouping: mixed loads and unallocable loads. Some of the commodities are clearly distinguished in both 1958 and 1962 (for example, coal coke and patent fuels, petroleum and petroleum products), but in others (for example, foodstuffs) broader groupings than is desirable had to be made because of the lack of comparability in the 1958 and 1962 commodity analyses.

Prices

There is no published information on prices charged for the transport of different commodities in road haulage contracting. Nor was it possible, because of the organisation of this sector of Measured Transport, to obtain aggregate receipts for each commodity carried from which an average 'price' could be estimated. The Road Haulage Association, to which approximately 40 per cent[2] of road haulage operators belong, was unable to supply any data on prices

---

1 'The Transport of Goods by Road', Ministry of Transport 1959.

2 'Operator' means here either 'A' or 'B' licence holder; such a licence holder may carry on a business of another kind and may undertake haulage contracting only in special circumstances. The Road Haulage Association estimates that their membership covers 90—95 per cent of operators who are engaged mainly in road haulage contracting.

charged for the carriage of different commodities. It was therefore decided to carry out a sample survey of road haulage operators in Great Britain using 33 of the 34 commodity groups[1] distinguished in the 1962 Ministry of Transport survey as a basis for the questionnaire.

A pilot survey was carried out initially in the Cambridge area and then in four towns in East Anglia early in 1967. From the information obtained in this pilot survey, a questionnaire on prices charged for transporting the 33 commodities was drawn up which road haulage operators could be expected to complete without much difficulty. The national survey was carried out later in 1967 on the basis of a random sample of operators drawn from the Ministry of Transport's register of 'A', Contract 'A' and 'B' licence holders. Vehicles operated by British Road Services were excluded from the sample, although their operations were taken into account at a later stage. The sample was a stratified one, the strata being (a) operators of 21 vehicles and over, (b) operators of 6–20 vehicles' (c) operators of 1–5 vehicles.

The sampling frame was based on a 45 per cent, 10 per cent, and 2 per cent coverage respectively giving a total of 2,143 operators in all with an estimated vehicle coverage of over 35,000 or approximately 15 per cent of all 'A' and 'B' licenced goods vehicles in 1966.[2] The number of questionnaires returned was 418 or approximately 25 per cent; of these, just under 200 (or 9 per cent) contained sufficient information to be used in the study; the vehicle coverage of the completed and usable questionnaires was 5,375 or 2.4 per cent of all 'A' and 'B' goods vehicles in 1966. As might be expected, the firms operating 21 vehicles and over appeared to keep better records and were more readily able to supply information than were the smaller operators; the usable response rate for the larger operators was 13 per cent.

From the information supplied by operators who completed the questionnaire it was possible to calculate an average price per ton mile for 31 of the 33 commodity groups distinguished. The groups for which it was not possible to work out the price per ton mile were (a) furniture removals and (b) empty containers. Hauliers were asked to give the prices charged in 1962 and in 1966. To obtain a single representative price for each commodity, individual prices were first combined in each of the different operator size groups: thus three average prices were obtained. These prices were weighted averages since the average price for each size group was obtained by weighting the individual prices by the number of vehicles operated by that haulier. These three average prices were then combined by weighting the prices by the number of vehicles operated by hauliers in the country as a whole in the operator size group concerned, and were then second weighted by the estimated average carrying capacity of vehicles in each size group. This was an approximation to tonnage moved for which

---

1 One of the commodity groups, laundry and dry cleaning, was not carried by 'A' and 'B' licence holders.

2 For full details of sampling methods used see appendix note to this chapter.

operators in each of the three size groups would be responsible, and by this method the bias in the sampling frame towards large hauliers was offset.

As explained earlier, it was not possible to apply price relative weights to all 33 commodity groups to obtain the movement of output in road haulage between 1958 and 1962; it was possible to distinguish only seven broad groups. A single price for each of these groups was obtained by combining the individual commodity prices using as weights the number of ton miles in each commodity group for which road haulage contractors were responsible in 1962. Prices were obtained, using this method, for the seven commodity groups in 1962 and in 1966 and these prices are used to obtain a weighted index of output in 1958 and 1962. Table 2.1 shows the results of the weighting procedure using 1966 prices as weights.[1]

The weighted index shows that output in road haulage contracting increased by nearly 31 per cent, while when the unweighted index is used the rate of growth is shown to be over 32 per cent. Over the four years, this indicates a difference between the two sides of 0.33 per cent each year on the continuously compounding growth rate calculation,[2] i.e. 7.00 per cent per annum as against 6.67 per cent per annum.

The category 'other goods', which includes a heterogeneous collection of commodities including among others such items as machinery and transport equipment, miscellaneous manufactured articles not otherwise specified, and furniture removals may, however, exaggerate or disguise some of the change that has taken place in the commodity pattern of output of road haulage contracting in the four years considered; for this group accounted for 29 per cent of total ton miles in 1958 and 28 per cent in 1962. Table 2.2 therefore has been included to show output weighted and unweighted for the six more homogeneous commodity groups. On this basis, an annual rate of growth of 7.24 is indicated using an unweighted index and 6.83 when a weighted index is used. The slower rate of growth of output when a weighted index is used is therefore even more evident when the six more homogeneous commodity groups are considered separately — an annual difference of 0.41 as against 0.33 — but even in these groups a good deal more aggregation was necessary than is desirable.

A similar weighted index was calculated using 1962 prices but there was little difference in the final result, indicating that *relative* prices have changed very little between the two years.

This is slightly different figure from that implied in Table 2.9 because the ton miles used were available with three places of decimals instead of one for 1958 and 1962. In Table 2.9 the rounded figure was used because figures for 1952 were available to only one decimal place. The rate of growth of output shown in Table 2.9 is 6.99 per cent per annum giving 0.32 per cent per annum difference between the weighted and unweighted indexes.

Table 2.1.   Output Weighted[a] and Unweighted, all Commodities, 1958–1962

Road Haulage Contracting

Commodity groups	Price (pence per ton mile in 1966)	Unweighted Output Quantity Ton miles million		Weighted Output Value (at 1966 prices) £ million	
		1958	1962	1958	1962
Food, drink and tobacco	7.05	2,999	3,414	88.10	100.29
Metals and metal work	4.97	1,754	2,292	36.32	47.46
Building and construction materials	4.94	2,452	3,582	50.47	73.73
Coal, coke and patent fuels	5.63	901	1,352	21.14	31.72
Petroleum and petroleum products	5.08	162	554	3.43	11.73
Chemicals	5.24	1,013	1,201	22.12	26.22
All other goods[b]	7.52	3,807	4,920	119.29	154.16
Total		13,087	17,315	340.87	445.31
Index		100.0	132.3	100.0	130.6

a Weighted by 1966 prices.

b Textile fibres and waste; other crude materials; wood, timber and cork;
electrical machinery and non-electrical machinery, transport equipment;
miscellaneous manufactured articles; unallocable loads; mixed loads;
furniture removals; empty containers.

Source: Ministry of Transport Road Goods Surveys 1958 and 1962, and DAE
field survey among road haulage operators in Great Britain.

This reduction in the rate of growth of output when a weighted index is used may
be interpreted as showing that the greatest increase in contractual road goods
transport was in those commodities which result in less value added per ton
mile. Table 2.3, summarised from Table 2.1, bears this out.

The commodity which was relatively cheapest to transport at 1966 average prices
building and construction materials, increased its share in total ton mileage
whereas the commodities which were relatively more expensive to transport,
food, drink and tobacco, and other manufactured goods, decreased their share.
The decline of food, drink and tobacco in the share of total ton mileage is shown
even more clearly if the specified commodities only are included and similarly,
the increase in the share of building and construction materials is even more
evident.

Table 2.2 Output Weighted[a] and Unweighted, Specified Commodities, 1958–1962

Road Haulage Contracting

Commodity groups	Price (pence per ton mile in 1966)	Unweighted Output Quantity Ton miles million		Weighted Output Value (at 1966 prices) £ million	
		1958	1962	1958	1962
Food, drink and tobacco	7.05	2,999	3,414	88.10	100.29
Metals and metal work	4.97	1,754	2,292	36.32	47.46
Building and construction materials	4.94	2,452	3,582	50.47	73.73
Coal, coke and patent fuels	5.63	901	1,352	21.14	31.72
Petroleum and petroleum products	5.08	162	554	3.43	11.73
Chemicals	5.24	1,013	1,201	22.12	26.22
Total		9,281	12,395	221.58	291.15
Index		100.0	133.6	100.0	131.4

a Weighted by 1966 prices.

Source: Ministry of Transport Road Goods Surveys 1958 and 1962, and DAE field survey among road haulage operators in Great Britain.

Table 2.3 Road Haulage Contracting

Shares of commodities in total ton mileage, 1958–1962

Commodity groups	Percentage share of ton miles		Percentage increase in ton miles, 1958–1962
	1958	1962	
Food, drink and tobacco	22.9	19.7	13.8
Metals and metalwork	13.45	13.3	30.7
Building and construction materials	18.7	20.7	46.1
Coal, coke and patent fuels	6.9	7.8	50.1
Petroleum and petroleum products	1.2	3.2	242.0
Chemicals	7.7	6.9	18.6
All other goods	29.1	28.4	29.2
	100.0	100.0	32.3[a]

a Average for all commodities. See Table 2.1.

2.   Rail freight transport

The railway authorities publish regularly partly disaggregated figures for ton miles and for freight receipts in three broad commodity groups: coal and coke, minerals, and general merchandise. Within the last two of these groups, however, a wide range of commodities are carried and an attempt is made in this study to apply the same methods used in disaggregating road goods traffic to railway goods traffic.

The railway authorities were able to supply more detailed information on (a) revenue receipts in 1962 and (b) tonnage carried in 1958 and 1962 for 14 specified commodities in the minerals group and 24 specified commodities in the general merchandise group.[1] The British Railways Board also supplied data on the 31 commodities distinguished in the 1962 Ministry of Transport Road Goods Survey, giving the average length of haul on the railways in 1966 for these commodities and the average rates per ton for their transport in 1962 and in 1966. The information on rates per ton was not used to calculate the price relatives by which output in the railways was weighted because the commodities and commodity groups approximate only very broadly to the usual rail freight classification of commodities. The information on average length of haul for each commodity was used, however, and applied to the tonnage figures for 1958 and 1962 given to us by the railway authorities for the 38 individual commodities within the minerals and general merchandise groups for which details of revenue receipts were available. (This method makes the assumption that there has been no drastic change in the average length of haul in the individual commodity groups between 1958 and 1966, but the railway authorities were unable to confirm or deny this from their available statistics. The published statistics on ton miles and on tonnage carried indicate that for the broad groups distinguished,[2] there has been very little change in average length of haul between 1958 and 1966, although this does not mean, of course, that there has been no change in average length of haul for individual commodities.) This information enabled us to calculate an estimated ton mileage in 1958 and in 1962 for each of the 38 specified commodities, and also an estimated average receipt per ton mile in 1962. This average receipt was used to weight the ton mileage of each of these commodities in the years 1958 and 1962.

---

1 These specified commodities in both minerals and merchandise groups taken together account for nearly 80 per cent of tonnage carried and just under 65 per cent of the revenue receipts in 1962. If the groups are taken separately the coverage is 85 per cent of minerals tonnage carried, 90 per cent of total receipts for minerals traffic, just over 70 per cent of total merchandise tonnage carried and 53 per cent of total merchandise receipts.

2 Railway freight statistics were amended in 1962 and instead of three groups, coal and coke, minerals, and general merchandise being distinguished the ton miles for coal and coke only are separated from all other freight train traffic. The average length of haul for all other freight train traffic shows little change between 1958 and 1962 and a small decline between 1962 and 1966.

50

The estimated ton mileage of the 38 specified commodities accounted for two-thirds of the total ton mileage estimated by the railway authorities in the minerals group and just under one-half in the general merchandise group of commodities[1] in the years for which the estimates were made. As there was no means of breaking down these residual groups further, an average receipt was calculated for the residual ton miles. This was done by subtracting the aggregate receipts obtained for transporting the 14 specified commodities in the minerals group from the total receipts for all minerals traffic to give receipts for

Table 2.4. Output Weighted[a] and Unweighted, 1958–1962

Rail Freight Transport – Minerals

Commodity	Price (pence per ton mile in 1962)	Unweighted Output Quantity Ton miles millions		Weighted output Value (at 1962 prices) £ million	
		1958	1962	1958	1962
Iron and steel	3.195	330.1	323.9	4.39	4.31
Iron and steel scrap	4.841	286.2	281.0	5.77	5.67
Iron Ore	2.936	772.2	709.8	9.45	8.68
Iron, pig	5.381	129.1	100.7	2.89	2.26
Lime and limestone	2.222	490.4	483.6	4.54	4.48
Bricks, clay and common	1.966	121.6	119.0	1.00	0.98
Bricks, refractory	3.615	85.3	33.8	1.28	0.51
Clay, common fire	4.566	33.1	24.4	0.63	0.46
Fertilisers and manure	3.758	234.9	163.0	3.68	2.55
O.T.W. Bitumen creosote	5.326	42.5	40.2	0.94	0.89
Roadstone	2.991	13.4	11.7	0.17	0.15
Sand, common	2.914	119.4	107.9	1.45	1.31
Slag, cinders and ashes	2.034	61.1	53.2	0.52	0.45
Sugar beet	1.263	153.2	112.9	0.81	0.59
Total of above		2,872.5	2,565.1	37.52	33.29
All other commodities	2.660	1,032.9	773.7	11.45	8.57
Total, all commodities[b]		3,905.4	3,338.7	48.97	41.86
Index, all commodities		100.0	85.5	100.0	85.5
Index, specified commodities only		100.0	89.3	100.0	88.7

a Weighted by 1962 prices.

b Excluding free hauled traffic

Source: Based on information supplied by the British Railways Board for the purposes of this study.

[1] Ton mileage figures have been adjusted to exclude free hauled traffic. See Chapter 2 appendix note (b) for details of adjustment.

Table 2.5. Output Weighted[a] and Unweighted, 1958–1962

Rail Freight Transport – General Merchandise

Commodity	Price (pence per ton mile in 1962)	Unweighted Output Quantity Ton miles millions		Weighted Output Value (at 1962 prices) £ million	
		1958	1962	1958	1962
Animal feeding stuffs	2.570	153.3	173.4	1.64	1.86
Beer	4.042	65.3	47.5	1.10	0.80
Butter, margarine, etc.	3.912	17.3	17.0	0.28	0.28
Cement	1.804	122.3	227.5	0.92	1.71
Chemicals not O.T.W.	4.427	109.8	123.1	2.03	2.27
Confectionery	4.227	131.5	162.8	2.32	2.87
Esparto grass & wood pulp	3.253	37.2	41.9	0.50	0.57
Fruit	4.481	106.6	108.2	1.99	2.02
Grain and flour	2.776	191.6	205.5	2.22	2.38
Iron & steel, other products	4.414	735.3	616.5	13.52	11.34
Machinery	7.504	71.6	57.0	2.24	1.78
Meat	8.188	29.7	30.4	1.01	1.04
O.T.W. – chemicals	3.396	86.1	104.8	1.22	1.48
O.T.W. – fuel and petrol	3.076	320.2	439.5	4.10	5.63
O.T.W. – other	5.534	30.4	33.7	0.70	0.78
Paper and cardboard	13.729	31.8	35.0	1.82	2.00
Potatoes	3.355	90.0	72.4	1.26	1.01
Soap and detergents	9.877	9.7	11.4	0.40	0.47
Sugar	2.144	69.9	55.5	0.62	0.50
Textiles and drapery	9.759	22.9	13.3	0.93	0.54
Timber and pitprops	5.605	45.6	23.3	1.06	0.54
Timber – other	5.768	40.9	41.9	0.98	1.01
Wines and spirits	6.696	41.6	45.7	1.16	1.28
Wool	12.723	7.8	8.3	0.41	0.44
Total of above		2,568.6	2,695.6	44.43	44.60
All other commodities	4.191	2,280.1	2,128.0	39.82	37.16
Total all commodities[b]		4,848.7	4,823.6	84.25	81.76
Index, all commodities		100.0	99.5	100.0	97.0
Index, specified commodities only		100.0	104.9	100.0	100.4

a Weighted by 1962 prices

b Excluding free hauled traffic

Source: Based on information supplied by the British Railways Board for the purposes of this study.

the residual minerals traffic. By dividing these receipts by the ton mileage figures for 'other' minerals an estimated average receipt per ton mile for 'other goods' in the minerals group was obtained. The same method was used to obtain the receipts per ton mile for 'other goods' in the general merchandise group.

Table 2.6.   Output Weighted and Unweighted, all Commodities, 1958–1962

Rail Freight Transport

Summary

Commodity group	Price (pence per ton mile in 1962)	Unweighted Output		Weighted Output	
		Quantity Ton miles millions		Value (at 1962 prices) £ million	
		1958	1962	1958	1962
Coal and coke	3.39	8,927	7,304	126.09	103.19
Minerals	a	3,905	3,339	48.97	41.86
General merchandise	b	4,849	4,825	84.25	81.76
Total		17,681	15,467	259.31	226.81
Index		100.0	87.5	100.0	87.5

a   See Table 2.4.

b   See Table 2.5.

Table 2.7.   Output Weighted and Unweighted, Specified Commodities, 1958–1962

Rail Freight Transport

Summary

Commodity group	Price (pence per ton mile in 1962)	Unweighted Output		Weighted Output	
		Quantity Ton miles millions		Value (at 1962 prices) £ million	
		1958	1962	1958	1962
Coal and coke	3.39	8,927	7,304	126.09	103.19
Minerals	a	2,873	2,565	37.52	33.29
General merchandise	b	2,569	2,696	44.43	44.60
Total		14,369	12,565	208.04	181.08
Index		100.0	87.4	100.0	87.0

a   See Table 2.4.

b   See Table 2.5.

Tables 2.4 and 2.5 show the average receipts per ton mile for the commodities in the minerals and in the general merchandise groups respectively, together with the estimated ton miles and an index of output as measured by ton miles with no differentiation of commodities carried, and an index in which the ton miles carried of each commodity are weighted by the average receipts per ton mile for that commodity. For general merchandise the weighted index of output is lower by 2½ per cent than the unweighted index, while in the case of minerals the weighted index shows no change from the unweighted index.

If the 'other goods' are omitted from the calculation, transport of general merchandise commodities in terms of unweighted ton miles is shown to increase by nearly 5 per cent between 1958 and 1962, while the weighted index shows an increase of less than half of one per cent in the same period. This indicates that most of the increase in aggregate ton miles was accounted for by those commodities which involve less value added. In the case of minerals traffic, the transport of the specified commodities in terms of undifferentiated ton miles declined less than *all* the commodities in this group taken together, but although there was a small difference between the weighted and unweighted index of 0.6 per cent the pattern of demand for transporting this group of commodities appears to have changed very little.

The total output of railway freight services includes, of course, coal and coke traffic and this type of traffic accounts for more than half of total rail freight transport in terms of ton miles. Table 2.6 shows the weighted and unweighted output of total rail freight transport in the years 1958 and 1962, including *all* commodities in the general merchandise and minerals categories. The difference in the weighted index shown for general merchandise in Table 2.4 is obscured when combined with the index for minerals and coal and coke. The weighted index, including all commodities, is shown to be the same as the unweighted one in comparing 1958 and 1962, and both show a substantial decline over the period. If specified commodities only are included for minerals and general merchandise in the summary table, together with coal and coke, the result shows a difference of 0.4 per cent between the weighted and unweighted indices, the unweighted index showing less of a decline than the weighted one, (Table 2.7).

3. Road passenger transport

The task of differentiating services provided by public road passenger transport proved to be more difficult than for the other two sectors because of the lack of information on passenger miles in the six different types of service which can be distinguished.

Annual estimates are available of total passenger receipts and of the number of passenger journeys, but estimates of the average length of journey (average stage) are available annually only for London urban stage bus services. However, estimates were obtained from unpublished material in the National Travel Survey, carried out in 1964, on the average length of journey on other types of service in other parts of the country and the Ministry of Transport kindly made this information available to us.

To obtain the price relatives by which to weight the various types of passenger transport, the following use is made of the data given in the 1964 National Travel Survey. From the published figures of number of passenger journeys and the estimates available on average length of journey, it was possible to calculate the number of passenger miles for each type of passenger service. From this derived figure and the published figure of passenger receipts in 1964, an estimate of the average price per passenger mile was obtained. This is shown in column 2 of Table 2.8.

Table 2.8. Output Weighted[a] and Unweighted, 1958–1962

Public Passenger Transport by Road

Type of Service	Price (pence per passenger mile in 1964)	Unweighted Output Quantity Passenger miles 000 m.		Weighted Output Value (in 1964 prices) £ million	
		1958	1962	1958	1962
Urban Stage Bus:					
a. London	2.987	5.63	4.70	70.1	58.5
b. Other main urban areas	2.322	12.45	11.33	120.5	109.6
Express bus	1.818	1.73	2.11	13.1	16.0
Excursion/tours	2.122	1.08	1.08	9.5	9.5
Contract	3.271	1.83	2.12	24.9	28.9
Non-urban stage bus	1.834	22.10	21.10	168.9	161.2
Total		44.80	42.40	407.0	383.7
Index		100.0	94.64	100.0	94.27

a Weighted by 1964 prices.

Source: Passenger Transport in Great Britain 1966; London Transport Annual Reports; 1964 National Travel Survey.

In order to make a comparison between the periods 1958 and 1962, however, certain assumptions had to be made about levels and movements in the average length of journey in types of passenger service other than the London urban bus stage services. For urban stage bus services in other main urban areas, which includes such large conurbations as Manchester and Birmingham, it was assumed that the average length of journey was unlikely to be very different from that in London. This is borne out by the 1964 figures given in the National Travel Survey. The average length of journey on express buses, excursion tours and contract buses was assumed not to have changed between 1962 and 1964 or between 1958 and 1962, and therefore the average length of journey for these services was taken to be the same as indicated in the National Travel Survey. These services are a small proportion of the total. The non-urban stage bus sector includes services operated in smaller urban, semi-urban and rural areas, and the estimated passenger mileage for this sector is found as a residual by subtracting estimated passenger mileage in the first five sectors from the published *total* passenger mileage figures for public service vehicles. Average length of journey can then be found from the passenger miles as estimated and the figure for number of passenger journeys in this sector, which is an estimate published by the Ministry of Transport.[1]

It must be stressed that some of the figures in Table 2.8, are estimates only, but it was thought worthwhile to indicate the way in which the output measure could be improved in public road passenger transport if sufficient and more accurate data were available. As it is, Table 2.8 shows little difference in the movement of output between the years 1958 and 1962 when a weighted index is used instead of an unweighted number of passenger miles. However, this may be due, first, to the fact that it was not possible to make a more detailed breakdown of passenger mileage in the so-called 'non-urban stage' bus services which accounted for one half of all public road passenger transport in both 1958 and in 1962 and, second, the need to assume constant the important variable, average stage, in four out of a total of six sectors.

C.   Shares and Trends in Output

The movement of output in the transport sector as a whole is shown in Table 2.9. This table uses the unweighted figures of output and shows the rate of growth of net output and the changing shares of each sector in the total for the period 1952 to 1962 and for the sub-periods 1952 to 1958 and 1958 to 1962.[2]

The position in 1952, as shown by the figures given in this table, was that the railways (passenger and freight services combined) accounted for just over one quarter of total output, and similarly public road passenger transport also accounted for approximately 26 per cent of the output of total Measured Transport. Road haulage contracting was at that time a relatively small sector as measured by its share of total output. Sea transport and port and inland water transport together accounted for just under one third of total output at that time; with air transport being a relatively insignificant part of total output.

At the end of the period, that is in 1962, the share of railways in total output had dropped to just under 20 per cent and road passenger transport had shown a similar decline in output share. The share of railway freight alone is estimated[3]

---

1 Passenger Transport in Great Britain, Table 42, 1966.

2 The basic data used in the calculations for Table 2.9 are given in the Statistical Appendix, Table A.1.

3 It is not possible to estimate with accuracy the net output of railway freight services. The estimate given above was calculated from the gross output values on the assumption that these reflect the share of freight services in total net output.

	Subsectoral Percentage Shares			Exponential rates of change per annum		
	1952	1958	1962	1952–62	1952–58	1958–62
Railways	27.5	23.6	19.7	-1.93	-1.62	-2.39
Road Passenger Transport	26.1	20.8	18.1	-2.30	-2.84	-1.49
Road Haulage Contracting	12.5	18.4	22.5	7.26	7.43	6.99 [b]
Sea Transport	20.7	21.1	20.5	1.23	1.20	1.29
Port and Inland Water Transport	10.7	11.4	11.7	2.26	2.00	2.67
Air Transport	2.5	4.7	7.5	12.58	11.86	13.67
TOTAL MEASURED TRANSPORT	100.0	100.0	100.0	1.65	1.39	2.04
Postal Services and Telecommunications	...	...	...	3.10	2.32	4.27
Private Road Passenger Travel	...	...	...	10.06	10.90	8.81
Non-Contractual Road Haulage	...	...	...	4.49	2.51	7.45

[a] The output indicators for the period 1952–1958 are 1954 weighted, and those for the period 1958–1962 are 1958 weighted. Details of weights and indicators used are given in the appendix to chapter 1. The concept of output is gross value added (including depreciation); subsidies and 'subsidy equivalents' are excluded.

[b] The 'unadjusted' figure for output. If the output is differentiated and weighted by price relatives, the exponential rate of change per annum is 6.67 over the period 1958–1962.

E

to have fallen from 16 per cent to 9 per cent of total output whereas road haulage contracting nearly doubled its share from 12.5 per cent in 1952 to 22.5 in 1962; in 1962 the share of road haulage contracting in total output was the largest of any sector in Measured Transport. The shares of sea transport and of port and inland water transport remained virtually unchanged in the period while that of air transport showed a threefold increase, although in relation to the total net output of Measured Transport it remained a relatively small sector.

A decline in a sector's share of total output does not, however, necessarily mean an absolute decline in output; if some sectors are growing at a faster rate than the industry average rate of growth, then other sectors' share of output will fall. On the right hand side of Table 2.9 the rates of growth of output in each sector are shown for the period as a whole and for the periods 1952 to 1958 and 1958 to 1962. It will be seen from this side of the Table that over the ten years 1952 to 1962 the most rapid rate of growth of output has been in air transport – the growth being somewhat faster in the period 1958 to 1962 than in the earlier period. Sea transport and port and inland water transport have grown steadily but not spectacularly over the whole period. Road haulage contracting has shown a very marked rate of increase over the period as a whole, although if the weighted output series is used, the annual rate of growth in the period 1958 to 1962 falls from 6.99 per cent to 6.67 per cent.

In both railways and public road passenger transport, however, there has been a steady decline in output over the whole period 1952 to 1962. This decline was faster in the period 1952–58 in road passenger transport than in the railways, but in the period 1958–62 the relative trends in those two sectors were reversed and it was the output of the railways which declined faster. (See also Figure 1).

Many factors may contribute to the changing shares of sectors within the total Measured Transport industry. External factors such as the decline of the coal industry, which has particularly affected rail freight output, or the growth of new industries may partly explain both changing shares and the rate of growth of output. Where the various transport services compete with each other, relative price differences and relative price changes are obviously important considerations but non-price factors such as speed, convenience, door-to-door service, reliability and handling are also important and may often outweigh price factors.

D.   Prices

1.   Road and rail freight transport

The results of this study, have made it possible to make a comparison of estimated prices in 1966 in road and rail freight transport. In Table 2.10 are

Figure 1. Index of Output at 1958 prices, 1952–1965

Index: 1958 = 100

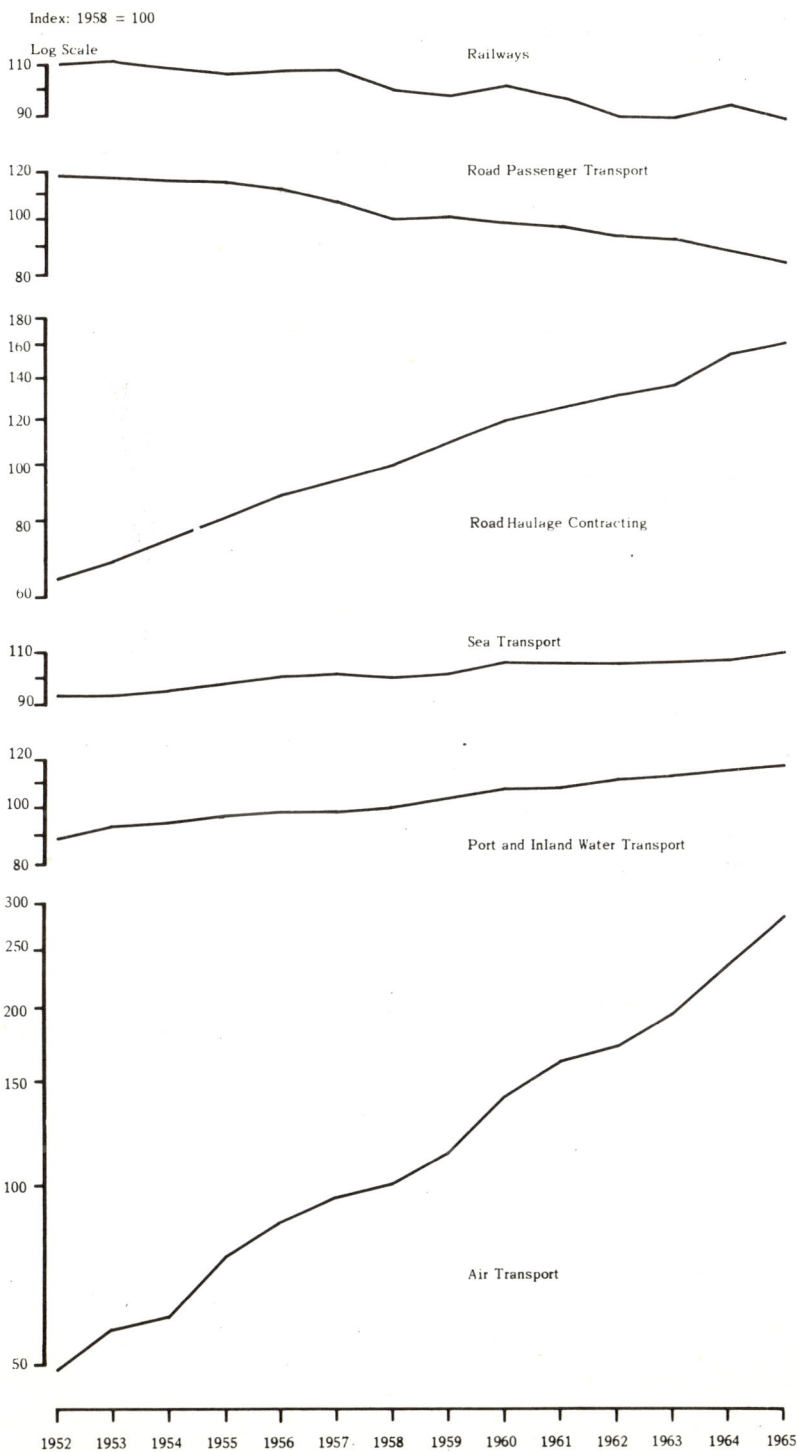

110
90

Railways

Log Scale

120
100
80

Road Passenger Transport

180
160
140
120
100
80
60

Road Haulage Contracting

110
90

Sea Transport

120
100
80

Port and Inland Water Transport

300
250
200
150
100
50

Air Transport

1952 1953 1954 1955 1956 1957 1958 1959 1960 1961 1962 1963 1964 1965

Table 2.10. Comparative Prices per ton mile, 1966
Rail Freight and Road Haulage Contracting

Commodity groups	Rail Freight Transport		Road Haulage Contracting	
	Average rate per ton-mile [a] (pence)	Average length of haul (miles)	Average rate per ton-mile (pence)	Average length of haul (miles)
Foodstuffs				
a. Cereals	2.09	205	4.93	77
b. Fresh fruit, vegetables, nuts and flowers	3.68	200	4.82	107
c. Meat and poultry	6.85	165	11.13	88
d. Fish	5.78	240	8.73	121
e. Dairy produce, eggs	4.79	135	6.76	85
f. Beverages	5.54	180	7.06	72
g. Flour	4.01	90	6.31	84
h. Animal feeding stuffs	2.53	130	5.80	68
i. Oilseeds, nuts and kernels; animal and vegetable oils and fats	6.00	120	-5.93	94
j. Other foods, tobacco	4.11	185	7.74	100
Metals and metal work; hardware				
a. Iron ore and scrap iron	3.46	50	5.84	76
b. Non-ferrous metal ores	3.48	40	5.05	98
c. Iron and steel finished and semi-finished products	3.71	85	4.53	133
d. Non-ferrous metals	5.27	60	5.03	134
e. Metal manufactures	8.64	140	6.78	87
Building and construction materials				
a. Cement	1.53	130	4.23	78
b. Crude minerals other than ore	2.81	70	4.92	34
c. Building materials	4.04	115	5.06	53
Coal, coke and patent fuels	3.64	50	5.63	57
Petroleum and petroleum products	1.72	85	5.08	98

a Including collection and delivery.

Table 2.10. (cont.)   Comparative Prices per ton mile, 1966
Rail Freight and Road Haulage Contracting

Commodity groups	Rail Freight Transport		Road Haulage Contracting	
	Average rate per ton-mile[a] (pence)	Average length of haul (miles)	Average rate per ton-mile (pence)	Average length of haul (miles)
Chemicals				
a. Lime	3.34	85	6.51	54
b. Crude and manufactured fertilisers	2.53	95	4.68	89
c. All other chemicals and plastic materials	3.94	125	5.11	122
d. Tars from coal and natural gas	4.67	55	6.48	69
Other goods				
a. Wood timber and cork	7.80	55	5.86	79
b. Textile fibres and waste	7.84	185	8.70	97
c. Other crude materials	6.44	70	9.50	85
d. Electrical and non-electrical machinery; transport equipment	6.33	170	6.10	102
e. Other manufactured articles	7.74	180	8.88	78

a Including collection and delivery.

Sources: Rail — information supplied by British Rail.

Road Haulage — calculated from results of D.A.E. survey.

given the comparative average prices per ton mile and the average length of haul for the transport of certain commodities by road and by rail.[1] (These prices it should be emphasised, are *average* prices or rates and therefore cannot *directly* take into account such factors as size of load or contract rates which may affect actual prices charged.) The length of haul is undoubtedly an important factor in the determination of price per ton mile. The transport of a commodity load for 100 miles compared to the transport of the same commodity load for a distance of

---

[1] The selection of commodities was determined by the groupings used in the Ministry of Transport, 1962 Road Goods Survey.

10 miles would mean that in the first case fixed costs such as loading and unloading and the waiting time involved are spread over a larger output of the transport service, or in simpler terms, that average terminal costs per ton mile would be declining. The length of haul shown for road goods transport is a weighted average of the average length of haul of road haulage contractors who responded to the survey carried out in connection with this study.

From the figures given in Table 2.10, it will be seen that of the 29 commodities compared[1] all except three (metal manufactures; wood, timber and cork; and machinery and transport equipment) have a lower average receipt per ton mile in railways than the average rate per ton mile charged by road haulage contractors. For two commodities, (oilseeds, nuts and kernels, etc.; and non-ferrous metals), there is little difference in average price or receipt per ton mile. One factor which would in part explain the price differential is differences in the average length of haul. Table 2.10 shows, however, that for 11 of the 24 commodities for which the average receipt per ton mile was lower in rail than in road haulage contracting the average length of haul was longer in road haulage than in rail; prima facie, it could be expected that the average rate per ton mile would be lower rather than higher for these commodities when transported by road haulage contractors. For six of the commodities compared, the average length of haul is very similar in road and rail but the average rate per ton mile is higher in road haulage contracting.

The price differential is shown even more clearly if a comparison is made of the total cost by road and by rail of transporting one ton of each commodity for the same length of haul. This is shown in Table 2.11 for those commodities where the average haul was the same or very nearly the same in both road and rail (the mean average length of haul of road and rail has been used in all cases, Table 2.10).

Table 2.11.   Comparative Cost of Transporting various Commodities by Rail and by Road, 1966

	Total cost of transporting one ton by:		
	RAIL s. d.	ROAD s. d.	Average length of haul (miles)
Flour	29. 1	45. 9	87
Coal, coke and patent fuels	16. 4	25. 4	54
Petroleum and petroleum products	13. 2	38.11	92
Crude and manufactured fertilisers	19. 5	35.10	92
All other chemicals and plastic materials	40. 8	52.10	124
Tars from coal and natural gas	24. 2	33. 6	62

[1]   Covering approximately 90 per cent of both rail freight tonnage and tonnage carried by contractual road haulage.

A comparison of prices in one year between road and rail freight services does not allow any definitive conclusion to be reached with regard to the share of road and rail in total Measured Transport or the growth of output in these sectors. In the first place, relative *changes* in price may be as important as, if not more important than, the relative *level* of prices in consumer choice of transport mode. Secondly, the direct comparison of average prices charged or average receipt per ton mile commodity by commodity could be made only for the year 1966 whereas for reasons explained in the introductory chapter, [1] our survey of productivity covered the years 1952–1962. If the analysis of output growth is extended to 1966, however, it can be shown that between 1962–66 output in rail freight continued to decline, although at a slower rate, while that of road haulage contracting continued to increase at an even faster rate than previously. Table 2.12 shows output trends for rail freight and road haulage contracting for the years 1952–1966.

Table 2.12.   Rail Freight and Road Goods Transport
Change in Output

| | Exponential rates of change per annum | | | |
	1952–66	1952–58	1958–62	1962–66
Road Haulage Contracting	7.53	7.43	6.99	8.29
Rail Freight	−2.46	−3.28	−3.34	−0.39

It is possible that the price differentials in favour of rail shown in Table 2.10 did not exist in earlier years. It is true that the *overall* average receipt per ton mile of freight has increased by 7.5 per cent in rail between 1962 and 1966 whereas in road haulage contracting the average price per ton mile for the 31 commodities increased by an overall average of approximately 20 per cent. [2] If *1962* road haulage average prices per ton mile for each of the 29 commodities are compared with *1966* rail average receipts per ton mile, however, considerable price differentials still exist in favour of the railways for 18 of the 29 commodities. This does suggest that factors other than price may have a considerable bearing on consumer choice of freight transport mode.

A comparison has been made here between the use of road haulage contracting and railway services for transporting commodities; a more complete study would

---

1 See p. 23.

2 Based on the results obtained from the D.A.E. survey.

need to bring in non-contractual road haulage services and to compare quantitative and qualitative factors in all three modes of freight transport. [1]

2. Road and rail passenger transport

In passenger transport, output in terms of passenger miles has declined absolutely in public road passenger services and in railway passenger services during the period 1952 to 1966; the *share* of public road passenger services in total passenger passenger miles has been more than halved as also has the share of British Rail and London Transport (Table 2.13). Private motoring, on the other hand, has more than doubled its share of total passenger miles and has grown at an annual exponential rate of nearly 10 per cent over the period as a whole.

Table 2.13.   Passenger Miles, 1952–1966   Great Britain

	Subsectoral Percentage Shares			Exponential rates of change per annum		
	1952	1958	1966	1952–66	1952–58	1958–66
Road passenger services						
Bus, coach, tram	44.7	30.6	17.9	−2.30	−2.39	−2.23
Private motoring	33.8	51.4	71.5	9.59	10.90	8.60
Rail passenger services						
British Rail	18.3	15.7	9.1	−0.74	1.33	−2.28
London Transport and others	3.2	2.3	1.5	−1.07	−1.45	−0.78
Total Land Passenger Transport Services	100.0	100.0	100.0	4.24	3.91	4.49

This is not altogether surprising since motor car and motor cycle ownership [2] has increased by an annual rate of more than 8 per cent over the same period. However, if the cost per passenger mile to the consumer of the service is compared for public passenger transport, road and rail, and private passenger

---

1 Similar information is not available for 'C' licence vehicles over a number of years. Such information as is available indicates that the average cost to user per ton mile for non-contractual road haulage is above that for both contractual road haulage and rail freight services. Estimates derived from data given on Table 6.1 in Chapter 6 show average cost to user as follows:

Freight Transport Mode	Average cost to user per ton mile in 1958 (pence)
Road Haulage Contracting	5.5
Non-Contractual Road Freight Transport	10.7
Rail Freight Transport	3.4

2 As measured by licences current.

transport by road, then there is some evidence that the cost per passenger mile is not the main determining factor when consumers make decisions on the mode of transport to be used. Table 2.14 shows average receipts per passenger mile on rail services (British Rail and London Transport separately), and on public road passenger services. Average expenditure (personal and business) per passenger mile on private motoring is also shown. Although average expenditure per passenger mile on private motoring (including an estimate for depreciation) has changed remarkably little over the period, the average expenditure in money terms in 1953 was approximately three times higher per passenger mile than it was in the other three types of passenger transport. In 1966 expenditure per passenger mile on private motoring was still nearly twice as much as it was on British Rail or public road passenger services and one third higher than the average receipt per passenger mile on London Transport.

The expenditure and receipts per passenger mile shown in Table 2.14 are in money terms and do not take account of the social costs which each mode of transport may cause and which are borne externally to the four modes considered collectively. The internally borne social costs, (which include some of the external social costs imposed by each of the sectors considered here), are to some extent taken account of in the figures for private motoring and public road passenger transport [1] (e.g. the additional petrol and other running costs incurred in traffic congestion), but no attempt has been made to assess social costs which are borne externally to the four modes considered collectively.

Expenditure per passenger mile may differ in these four modes of transport because of the different lengths of journey undertaken. A comparison of expenditure (or receipts) per passenger mile should therefore take this factor into account. From the information which is available,[2] it has been estimated that the average length of journey by British Rail is 20 miles for all services, and by public road passenger transport it is estimated at 3.25 miles in 1962. Both averages include, however, inter-city services, suburban commuter services and express services by road and by rail; a more complete comparison would need to distinguish between average cost per passenger mile and average length of journey on each different type of service provided by road and rail. On the other hand, terminal costs are likely to be a lower proportion of total costs for a comparable length of journey in passenger than in freight transport services, because in passenger services the terminal and stage waiting time is shorter and loading and unloading passengers costs less than unloading and loading freight. A comparison of price per passenger mile, even though the length of journey differs in each case, is therefore more meaningful for passenger services than for freight services.

It may also be noticed that not all passenger transport services are substitutes for one another. Locational imperfections and lack of flexibility in public rail

---

1 There are no internally borne social costs in rail passenger transport.

2 Statistical Appendix, Table F.2.

Table 2.14 Expenditure on Rail and Road Passenger Transport 1952–66

Great Britain

	British Rail			London Transport (Rail)			Public Road Services[a]			Private Motoring[b]		
	Total receipts	Passenger miles	Average receipt per passenger mile	Total receipts	Passenger miles	Average receipt per passenger mile	Total receipts	Passenger miles	Average receipt per passenger mile	Total expenditure	Passenger miles	Average expenditure per passenger mile
	(£ million)	(000 million)	(pence)	(£ million)	(000 million)	(pence)	(£ million)	(000 million)	(pence)	(£ million)	(000 million)	(pence)
1952	111.9	20.5	1.31	18.0	3.6	1.20	250.2	50.1	1.20	...	37.9	...
1953	114.7	20.6	1.34	18.3	3.5	1.25	260.7	50.7	1.23	627.2	42.1	3.58
1954	116.6	20.7	1.35	19.2	3.5	1.32	262.2	50.0	1.26	735.0	47.2	3.74
1955	118.2	20.3	1.40	20.6	3.5	1.41	276.8	49.8	1.33	774.2	54.3	3.42
1956	127.5	21.1	1.45	22.2	3.4	1.57	289.1	48.6	1.43	833.0	59.5	3.36
1957	138.9	22.6	1.48	23.2	3.3	1.69	301.7	45.9	1.58	842.8	59.9	3.38
1958	138.0	22.1	1.50	24.4	3.3	1.77	297.8	43.4	1.65	1,038.8	72.9	3.42
1959	140.0	22.3	1.51	24.1	3.2	1.81	305.5	44.1	1.66	1,156.4	82.1	3.38
1960	151.3	21.5	1.69	26.4	3.2	1.98	314.7	43.9	1.72	1,283.8	88.9	3.47
1961	157.5	21.1	1.79	28.5	3.1	2.21	329.4	43.1	1.83	1,479.8	97.7	3.64
1962	161.1	19.7	1.96	29.8	3.1	2.31	341.0	42.4	1.93	1,607.2	103.7	3.72
1963	161.8	19.2	2.02	32.1	3.1	2.49	349.4	41.5	2.02	1,754.2	110.5	3.81
1964	167.2	19.9	2.02	34.6	3.1	2.68	364.4	40.3	2.17	1,999.2	125.5	3.82
1965	173.0	18.7	2.22	35.6	3.0	2.85	373.9	37.6	2.39	2,256.0	134.8	4.02
1966	179.4	18.5	2.33	39.1	3.1	3.03	391.6	36.3	2.59	2,493.1	145.1	4.12

a Including London Transport and all bus, coach and tram services.

b Includes consumer and business expenditure, taxes and estimated depreciation of vehicles, but excludes the purchase of new vehicles. Local and central government expenditure on roads is also excluded. A deduction of 2 per cent each year for expenditure in Northern Ireland has been made from the published figures.

Source: Highway Statistics 1963 and 1966; Passenger Transport in Great Britain 1963 and 1967: Ministry of Transport.

and road passenger services make them less than perfect substitutes for private motoring. There are, of course, many instances where public road and rail services are perfectly substitutable for one another (e.g. long distance coach or rail services between London and Edinburgh) and in these instances the price factor may be more important in consumer decision-making than any qualitative factors such as speed.

In passenger transport, as in freight transport, insufficient information is available to make any quantitative assessment of the non-price factors which enter into the decision to use different types of transport services. In a recent report by the Prices and Incomes Board[1] an assessment of one factor, speed, was made, together with actual average fares or costs based on 12 inter-city routes of an average distance of 200 miles, by different types of transport. The results are given below:

	Rail	Coach	Motor car
Average journey time	3 hrs. 35 min.	8 hours	5 hours [a]
Average actual fare	46s. 11d.[b]	30s.	66s. 8d. [c]

a Based on an average speed of 40 m.p.h.

b Second class.

c Running costs only (assuming one person per car).

This indicates that railways have had an advantage in both price and speed over the motor car and in speed over coach services, and the decline in the share of public road and rail passenger services must be explained by other non-price factors, such as door to door service, flexibility and the general increase in motor car ownership, which outweigh considerations of both price and speed.

Summary

In this chapter, two main aspects of output in Measured Transport were considered. First, the accuracy of the output measure in three of the six sectors was examined more closely and, second, the trends in output and the output shares in all six sectors of Measured Transport for the period 1952–1962 were considered. An attempt was also made to assess the relative importance of price and non-price factors as determinants of consumers' choice of transport service.

---

1 National Board for Prices and Incomes, Report No. 72. Proposed Increases by British Railways Board in Certain Country-wide Fares and Charges. HMSO. Cmnd. 3656, 1968.

Measurement of output

Where physical indicators of net output movements are in terms of undifferentiated ton miles or passenger miles — as is the case in most of the national income data on transport — they are likely to be more or less inaccurate indicators of output movements. The main reason for this is that the units of the indicator are non-homogeneous in character and in the amount of output they represent. As the pattern of demand for these transport services changes through time, units of service of different types will account for changing proportions of the total value added. An undifferentiated aggregation of physical units of output will not take account of such changes in the pattern of demand and output.

The method employed in this chapter to differentiate ton miles and passenger miles is to use a system of price relative weights whenever the required data could be assembled. Relative prices in a base year are assumed to reflect relative differences in the value of net output and they are used as proxies for this. This process of differentiation and weighting which recognises the heterogeneous nature of transport services and goes some way to take account of it, is attempted in road haulage contracting, rail freight transport and public road passenger transport for the years 1958 and 1962.

In road haulage contracting in the period 1958—1962 the differentiated measure of output movements indicates an exponential rate of change of output of 6.67 per cent per annum (6.99 per cent in the case of undifferentiated aggregation). The undifferentiated and unweighted indicator therefore exaggerates the increase in output and suggests that the pattern of demand for contractual road haulage services is changing in favour of services which require less value added per physical unit of output.

In the case of rail freight transport, very small differences were found between the differentiated and undifferentiated indexes, and in public road passenger transport the not too well founded data and the slight degree of differentiation and weighting by type of service which was found to be possible did not permit any definitive conclusion to be drawn.

Output shares and trends

Table 2.15 summarises the movements in output in the six sectors of Measured Transport together with the three other sectors in Transport and Communication. It shows that output in air transport, road haulage contracting, and private road passenger travel increased at a relatively fast rate throughout the whole period, whereas in the railways and in public road passenger transport output declined at an annual rate of 1.9 per cent and 2.3 per cent respectively. The provisional figures for the period 1962—65 indicate that the trend of output noticeable in the years 1952—62 has continued in the later period. In railways, the rate of decline in output has slackened but public road passenger transport has declined even more rapidly than in the previous period while the fast growing sectors (air, road haulage contracting and private road passenger transport) have continued to grow as fast as, or faster than, in the previous sub-period 1958—62.

Table 2.15. Movements and Levels of Net Output, 1952–1962, 1952–58, 1958–62, 1962–65 and 1958

Sectors of Measured Transport in Ranking Order of Output Movements 1952–62	Movements				Levels
	Percentages at exponential rates of change per annum				£ millions at 1958 prices
	1952–62	1952–58	1958–62	1962–65 (Provisional) [a]	1958
Air Transport	12.58	11.86	13.67	16.65	55
Road Haulage Contracting	7.26	7.43	6.99 [b]	6.90	214
Port and Inland Water Transport	2.26	2.00	2.67	1.92	133
Sea Transport	1.23	1.20	1.29	1.47	245
Railways	– 1.93	– 1.62	– 2.39	– 0.18	274 [c]
Road Passenger Transport	– 2.30	– 2.84	– 1.49	– 3.74	242
MEASURED TRANSPORT	1.65	1.39	2.04	3.08	1,163
Postal Services and Telecommunications	3.10	2.32	4.27	6.28	377
Private Road Passenger Travel [d]	10.06	10.90	8.81	8.75	–
Non-contractual Road Haulage [d]	4.49	2.51	7.45	6.32	–
GROSS DOMESTIC PRODUCT	3.02	2.32	3.17	3.90	20,130

a Provisional because the output indicator for road haulage contracting is only an extrapolation, cf. 'Highway Statistics 1967', Table 32, footnote. Ministry of Transport, London.

b Before correction for aggregation bias of 0.32 per cent, and using ton mileage figures to one place of decimals only.

c Excluding subsidies and 'subsidy equivalents'.

d Output as measured in terms of estimated passenger miles and ton miles, in both cases unweighted.

Relative prices

Many factors will contribute to the growth of output and the share of sectors within the Measured Transport industry. In this study, it was possible to make a comparison for the year 1966 of estimated prices per ton mile for 29 commodities in road and rail freight transport and in passenger travel by a comparison of expenditure per passenger mile on rail, public road passenger transport and private motoring for the period 1952–1966. In freight transport, the railways appear to have had a more competitive price structure in 1966 than road haulage contracting for transporting most of the 29 commodities. For seven of the commodities or commodity groups, the average length of haul was longer on the railways than it was road haulage contracting, and this helps to explain the price differential in favour of rail. For eleven of the 29 commodities, however, the average haul was longer by road but the average rate per ton mile was higher than on the railways. For those commodities where the average haul was the same (or very nearly the same) in both road and rail, the price differential was in favour of railways.

Similarly, the level of expenditure per passenger mile on publicly provided passenger transport was at a lower level throughout the period than the level of expenditure per passenger mile on private motoring. The rate of increase in expenditure per passenger mile between 1952 and 1962 was greater, however, in publicly provided passenger transport services than in private motoring. Even allowing for the fact that rates of change in prices may be as important in consumer choice as the relative levels of prices, the evidence nevertheless does suggest that factors such as speed, flexibility, convenience, door-to-door service, reliability and handling have been sufficient to outweigh relative price as the determining factor in consumers' choice of transport mode.

Appendix to Chapter 2

Survey of road haulage contractors carried out by the Department of Applied Economics

(a)   Sampling procedure

The basis of the sample was a one per cent sample of all operators in each of the size groups. This one per cent sample was then weighted by the ratio of the average fleet size of each group divided by the average fleet size of the base group (in this instance, the 1–5 fleet size group). The average fleet size shown below was obtained from the Ministry of Transport's published figures of public haulage operators as at 31st December 1963.

Fleet size	Average number of vehicles per operator	
1–5 vehicles	1.77	(2)
6–20 vehicles	9.97	(10)
21 vehicles and over	45.16[a]	(45)

a Excluding Transport Holding Company and British Railways fleets.

The percentage of operators to be included in the sample in each size group was calculated using the above average number of vehicles. This was done on the assumption that there had been no drastic change in the distribution of the average fleet size between 1963 and 1967. The basic sampling frame was therefore as follows:

1–5 size group $\qquad 1\% \times \dfrac{2}{2} = 1\%$ of operators

6–20 size group $\qquad 1\% \times \dfrac{10}{2} = 5\%$ of operators

21 and over size group $\qquad 1\% \times \dfrac{45}{2} = 22.5\%$ operators

The response from the initial sample of operators selected on the above basis was, however, rather unsatisfactory partly because many of the adressees had moved. It was therefore decided to double the sample size in all three groups. The final sampling frame was therefore as follows:

Fleet size	Operators in sample	Percentage of operators	Estimated number of vehicles in sample	Percentage of vehicles (1963)
1–5 vehicles	878	2	1,550	2
6–20 vehicles	666	10	6,640	11
21 vehicles and over	698	45	31,520	41
	2,242		39,710	

(b) Estimation of ton mileage of free-hauled traffic by rail, 1958 and 1962

Railway Freight Tonnage and Ton Mileage

(1)	(2)	(3)	(4)	(5)	(6)
Ton-miles (000 m)	Average haul (miles)	Tonnage forwarded (1) ÷ (2) (millions)	Tonnage (millions)	Tonnage (millions)	Ton-miles (millions)
(including free hauled on revenue earning trains)			(Revenue earning)	(Free hauled on revenue earning trains)	
General Merchandise					
1958	5,231	131.7	39.7	36.8	2.9	381.9
1962	5,200	134.3	38.7	35.9	2.8	376.0
Minerals					
1958	4,268	73.9	57.8	52.9	4.9	362.1
1962	3,600	70.9	50.8	47.1	3.7	262.3

Sources: Col. 1. British Transport Commission, Annual Report and Accounts, 1962. Vol. II.

Col. 2. British Transport Commision, Annual Report and Accounts, 1962. Vol. II

Col. 3. Derived by dividing Col. 1 by Col. 2, since $T = \dfrac{TM}{AH}$

Col. 4. Annual Abstract of Statistics, 1963.

Col. 5. Derived by subtracting Col. 4 from Col. 3.

Col. 6. Derived by multiplying Col. 2 by Col. 5. (This makes the assumption that the average haul for free-hauled traffic is the same as that for revenue earning traffic).

(c) Commodity classifications used in the 1958 and 1962 ministry of transport surveys of the transport of goods by road

1958

Group 1. Groceries, fish, etc. (groceries, bread and confectionery, fish, eggs, school meals, etc.).

2. Meat and animal products.

3. Fruits and vegetables, flowers

4. Fresh milk and cream, milk powder.

5. Live animals.

6. Other agricultural produce and requirements (grain, potatoes, flour, beet, feeding stuffs for animals, linseed oil).

Group 7. Beverages and tobacco.

8. Wood, lumber and cork (including manufactures other than furniture).

9. Metals and metalwork (including girders, castings, ingots, sanitary, plumbing, heating and lighting fixtures and fittings if mainly of metal), hardware.

10. Building and constructional materials (excluding iron and steelwork, timber, sanitary, plumbing, lighting and heating fixtures and fittings): including sand, gravel, cement, bricks, slates, tiles, rubble and hardcore.

11. Other crude materials not elsewhere specified (including leather, rubber, fibres, china clay, wood pulp).

12. Coal, coke, and patent fuels.

13. Petroleum, oils, lubricants and related materials.

14. Chemicals and chemical products (including manufactured fertilisers, plastics, paint, lime).

15. Machinery (including electrical apparatus, wireless and television sets, motor car parts, instruments).

16. Furniture.

17. Manufactured goods not elsewhere specified (cloth, clothing, footwear, glass, pottery, fancy goods, paper, newspaper, laundry).

18. Unallocated (homogeneous loads).

19. Unallocated (mixed loads).

20. Residuals and not known.

1962

Foodstuffs

1.	Cereals	Wheat, spelt, maslin, rice, barley maize, rye, oats, unmilled cereals
2.	Fresh fruit, vegetables, nuts and flowers	
3.	Meat and Poultry	Fresh, frozen, dried, salted, smoked or preserved meat
4.	Fish	Fresh, frozen, dried, salted, smoked, preserved or canned fish
5.	Live animals	
6.	Dairy produce, eggs	Milk and cream (whether fresh, evaporated, condensed or powdered), butter, cheese
7.	Beverages	Beer, wine, spirits for drinking, other alcoholic beverages; table waters, mineral waters, lemonade, soft drinks
8.	Flour	

F

Foodstuffs (cont.)

9.	Animal feeding stuffs	Hay, straw, husks, oil-seed cake, fodder, bran, shapes, food wastes, prepared animal feed
10.	Oil seeds, nuts and kernels; animal and vegetable oils and fats	Derivations of animal and vegetable oils and fats such as stearine and stearine pitch
11.	Other foods; tobacco	Cereal flakes and other cereal preparations, malt, sugar beet, dried or de-hydrated fruits, preserved fruits, fruit juices, dry pulses, hops, preserved vegetables, edible vegetable preparations, sugar (refined or not), molasses, glucose, dextrose, other sugars, sugar confectionery, sugar preparations, natural honey, coffee, cocoa, chocolate, tea, spices, margarine, lard, ice cream; tobacco (manufactured or unmanufactured)

Metals and metal
work; hardware

12.	Iron ore and scrap iron	Hematites, roasted iron pyrites, slag for re-smelting, flue dust, ferrous scrap
13.	Non-ferrous metal ores	Bauxite, cryolite, non-ferrous metal scrap
14.	Iron and steel finished and semi-finished products	Crude steel, pig-iron, ferro alloys, iron and steel billets, slabs, sheets, bars, coils, rods, wires, plates, extrusions, angles, shapes, sections, hoops, strips, rails, tubes, pipes, fittings, castings, forgings
15.	Non-ferrous metals	Unwrought aluminium and aluminium alloys, unwrought lead and lead alloys, unwrought zinc and zinc alloys, unwrought silver and platinum, non-ferrous bars, rods, plates, sheets, wire, pipes, tubes, castings and forgings
16.	Metal manufactures	Metal structural parts and frameworks, cables of any metal, sanitary, lighting, plumbing and heating fixtures and fittings made of metal

Building and
construction materials

17.	Cement	Portland Cement
18.	Crude minerals other than ore	Sand, gravel, crushed stones, granite chips, pebbles, macadam, pumice, clay, bentonite, chamotte, sillimanite, cyanite, building and monumental (demension) stone, plaster, limestone for industry, sulphur, unroasted iron pyrites, salt (crude or refined), slag for civil engineering use, chalk, quartz, quartzite, asphalt

19. Building materials — Bricks, tiles, other clay construction materials, refractory construction materials, pieces of concrete or cement, premixed cement, asbestos, cement and fibro-cement and other fabricated building materials, pumiceous agglomerates, glass, ceramic sanitary fixtures, glassware, pottery ceramics

20. Coal and coke — Patent solid fuel, briquettes, lignite, peat

21. Petroleum and petroleum products; gas — Petroleum (crude or refined) motor spirit, light oils, lamp oil, kerosene, paraffin, white spirit, gas oil, fuel oil, diesel oil, distilled oil, lubricants, bitumen, bituminous mixtures, paraffin wax, gaseous hydrocarbons (methane, propane, butane, calor gas, bottogas propogas, etc., whether liquefied or compressed, in bulk or in cylinders)

Chemicals

22. Lime — Quick lime, builders' lime, slaked lime, agricultural lime

23. Crude and manufactured fertilisers — Sodium-nitrate (chile saltpetre), crude phosphates, crude potash salts, basic slag, other phosphatic fertilisers, potassic fertilisers, nitrogenous fertilisers, composite fertilisers

24. All other chemicals and plastics materials — Sulphuric acid, sodium hydroxide, caustic soda, soda lye, sodium carbonate, sodium bicarbonate, calcium carbide, alumina, glycerine lyes, alcohol, acetates, plastic in bulk, plastic sheet, plastic extrusions, colouring and tanning materials, medicinal and pharmaceutical products, perfumes, polishing preparations, hunting ammunition, starch, dextrin, starchy substances, gluten, oxygen, hydrogen, nitrogen, acetylene, carbon dioxide

25. Tars from coal and natural gas — Benzol, pitch mineral tar, napthalene, tar oils

Other goods

26. Wood, timber and cork — Sawn, squared, or prepared timber, railway sleepers, pit props, poles, logs, wood for pulping, pulp wood, fire wood, charcoal, wood waste, cork, cork chips, cork waste

Other goods (cont.)

27.	Textile fibres and waste	Wool, cotton, silk, jute, flax, sisal, hemp and other vegetable textile fibres; artificial and synthetic fibres; waste materials from textile fabrics; rags
28.	Other crude materials	Hides, skins, furs (undressed), crude rubber, synthetic rubber, reclaimed rubber, cellulose, pulp, wood pulp, waste paper, old paper, non-edible animal and vegetable raw materials, and crude materials not elsewhere specified
29.	Electrical and non-electrical machinery; transport equipment	Tractors, agricultural machines (assembled or dismantled), electrical equipment, transport equipment including motor vehicles (assembled or dismantled); parts for these items. All other electrical and non-electrical machinery
30.	Furniture removals	
31.	Other manufactured articles	New furniture, leather goods, rubber manufactures, wood manufactures, cork manufactures, paper and paperboard and manufactures thereof, printed matter, textile fabrics and yarns, clothes, optical and precision goods, clocks, watches, jewellery, veneer sheets, plywood, wood panels, travel goods, handbags, hosiery, footwear
32.	Mixed loads	
33.	Empty containers	

3   Factor Inputs

The primary aim in this Chapter is to study trends in employment and, in various more refined senses, labour input; and then to make a similar study of trends in capital stock and capital input. The employment and capital input trends are then brought together for the purpose of studying trends in capital intensity (capital stock per person employed). An analysis is then made by sector and by industry of labour and capital requirements per unit of output and, finally, of combined factor requirements per unit of output.

The chief concern is with time trends and less attention is paid to the absolute levels of employment and capital stock, although these figures are provided in the Statistical Appendix (Sections B and C). In relative terms, employment, labour input and capital input are analysed by sector shares, and an index of capital intensity shows the positions of the sectors in relation to the average for Measured Transport as a whole (Table 3.6.).

A comparative study of absolute levels is deferred until the productivity ratios themselves have been calculated, and as these, to be meaningful, must be in terms of net output per unit of combined labour and capital input, there seems little point in analysing labour and capital inputs *separately* in absolute terms.

A.   Labour Input

The analysis is sequential and four stages may be distinguished. The form of the first three stages is in terms of shares and trends presented in adjacent format. The trends are exponential over short run periods 1952 to 1958 and 1958 to 1962, and over the medium run period 1952 to 1962. The shares are for 1952, 1958 and 1962. The first stage of the analysis is of employment in terms of manpower in work and is shown on Table 3.1. The second stage (Table 3.2) is an analysis of labour input in terms of standardised labour units, by this means an allowance is made for the *intra*-sectoral labour 'quality' shift, as defined,[1] over time. The third stage (Table 3.3) brings into account the effect of changes in weekly hours of work and in public and annual holidays

---

[1] See Chapter 1, page 24, and also the Statistical Appendix, Table B2 and note 1 to Table B2. The term 'quality', as applied here and elsewhere in this paper to labour shifts, carries the meaning given on page 25. A methodological note on the *inter*-sectoral 'quality' shifts in Measured Transport may be found at the end of this Chapter, page 108.

allowed. The fourth stage, shown in Table 3.4, brings together the trends analysed in the three earlier stages and presents them in sequential form. This starts with a simple count of the number of people (whether adult males, females, youths or boys) in work, and ends with labour input in terms of standardised male equivalent hours per annum after allowing for and separately distinguishing the *intra*-sectoral labour 'quality' shifts, changes in the weighted average of weekly hours worked per standard labour unit, changes in public and annual holidays allowed and, finally, for the Measured Transport and Transport and Communication industries only, the *inter*-sectoral labour 'quality' shift. These analyses are supplemented by graphs (Figures 2A to G), and by more detailed data, accompanied by explanatory notes, in the Statistical Appendix.

1. Manpower

In terms of manpower in work, the analysis in Table 3.1 shows a decline of −0.94 per cent per annum in employment in the Measured Transport industry over the period 1952 to 1962. The evidence presented by the differentiation of this trend by sub-periods indicates a faster rate of decline in the more recent sub-period, 1958 and 1962, than in the earlier one, and the evidence from Figure 2G (which is on a logarithmic scale) shows a further quickening in the rate of decline over the years 1962 to 1965. The sectoral components of this movement are a rapid rise in employment in air transport, a relatively small sector in terms of labour requirements, and a slower upward movement in the larger road haulage sector. These upward movements are more than offset by an increasingly rapid decline in labour demand by the railways, by far the largest employer of labour in the industry, and by a more moderate rate of decline in employment in sea transport and in ports and inland water transport. The rate of decline of employment in road passenger transport is greater than the industry average in the first sub-period, but less in the second.

The analysis of sectors outside the Measured Transport industry shows that miscellaneous transport services and storage, a relatively small sector, is increasing its labour force at a comparatively rapid rate, faster even than the rate for air transport. Postal services and telecommunications, a relatively large sector, is also increasing its demand for labour but at a lower rate than this, although it is high in relation to the Measured Transport industry as a whole.

The Measured Transport industry corresponds in scope to all 'organised' transport in the economy. 'Organised' is used in the economic sense of organisation on an enterprise basis with specialisation in the provision of transport services which enter a market. The transport services which are excluded by this definition are the miscellaneous services already mentioned, the non-contractual road haulage transport and private passenger transport by motor car, motor cycle and pedal cycle. Using this definition of the Measured Transport industry, it is now possible to set its demand for labour in context with the demand for labour in the service industries as a whole. A comparison of rates of change of labour input shows that the rate for Measured Transport

Table 3.1. Labour Input, Crude[a]

United Kingdom SIC 1958

	Sectoral shares, percentages			Exponential rates of change per annum		
	1952	1958	1962	1952–62	1952–58	1958–62
Railways	37.0	36.1	33.7	-1.86	-1.34	-2.64
Road Passenger Transport	23.3	22.3	22.5	-1.31	-1.62	-0.84
Road Haulage Contracting	14.5	15.0	17.0	0.70	-0.33	2.23
Sea Transport	11.6	12.3	12.0	-0.62	0.10	-1.70
Port and Inland Water Transport	11.6	11.6	11.2	-1.28	-0.82	-1.97
Air Transport	2.0	2.7	3.6	4.82	3.61	6.67
TOTAL MEASURED TRANSPORT	100.0/77.8	100.0/76.0	100.0/72.9	-0.94	-0.91	-1.00
Miscellaneous Transport Services and Storage	2.6	3.3	4.4	4.99	3.44	7.30
Postal Services and Telecommunications	19.6	20.7	22.6	1.12	0.41	2.19
TOTAL TRANSPORT AND COMMUNICATION	100.0	100.0	100.0	-0.31	-0.52	0.03

a Manpower in work. The self-employed, employees in work and those temporarily stopped are included; the longer term unemployed are excluded.

Table 3.2. Labour Input, Standardised Units[a]

United Kingdom SIC 1958

	Sectoral shares, percentages			Exponential rates of change per annum		
	1952	1958	1962	1952–62	1952–58	1958–62
Railways	36.7	35.8	33.5	−1.78	−1.20	−2.65
Road Passenger Transport	23.8	22.7	22.9	−1.30	−1.61	−0.86
Road Haulage Contracting	14.5	15.0	17.1	0.73	−0.25	2.19
Sea Transport	11.5	12.2	11.8	−0.66	0.11	−1.79
Port and Inland Water Transport	11.7	11.8	11.4	−1.18	−0.74	−1.85
Air Transport	1.8	2.5	3.3	5.19	4.11	6.80
TOTAL MEASURED TRANSPORT	100.0/79.2	100.0/77.3	100.0/74.7	−0.90	−0.83	−1.00
Miscellaneous Transport Services and Storage	2.4	3.1	4.1	4.81	3.56	6.71
Postal Services and Telecommunications	18.4	19.6	21.2	1.09	0.66	1.74
TOTAL TRANSPORT AND COMMUNICATION	100.0	100.0	100.0	−0.32	−0.43	−0.16

a Standard 'male equivalent' labour units.
See Statistical Appendix Section B. Technical Note 1 to Table B.2 for methods of calculation.

over the period 1952 to 1962 was 2.40 per cent per annum[1] lower than that in all Civilian Service industries excluding Measured Transport, and this differential has been higher in the more recent period, 1958–62. The trend of demand for labour by the Measured Transport industry is therefore markedly lower and divergent from the demand for labour in the Service industries as a whole. In part this is due, on the transport side, to the substitution of 'own account' transport, both freight and passenger, for contractual, marketed transport. It has been indicated that the labour content of 'own account' transport output is indeterminable.[2] The measurement problems are such that no estimate can at present be made of the demand for labour by all transport services.

2. Standardised labour units

In Table 3.2 the analysis of labour demand is in terms of standard labour units, and the intra-sectoral labour 'quality' shift is represented by the difference between Table 3.1 and Table 3.2, and is in fact the exponential rates of change in Table 3.2 minus the corresponding rates in Table 3.1. The values of the sectoral and industry 'quality' shifts on this basis are shown in Table 3.4, Row 3. They are of significant size, defined as accounting for five per cent or more of the rate of change of demand for labour in terms of manpower in work, in the following sectors in the periods shown.

Decline, in intra-sectoral labour 'quality':

Road Haulage Contracting, 1952–58

Sea Transport, 1958–62

Postal Services and Telecommunications, 1958–62

Miscellaneous Transport Services and Storage, 1958–62

Increase

Railways, 1952–58

Road Haulage Contracting, 1952–58

---

1 This is a differential rate of change of manpower in work in exponential terms. It is the rate for total Civilian Services (excluding Measured Transport) minus the rate for Measured Transport. The rates for each variable are as follows:

	1	2	3
	Total Civilian Services (excl. Measured Transport)	Measured Transport	Differential (Col. 1–Col. 2)
1952–62	1.46	−0.94	2.40
1952–58	1.13	−0.91	2.04
1958–62	1.96	−1.00	2.96

2 The labour involved in 'own account' freight and passenger transport services is only engaged in transport work for a fraction, and often only a small fraction, of the total normal working period, and it is indeed arguable whether the driver of a private passenger motor car is working at all, in any meaningful sense.

Sea Transport, 1952–58

Air Transport, 1952–58 and 1958–62

No significant change

Road Passenger Transport

A decline in intra-sectoral labour 'quality' reflects a shift towards the employment of workers with lower net productivity, as measured by their average remuneration per hour of work,[1] and, similarly in the opposite direction, for an increase in intra-sectoral labour 'quality'.

The pattern which emerges from this sectoral analysis is that of increasing labour 'quality' in the earlier period, 1952–58, and declining 'quality' in the more recent period, 1958–62. These changes by sector are reflected in significant terms in the figures for the Transport and Communication industry (Table 3.4 Row 3). In the Measured Transport industry there occurs a significant increase in the period 1952–58, but no change at all in the more recent period, 1958–62.

The standardisation of labour input affects the shares of the various sectors of the Measured Transport industry in the following differential way.

Sectors where the share of total labour input is *greater* in standardised terms than in crude terms in 1952, 1958, 1962.

Road Passenger Transport

Port and Inland Water Transport

Sectors where the share of total labour input is *less* in standardised terms than in crude terms in 1952, 1958 and 1962.

Railways

Sea Transport

Air Transport

In Road Haulage Contracting there is virtually no change in the sector's share of total labour input in crude terms and in standardised terms.

In standardised terms, the share of Measured Transport as a whole in total labour input in the Transport and Communication industry is significantly greater in each year examined than it is in crude terms. A clearly important factor in these differences of share is the large labour force in postal services and telecommunications, coupled with the relatively low proportion of adult male workers in this labour force compared with the Measured Transport industry as a whole.

---

[1] On the principle, described in Chapter 1, that the wage is equal to the net marginal product of labour, and all workers of the grade concerned are paid according to the net product of the marginal worker.

Figure 2A. Railways

Index 1952 = 100
Log Scale

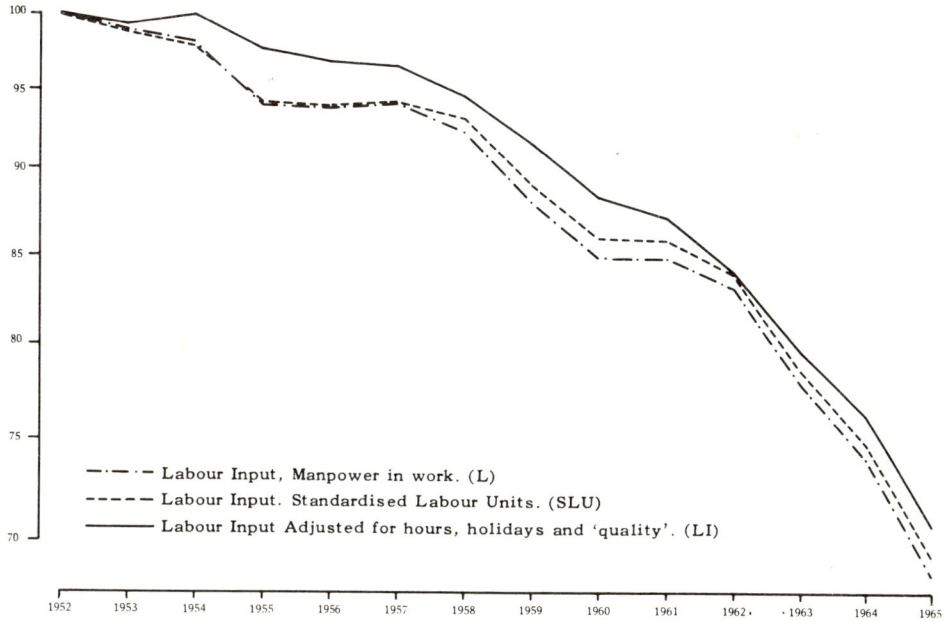

Labour Input, Manpower in work. (L)
Labour Input. Standardised Labour Units. (SLU)
Labour Input Adjusted for hours, holidays and 'quality'. (LI)

Figure 2B. Road Passenger Transport

Index: 1952 = 100
Log. Scale

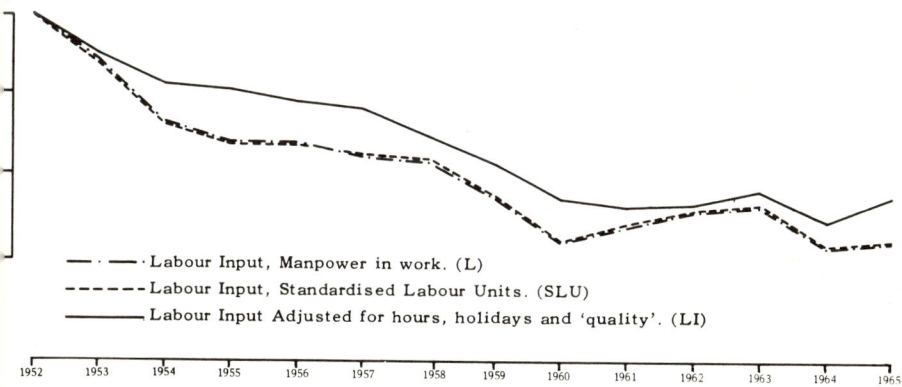

Labour Input, Manpower in work. (L)
Labour Input, Standardised Labour Units. (SLU)
Labour Input Adjusted for hours, holidays and 'quality'. (LI)

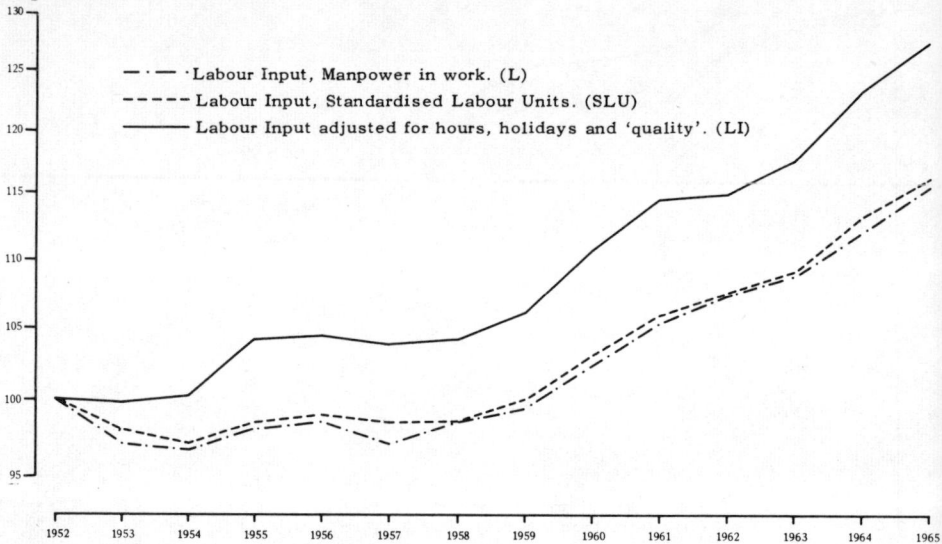

Figure 2C.   Road Haulage Contracting

Index: 1952 = 100
Log. Scale

--- · --- · Labour Input, Manpower in work. (L)
- - - - Labour Input, Standardised Labour Units. (SLU)
——— Labour Input adjusted for hours, holidays and 'quality'. (LI)

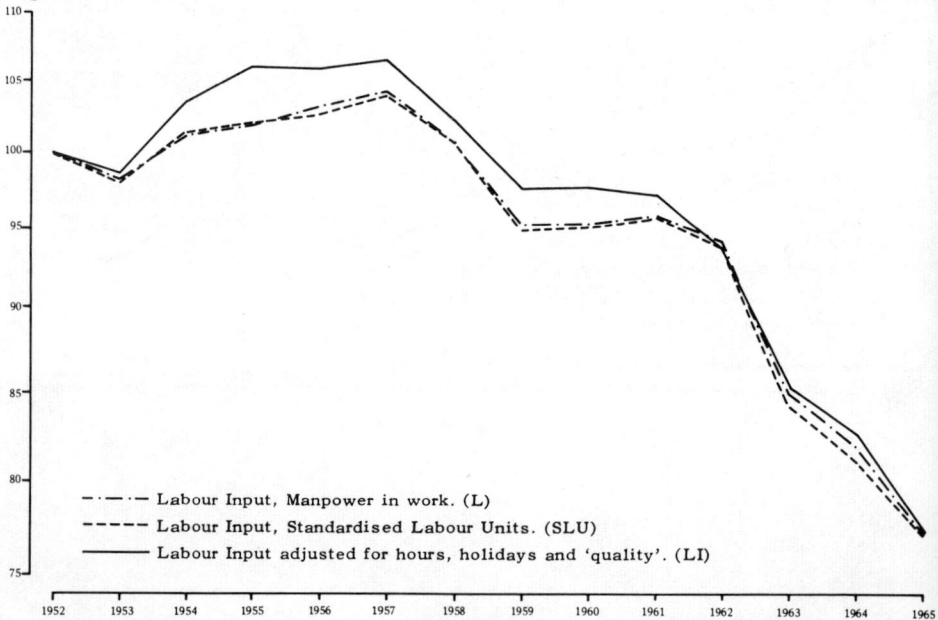

Figure 2D.   Sea Transport

Index: 1952 = 100
Log. Scale

--- · --- Labour Input, Manpower in work. (L)
- - - - Labour Input, Standardised Labour Units. (SLU)
——— Labour Input adjusted for hours, holidays and 'quality'. (LI)

Figure 2E.   Air Transport

Index: 1952 = 100
Log. Scale

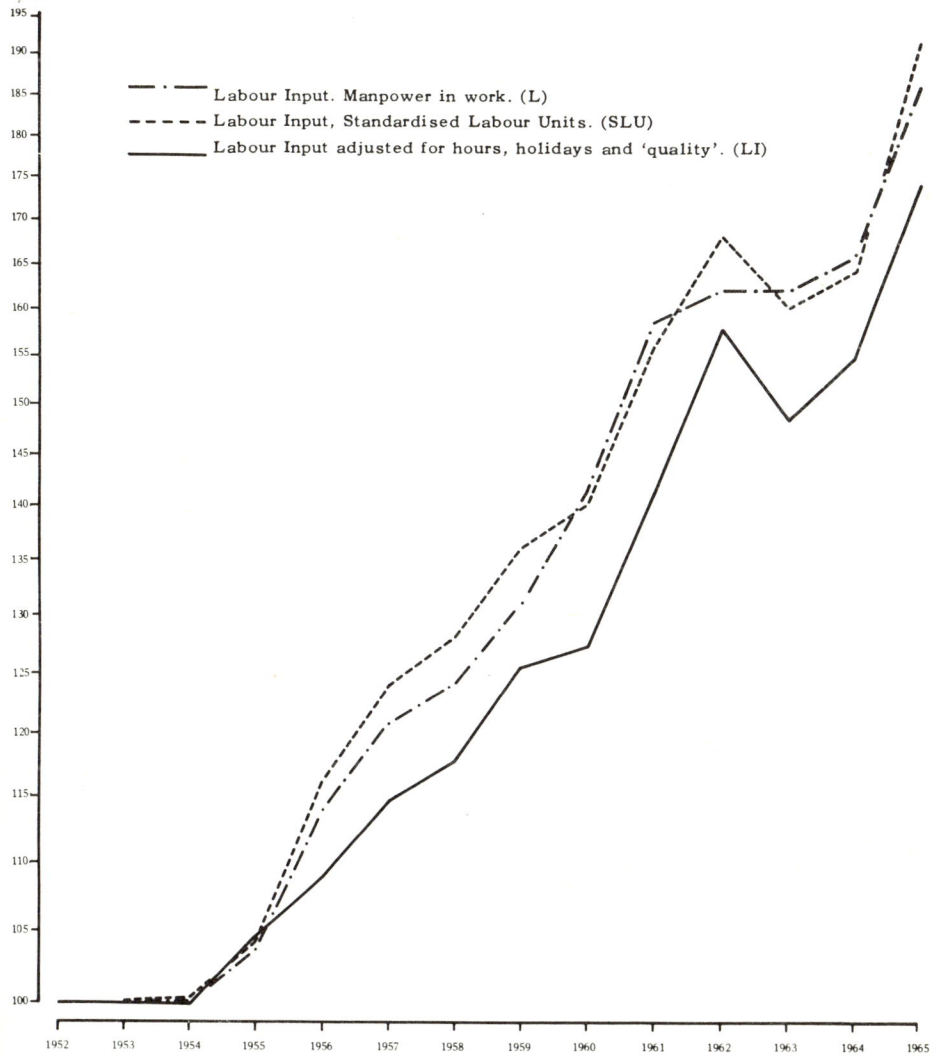

Labour Input. Manpower in work. (L)
Labour Input, Standardised Labour Units. (SLU)
Labour Input adjusted for hours, holidays and 'quality'. (LI)

Figure 2F.   Port and Inland Water Transport

Index: 1952 = 100
Log. Scale

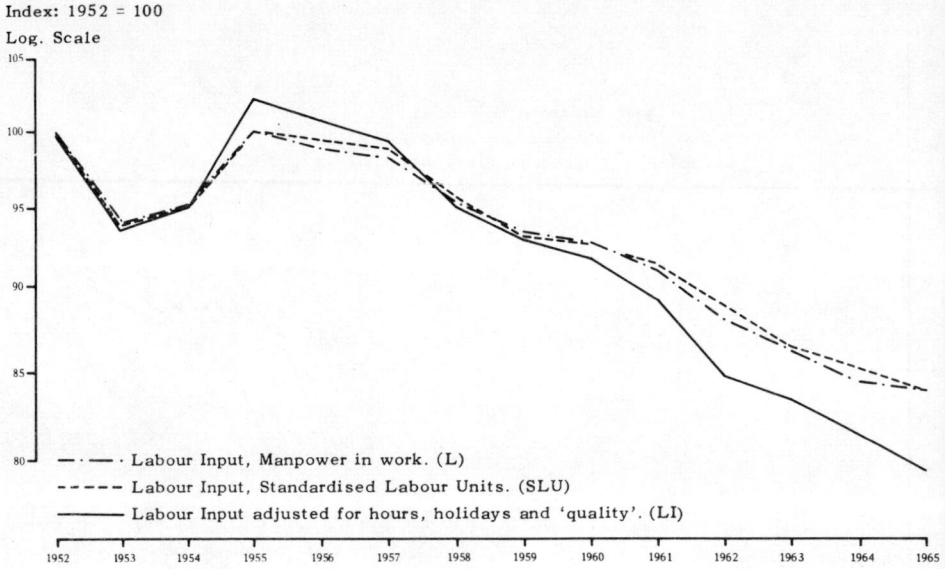

— · — · Labour Input, Manpower in work. (L)
- - - - - Labour Input, Standardised Labour Units. (SLU)
——— Labour Input adjusted for hours, holidays and 'quality'. (LI)

Figure 2G.   Total Measured Transport

Index: 1952 = 100
Log. Scale

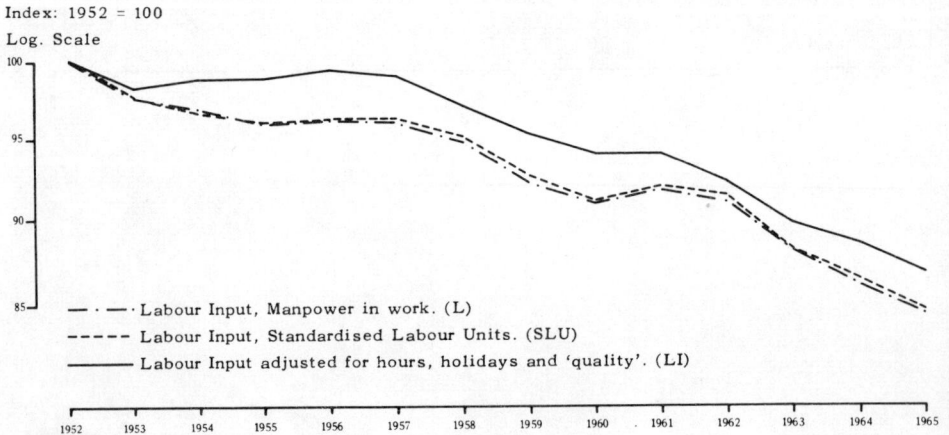

— · — · Labour Input, Manpower in work. (L)
- - - - - Labour Input, Standardised Labour Units. (SLU)
——— Labour Input adjusted for hours, holidays and 'quality'. (LI)

86

3. Hours of work and holidays allowed

In nearly every transport sector and industry the movement of average weekly hours of work and of public and annual holidays allowed has a significant effect upon the movement of labour input in each of the two short run periods. But in railways, road passenger transport and sea transport the effect of movements in the two short run periods virtually cancel each other out; there having been an increase in hours of work per standard labour unit per year in the earlier period, 1952–58, and a decline in the more recent period, 1958–62. In road haulage contracting the net movement is positive throughout the period, but is greater in the first than in the second period. In port and inland water transport there has been an accelerating decline in hours worked over the whole period, and in air transport a sharp fall has been later reversed.

The adjustment to the trend of labour input in terms of standard labour units to bring into account changes in average weekly hours of work and also changes in the length of public and annual holidays allowed is of significance in most sectors and periods. Over the time periods examined it would not have been realistic to have ignored the changes in these aspects of labour input which have occurred in these years.

4. Labour input adjusted

The final measure of labour input (Table 3.3) is adjusted in several respects as follows.

For changes in hours of work and in public and annual holidays allowed; for the *intra*-sectoral labour 'quality' shift change; for the *inter*-sectoral labour 'quality' shift change which applies only to labour input into the Measured Transport and the Total Transport and Communication industries.

The magnitude of each type of adjustment is shown in the sequential analysis of labour input (Table 3.4). If, for sectors, Row 1 is subtracted from Row 5, the movement of labour input per person employed is obtained. For industries this measure is obtained by subtracting Row 1 from Row 7. The measure indicates the movement in the amount of labour input which on average is contributed by each person employed after all the adjustments which have been mentioned have been made.

In both Measured Transport and Total Transport and Communication 'labour input per person employed' has increased in the earlier period (1952–58) and declined in the more recent period (1958–62). The increase was greater and the decline less steep in Measured Transport than in the larger industry, due to a marked decline in the postal services sector.

One general conclusion that may be drawn is that in the Measured Transport industry there was a tendency over time for each person employed to contribute, on average, less labour input each year when changes in all the factors named earlier have been brought into account. The only exceptions to this trend among the sectors are in air transport where, since 1958, labour input per person

cont. on p. 91

Table 3.3. Labour Input, Standardised Hours per Year[a]

United Kingdom SIC 1958

	Sectoral shares, percentages			Exponential rates of change per annum		
	1952	1958	1962	1952–62	1952–58	1958–62
Railways	34.8	33.9	31.6	-1.77	-0.93	-3.03
Road Passenger Transport	23.0	21.8	22.0	-1.25	-1.36	-1.12
Road Haulage Contracting	14.8	15.9	18.4	1.39	0.68	2.43
Sea Transport	14.0	14.8	14.2	-0.65	0.38	-2.17
Port and Inland Water Transport	11.6	11.4	10.7	-1.66	-0.85	-2.88
Air Transport	1.8	2.2	3.1	4.56	2.71	7.34
TOTAL MEASURED TRANSPORT	100.0/80.4	100.0/79.2	100.0/76.6	-0.81	-0.51	-1.27
Miscellaneous Transport Services and Storage	2.3	3.0	4.1	5.41	4.14	7.33
Postal Services and Telecommunications	17.3	17.8	19.3	0.72	0.15	1.58
TOTAL TRANSPORT AND COMMUNICATION	100.0	100.0	100.0	-0.33	-0.27	-0.43

a 'Crude' labour input converted to standard labour units and then adjusted for weighted average weekly hours of work and for public and annual holidays allowed.

Table 3.4

Table 3.4 Labour Input Adjusted for Hours and 'Quality'

United Kingdom
SIC 1958

Exponential rates of change per annum

	RAILWAYS			ROAD PASSENGER TRANSPORT			ROAD HAULAGE CONTRACTING			SEA TRANSPORT			PORT AND INLAND WATER TRANSPORT			TOTAL TRANSPORT AND COMMUNICATION[a]		
	1952–62	1952–58	1958–62	1952–62	1952–58	1958–62	1952–62	1952–58	1958–62	1952–62	1952–58	1958–62	1952–62	1952–58	1958–62	1952–62	1952–58	1958–62
1. Labour Input, crude, ΔL	-1.86	-1.34	-2.64	-1.31	-1.62	-0.84	0.70	-0.33	2.23	-0.62	0.10	-1.70	-1.28	-0.82	-1.97	-0.31	-0.52	0.03
2. Labour Input, Standard Labour Units, ΔSLU	-1.78	-1.20	-2.65	-1.30	-1.61	-0.86	0.73	-0.25	2.19	-0.66	0.11	-1.79	-1.18	-0.74	-1.85	-0.32	-0.43	-0.16
3. Intra-sectoral labour 'quality' shift, ΔLQ_s (Row 2 – Row 1)	0.08	0.14	-0.01	0.01	0.01	-0.02	0.03	0.08	-0.04	-0.04	0.01	-0.09	0.10	0.08	0.12	-0.01	0.09	-0.13
4. Average hours worked per Standard Labour Unit per year, $\Delta SLU/H$	0.01	0.27	-0.38	0.05	0.25	-0.26	0.66	0.93	0.24	0.01	0.27	-0.38	-0.48	-0.11	-1.03	-0.01	0.16	-0.27
5. Labour Input to the sector, adjusted for hours, holidays and the intra-sectoral 'quality' shift, ΔLI_s (Row 2 + Row 4)	-1.77	-0.93	-3.03	-1.25	-1.36	-1.12	1.39	0.68	2.43	-0.65	0.38	-2.17	-1.66	-0.85	-2.88	-0.33	-0.27	-0.43
6. Labour Input per person employed, ΔLI_L (Row 5 – Row 1)	0.09	0.41	-0.39	0.06	0.26	-0.28	0.69	1.01	0.20	-0.03	0.28	-0.47	-0.38	-0.03	-0.91	-0.02	0.25	-0.46
7.																-0.15	-0.12	-0.20
																0.18	0.15	0.23
																0.16	0.40	-0.23

	AIR TRANSPORT			TOTAL MEASURED TRANSPORT			MISC. TRANSPORT SERVICES AND STORAGE			POSTAL SERVICES AND TELECOMMUNICATIONS		
	1952–62	1952–58	1958–62	1952–62	1952–58	1958–62	1952–62	1952–58	1958–62	1952–62	1952–58	1958–62
1. Labour Input, crude, ΔL	4.82	3.61	6.67	-0.94	-0.91	-1.00	4.99	3.44	7.30	1.12	0.41	2.19
2. Labour Input, Standard Labour Units, ΔSLU	5.19	4.11	6.80	-0.90	-0.83	-1.00	4.81	3.56	6.71	1.09	0.66	1.74
3. Intra-sectoral labour 'quality' shift, ΔLQ_s (Row 2 – Row 1)	0.37	0.50	0.13	0.04	0.08	—	-0.18	0.12	-0.59	-0.03	0.25	-0.45
4. Average hours worked per Standard Labour Unit per year, $\Delta SLU/H$	-0.63	-1.40	0.54	0.09	0.32	-0.27	0.60	0.58	0.62	-0.37	-0.51	-0.16
5. Labour Input to the sector, adjusted for hours, holidays and the intra-sectoral 'quality' shift, ΔLI_s (Row 2 + Row 4)	4.56	2.71	7.34	-0.81	-0.51	-1.27	5.41	4.14	7.33	0.72	0.15	1.58
6. Labour Input per person employed, ΔLI_L (Row 5 – Row 1)	-0.26	-0.90	0.67	0.13	0.40	-0.27	0.42	0.70	0.03	-0.40	-0.26	-0.61
7. Labour Input to the industry, adjusted for hours, holidays and the intra- and ... ΔLI				-0.69	-0.42	-1.11						
				0.12	0.09	0.16						

Figure 3. Capital Stock

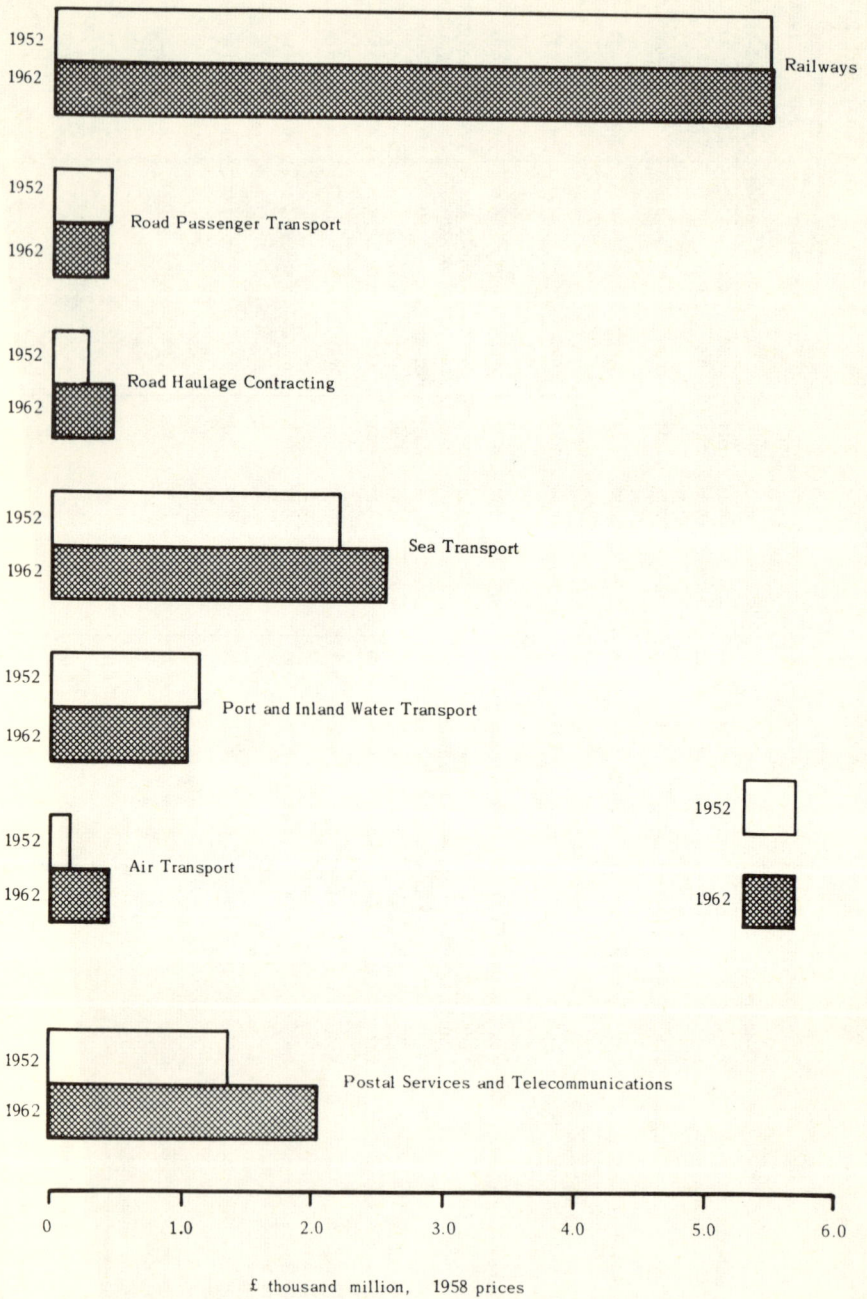

£ thousand million, 1958 prices

Figure 4.   Trends in Capital Stock, 1952–1965

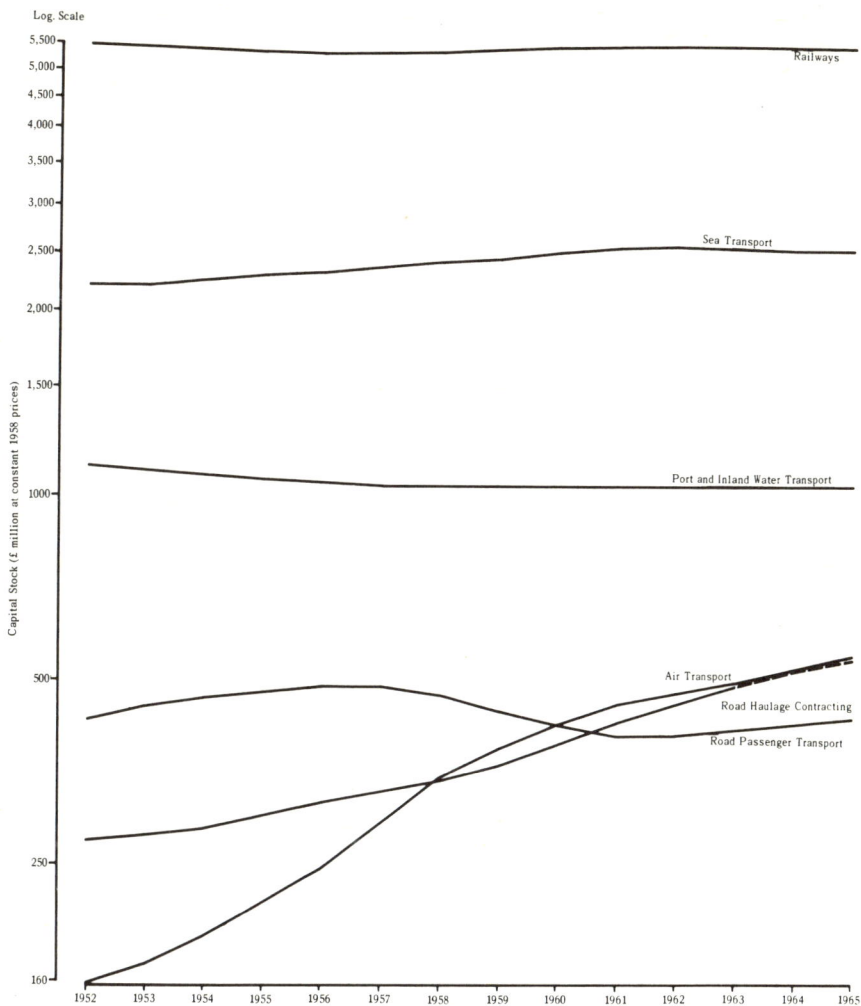

employed has been increasing; and in road haulage contracting and miscellaneous transport services and storage where there has been a rising trend over the whole period, although it was slight between 1958 and 1962.

B.   Capital Input

There are two main stages in the analysis of capital input. The first is concerned with the sectoral trends and shares in gross capital stock, at 1958 replacement cost, in the Measured Transport industry and in postal services and telecommunications. The analysis is set out in Table 3.5 and illustrated further in Figures 3 and 4. The basic data for the analysis are given in Table C.1 of the Statistical Appendix. The second stage of the analysis has the same coverage

91

Table 3.5. Capital Input, Gross Stock, at 1958 Replacement Cost

United Kingdom SIC 1958

	Sectoral Percentage Shares			Exponential rates of change per annum		
	1952	1958	1962	1952–62	1952–58	1958–62
Railways	56.6	53.7	52.6	0.05	-0.39	0.72
Road Passenger Transport	4.5	4.7	3.9	-0.60	1.49	-3.72
Road Haulage Contracting	2.8	3.4	4.4	5.19	3.67	7.47
Sea Transport	22.8	24.2	24.6	1.55	1.49	1.66
Port and Inland Water Transport	11.6	10.5	10.0	-0.74	-1.23	0
Air Transport	1.6	3.5	4.6	11.20	13.33	7.99
TOTAL MEASURED TRANSPORT	100.0	100.0	100.0			
a. Capital Input, Crude, into the Measured Transport industry, ΔK				0.80	0.51	1.24
b. Capital Input into the industry, adjusted for the inter-sectoral 'quality' shift, ΔKI_i				1.91	1.94	1.87
c. Inter-sectoral capital 'quality' shift, ΔKQ_i (Row b – Row a)				1.11	1.43	0.63
Postal Services and Telecommunications ...	...		...	4.10	3.79	4.56

Figure 5.   Trends in Capital Intensity, 1952—1965

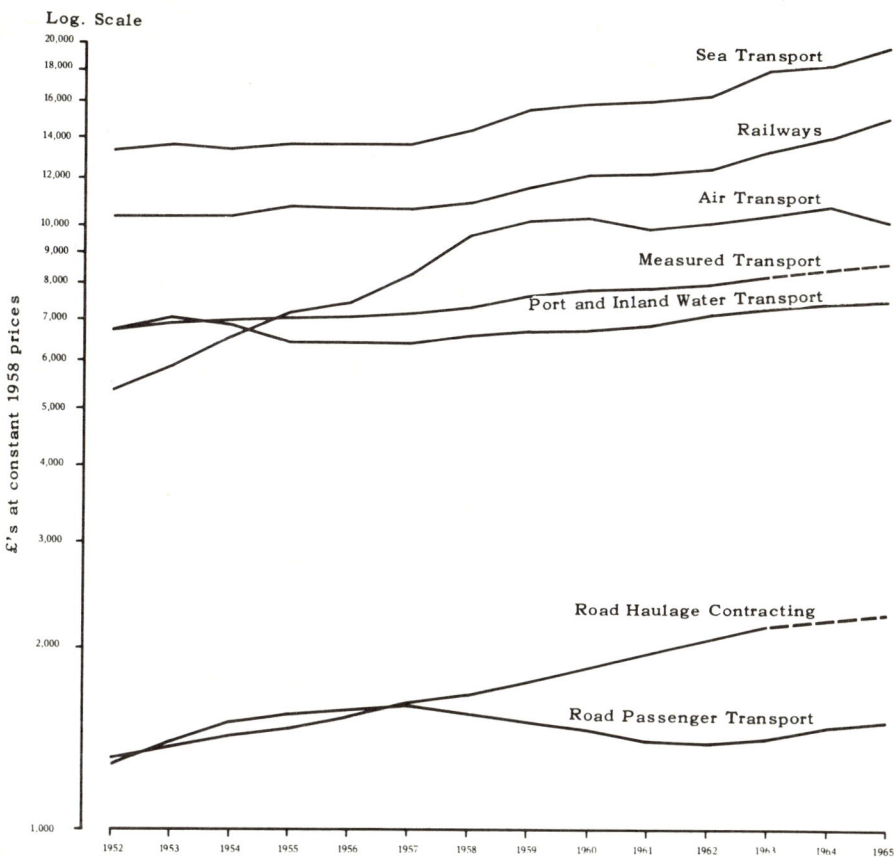

of activities and is concerned with sectoral trends in capital intensity (capital per person in employment or self-employment), and with a comparative scale of capital intensity of sectors in relation to the industry average in three separate years. The analysis is set out in Table 3.6, illustrated in Figure 5, and the basic data are given in the Statistical Appendix in Table C.1.

1.   Capital stock

Two sectors where the growth of capital input has been most marked are also the sectors in which labour input (in standardised manhours) has also been increasing over the same period. These sectors are air transport and road haulage contracting. In the more recent sub-period, 1958—62, there has been a notable reduction in the rate of increase in capital in air transport and an opposite, accelerating trend in road haulage contracting in the same period. Some steady growth of capital has occurred at a relatively low rate in sea transport, and in railways an almost imperceptible, positive rate has prevailed in the more recent period. The other transport sectors show slight declines in capital input. In postal services and telecommunications the growth rate of capital input is

93

relatively high and stable over the whole period studied. In the Measured Transport industry a rather less than one per cent per annum exponential growth rate for the whole period shows, when differentiated by sub-periods, some tendency to accelerate.

An adjustment to capital input to the Measured Transport industry is made in order to take account of the inter-sectoral capital 'quality' shift. The method of measuring this qualitative element in the industry's capital input has already been explained.[1] The magnitude of this shift is large, particularly so in the sub-period 1952 to 1958.[2] The chief reason is the very low rate of return (after subsidy) on the very large amount of capital stock in place in the railways. The method of measuring the shift brings the rate of profit on capital into account, thus giving less weight to the low profitability sectors, particularly the railways where the gross rate of return to capital was only 1.7 per cent in 1958, and considerably greater weight to the higher profitability sectors: road haulage contracting (18.8 per cent in 1958) and road passenger transport (14.9 per cent).[3]

Before allowing for the inter-sectoral 'quality' shift, the rate of capital input to the Measured Transport industry is on an accelerating trend, but this is not so when the shift is brought into the calculation.

In absolute terms, as shown in Figure 3 and Table 3.5 (first panel), more than three-quarters of the gross capital stock in place in Measured Transport is in the railways and in sea transport (a combined percentage share of 77.2 in 1962). The reasons for the high capital concentration in rail and sea transport are clear enough in general, absolute terms, but in relation particularly to road freight and passenger transport the heavy *relative* preponderance of the railways is due in part to the inclusion of the capital invested in rail track and the exclusion from the two road transport sectors of the capital, or of any share of it, invested in roads.

What order of difference would it make to include appropriate shares of road capital with road passenger transport and road haulage contracting? Appropriate shares in total capital have been derived from the shares of these sectors in total road vehicle mileage weighted by 'passenger car units' (PCU). The weighting is necessary in order to take account of differences between types of traffic in road use, that is, differences in wear and tear on the road surface inflicted by different vehicle types, and differences in road occupancy in the sense of relative size, speed and congestion-causing factors.[4] The result of this weighting exercise for

---

1 Chapter 1., pp26–27, and the methodological note at the end of this Chapter, page 108.

2 See Table 3.5.

3 See Table 4.9 in Chapter 4.

4 'Passenger car unit' values used in this weighting are motor-cars and light vans, 1; motor-cycles, ½; buses and coaches, 3; goods vehicles exceeding 30 cwt unladen weight, 3.

1962 is that 7.4 per cent of the total gross capital stock in roads is assigned to public road passenger transport, and 19.1 per cent to road haulage contracting. Sectoral shares for 1962, recalculated to include the road track capital assigned to Measured Transport on this basis, are set out below and compared with the sectoral shares excluding the appropriate portions of the total capital invested in roads.

	Capital Stock, gross at 1958 replacement cost. Sectoral shares for 1962 (percentages)	
	Excluding share of Capital in Roads[a]	Including share of Capital in Roads
Railways	52.6	49.9
Road Passenger Transport	3.9	5.1
Road Haulage Contracting	4.4	7.8
Sea Transport	24.6	23.4
Port and Inland Water Transport	10.0	9.5
Air Transport	4.6	4.3
Total Measured Transport	100.0	100.0

[a] The total gross capital stock in roads was £2.1 thousand million in 1962 (1.6 in 1951 and 1.7 in 1958), 'excluding the non-renewable element more than 75 years old'. (Source: National Income and Expenditure, 1967, CSO.) Of this total, £0.56 thousand million has been assigned to the Measured Transport industry in the way already described.

Although the share for road haulage contracting is nearly doubled when its portion of total capital in roads is included, the railways easily maintain their dominant position. The answer to the question posed earlier is that the inclusion of an appropriate portion of the total capital in roads does significantly alter the shares of the road using transport sectors, particularly road haulage contracting, but the relative positions of the various transport sectors are changed only to the extent that shares of the two road transport sectors rise above the share of air transport.

2.   Capital intensity

The analysis of trends in capital intensity is shown on the second panel of Table 3.6. The measure is $\Delta K - \Delta L$ (that is, exponential rate of growth of capital less exponential rate of growth of labour unadjusted), which involves the concept of capital in place per person in employment or self-employment. No allowance is made here for changes in labour quality, hours of work or holidays. The measure of capital employed in this study is capital in place, rather than

Table 3.6. Capital Intensity[a]

United Kingdom SIC 1958

	Relative Capital Intensity Index			Exponential rates of change per annum		
	1952	1958	1962	1952–62	1952–58	1958–62
Railways	153.0	148.9	155.8	1.92	0.96	3.36
Road Passenger Transport	19.1	21.2	17.3	0.71	3.11	-2.88
Road Haulage Contracting	19.5	22.8	25.7	4.49	3.99	5.24
Sea Transport	197.0	196.7	205.9	2.17	1.39	3.36
Port and Inland Water Transport	100.3	89.9	89.0	0.54	-0.41	1.97
Air Transport	79.5	130.9	126.3	6.37	9.73	1.33
TOTAL MEASURED TRANSPORT	100.0	100.0	100.0	1.74	1.42	2.24
Capital Intensity in Measured Transport, adjusted for the intersectoral shift in capital 'quality', $\Delta(KI_i/L)$				2.85	2.85	2.87
Postal Services and Telecommunications	56.4	63.5	63.9	2.98	3.38	2.37

[a] Capital Stock, gross, at 1958 replacement cost divided by manpower in work.

capital in use.[1] The corresponding labour measure to capital in place is the one stated above.

With only two exceptions, in sub-periods, in road passenger transport and port and inland water transport, the sectoral and industry trends of the K/L ratios are positive. A distinction needs to be made, however, between an increase in the K/L ratio due *predominantly* to an increased input of capital and an increase in K/L due predominantly to a decline in the input of labour.

A. Sectors where a decline in labour input has been predominant in raising K/L in 1952–1962.

Railways
Road Passenger Transport
Port and Inland Water Transport

B. Sectors where an increase in capital input has been predominant in raising K/L in 1952–1962.

Road Haulage Contracting
Sea Transport
Air Transport

Postal Services and Telecommunications

In the Measured Transport industry the influence of declining labour input in the period 1952–1962 has been the marginally dominant influence determining the trend of the K/L ratio for the industry, although the increase in capital input became dominant in the sub-period, 1958–1962.

The significant point about the B group of sectors is that it is known that net new capital formation has contributed to the higher K/L ratio and, although there is no certainty about it, positive net capital formation is likely to embody the latest available and applicable technical knowledge. Where, as in the first group of sectors distinguished, a decline in labour input has been the dominant influence, there exists the possibility that the K/L ratio has risen because capital has been scrapped at a rate which is slower than the decline in the labour force, and each case has to be examined to discover whether this is so or not. In railways the growth of capital input has been very slow over the period as a whole. The rise in the K/L ratio has therefore been due almost completely to the decline in the labour force. This does not mean, of course, that no new capital equipment embodying improved technology has been introduced. This could have been done in the normal course of renewal and replacement. But with virtually no net additions to the capital stock taking place, the opportunities for applying new techniques which require the 'vehicle' of new capital equipment were accordingly less. In road passenger transport and in port and inland water transport both the capital and labour inputs declined over the period 1952 to 1962.

---

[1] See Chapter 1, p. 27 and Chapter 4, p. 114 for the reasons for the use of this concept.

There was an accelerating decline in capital in road passenger transport, and as labour input declined faster than capital input over the period 1952–62, the K/L ratio rose, and therefore the opportunities for the introduction of new capital equipment embodying modern techniques were even less, in these circumstances, than they were in the railways.

The implications for the contributions of movement in K/L to movement in labour productivity are clearly that such contributions are more likely to come from the B rather than the A sectors.[1] It is also true (as shown in Chapter 2) that in terms of output the A sectors are contracting, except for port and inland water transport where labour input is falling rather faster than capital input, and the B sectors are expanding.

In the Measured Transport industry the trend of the K/L ratio, unadjusted for the inter-sectoral capital 'quality' shift, was influenced chiefly by the decline in manpower rather than by net additions to capital stock in the whole period considered; although the increase in net capital formation reversed the position in the more recent sub-period. However, a more realistic picture emerges when the effect of the capital 'quality' shift is taken into account. Then, as shown on Tables 3.1 and 3.5, the increase in capital stock becomes the dominant factor in the trend of the adjusted K/L ratio which rose at a faster pace than the unadjusted ratio.

The capital intensity index, shown in the first panel of Table 3.6, sets the capital intensity of the sectors in relationship to the average capital intensity of the Measured Transport industry. The railways and sea transport sectors, of massive importance in terms of capital stock are also high in scale of capital intensity; whereas air transport, of minor importance in terms of capital stock, is approaching the scale of capital intensity found, on average, in the railways. Capital intensity in the two road-using sectors was relatively very low. If, as in the analysis of capital stock, the appropriate portion of the capital stock invested in roads is added to the numerator of the K/L ratios[2] in 1962, the result, in terms of the index of relative capital intensity is as follows:

	Relative Capital Intensity Index, Measured Transport = 100, 1962	
	Excluding share of Capital in Roads	Including share of Capital in Roads
Railways	155.8	147.8
Road Passenger Transport	17.3	22.7
Road Haulage Contracting	25.7	45.8
Total Measured Road Transport	21.7	34.0

1 And they do. See Chapter 5, Table 5.4.

2 The appropriate addition is made to K in respect of each sector considered and to the base, for the comparison, the Measured Transport industry.

The indexes for the two road sectors, including capital in roads, are overstated to the extent that an unknown quantity of labour employed in roads has been omitted from the calculation. Even so, if the two road sectors are considered together in relation to the railways it is found that excluding road capital 7.2 times the amount of capital per head was employed on average in 1962 in the provision of rail passenger and freight services than in the provision of public road transport services of both these types. Including capital in roads the figure is 4.3 times. The high relative level of capital intensity of the railways, shown in Table 3.6, first panel, is therefore only to a very small extent (as shown) due to the exclusion of capital in road tracks from the calculations.

Even when roads are excluded, capital intensity in the Measured Transport industry is relatively very high when compared with the averages for the goods and service sectors of the United Kingdom economy. In 1962 the K/L ratio in Measured Transport was £8,006; in all civilian services (excluding private dwellings) it was £3,252, and only £2,791 in the goods industries.

C. Factor Requirements per Unit of Output

There are obvious limitations in any analysis of factor input which is unrelated to output and which treats the factors of labour and capital separately. A study of the level and movement of factor employment by sector and industry is necessary where adjustments to the data are needed, as they are in the case of transport, in order to try to improve the accuracy of all the measures involved. That having been done, it is now informative to relate movements in factor input to movements in output, but it is emphasised that at this stage there is no intention to reach or imply any conclusions concerning productive efficiency. The inverse of the traditional productivity ratio of output per unit of labour input is being used here, in the way suggested earlier,[1] in order to measure the saving or dissaving in the input of the labour factor over time which is due to *all* causes.

Movements in factor requirements per unit of output are set out on Table 3.7 in terms of labour requirements, and of capital and capital per head requirements.

1. Labour requirements

There are movements which are indicative of labour saving in all but two sectors of the Measured Transport industry, and in this industry as a whole, over the whole period examined, and this is true on the basis of a measure which is unadjusted and in respect of one which is adjusted for the intersectoral 'quality' shift which is described elsewhere.[2] The two sectors where an increasing amount of labour input per unit of output has been required over this period are railways

---

[1] See Chapter 1, page 17 and footnote 3.

[2] See Chapter 1, page 24, and the methodological note at the end of this Chapter, page 108.

Table 3.7. Movements in Factor Requirements per Unit of Output, 1952–1962, 1952–1958 and 1958–1962   United Kingdom SIC 1958

Exponential rates of change per annum

	1952–1962			1952–1958			1958–1962		
	Labour, $\Delta LI - \Delta Y$	Capital, $\Delta K - \Delta Y$	Capital per head, $\Delta\left(\frac{K}{L}\right) - \Delta Y$	Labour, $\Delta LI - \Delta Y$	Capital, $\Delta K - \Delta Y$	Capital per head, $\Delta\left(\frac{K}{L}\right) - \Delta Y$	Labour, $\Delta LI - \Delta Y$	Capital, $\Delta K - \Delta Y$	Capital per head, $\Delta\left(\frac{K}{L}\right) - \Delta Y$
Railways	0.16	1.98	3.85	0.69	1.23	2.58	-0.64	3.11	5.75
Road Passenger Transport	1.05	1.70	3.01	1.48	4.33	5.95	0.37	-2.23	1.39
Road Haulage Contracting	-5.87	-2.07	-2.77	-6.75	-3.76	-3.44	-4.56	0.48	-1.75
Sea Transport	-1.88	0.32	0.94	-0.82	0.29	0.19	-3.46	0.37	2.07
Port and Inland Water Transport	-3.92	-3.00	-1.72	-2.85	-3.23	-2.41	-5.55	-2.67	-0.70
Air Transport	-8.02	-1.38	-6.21	-9.15	1.47	-2.13	-6.33	-5.68	-12.34
TOTAL MEASURED TRANSPORT									
1. Unadjusted	-2.46	-0.85	0.09	-1.90	-0.88	0.03	-3.31	-0.80	0.20
2. Adjusted for inter-sectoral 'quality' shifts in labour and capital	-2.34	0.26	1.20	-1.81	0.55	1.46	-3.15	-0.17	0.83
Postal Services and Telecommunications	-2.38	1.00	-0.12	-2.17	1.47	1.06	-2.69	0.29	-1.90

and road passenger transport, but in these sectors the position changed in the period 1958 to 1962 when labour saving occurred in the railways and the rate of dissaving or using, in labour terms, in road passenger transport was lower than it was for the earlier sub-period. In the Measured Transport industry there was an acceleration of movements in labour saving, whether or not adjustment is made for the inter-sectoral labour 'quality' shift over the whole period, in spite of lower rates of saving in the two growth sectors: air transport and road haulage contracting, in the period 1958–1962 (the third panel of Table 3.7).

2. Capital requirements

Movements in capital requirements per unit of output were generally less factor saving than has been seen to be the case with labour input. The two main growth sectors (air and road haulage contracting) were capital saving per unit of output over the whole period, but road haulage contracting became capital using in the more recent sub-period and air transport was capital using in the earlier sub-period. The aggregate industry movement is seen to have been capital saving over the whole period if no adjustment is made for the marked inter-sectoral capital 'quality' shift; but when this is introduced there is seen to have been a capital using trend in the first sub-period and capital saving one in the second.

More capital per head per unit of output i.e. more 'deep' capital was required by the railways, road passenger transport, sea transport and the Measured Transport industry (both with and without the effect of the 'quality' shift) in all periods, and less capital per head was required in all other transport sectors in all periods. It is however important that the distinction be made here between those sectors where an increase in capital intensity has occurred *predominantly* because of a decrease in the number of persons in employment and self-employment and those sectors where the K/L ratio has increased chiefly because of an increase in capital input. The position over the 1952–62 period is given earlier (page 97) where the implications of this are also explained.

3. Total factor requirements

The general picture which begins to emerge is that there is a tendency, on the evidence of the 1952–62 period, for the Measured Transport industry to be labour saving and capital using, particularly in the sense of more capital *per man* per unit of output. There may be many reasons for this behaviour. For example, movements in relative factor prices, the nature and method by which technical and organisational knowledge has been applied, or disproportionate downward adjustments of labour and capital inputs as demand for the output of services has fallen – it is certainly true that some classes of transport equipment are relatively indivisible and specific to their designed uses and this may be an important contributory cause of such disproportionate adjustments to factor inputs.

One aspect of this analysis which unequivocally invites further investigation is the increase in requirements, per unit of output, of both labour *and* capital in the railways and in road passenger transport over the whole period 1952–1962. Both these sectors experienced declining demand for their output of services over the

Table 3.8. Movements in Total Factor Requirements per Unit of Output

	Exponential rates of change per annum		
	1952–62	1952–58	1958–62
Railways	0.64	0.93	0.20
Road Passenger Transport	1.25	2.42	−0.50
Road Haulage Contracting	−4.46	−5.43	−2.99
Sea Transport	−0.92	−0.20	−2.01
Port and Inland Water Transport	−3.79	−2.92	−5.11
Air Transport	−5.47	−5.21	−5.87
MEASURED TRANSPORT			
1. Unadjusted	−1.93	−1.46	−2.62
2. Adjusted for inter-sectoral 'quality' shifts in labour and capital[a]	−1.46	−0.92	−2.26
Postal Services and Telecommunications	−1.68	−1.42	−2.06

a See methodological note at the end of this Chapter.

whole of this period, and there is evidence from this analysis that downward adjustments in factor inputs lagged behind the decline in output. When the cut-back in factor employment came in these two sectors in the period 1958–62, it took the form of a reduction in labour requirements per unit of output in the railways, and it was accompanied by an increase in capital requirements. In road passenger transport, labour requirements per unit of output moved up at a much lower rate than in the earlier period and capital requirements were much reduced.

In Table 3.8 are set out the combined labour and capital requirements per unit of output. All sectors except the railways were total factor saving per unit of output in the more recent period; the comparatively very high rate of factor using by the road passenger transport sector in 1952–58 was radically reversed in the later years. The rate of total factor saving was higher (or rate of total factor using lower, as the case may be) in the more recent period than in the earlier period in all sectors (and in the Measured Transport industry on both an unadjusted and adjusted basis) except road haulage contracting, where capital using occurred during the years 1958–62. Over the same period, postal services and telecommunications reduced their usage of factors per unit of output rather faster than the Measured Transport industry (after adjustment).

These are the main results from the measurement and interpretation of factor input. For explanations it is necessary to invert the final set of ratios studied here, to reverse the signs on the exponential rates of change shown in Table 3.8, to examine the resultant total factor productivity ratios and trends, and to test a number of hypotheses.[1] This process is attempted in Chapters 5 and 6, where a

1 See Chapter 1, page 33.

full account is also given of the methods used to combine labour and capital inputs.

Summary

The philosophy behind the measures applied here to the measurement and adjustment of factor input have their origin in the use made in this Paper of a production function as a method of interpreting productivity movements. The obvious defects of the 'partial' productivity ratios of output per unit of labour input or output per unit of capital input are thus avoided.

A production function, of the type used, attributes labour productivity movement to movements in capital intensity (capital stock per person employed) and technical change (a residual term). It would obviously be useful to be able to be specific about the meaning of this residual term, but unless various shift changes in factor input are previously removed, or added back, they will affect (positively or negatively) the residual term and make it that much less specific. So, to avoid this happening, labour and capital inputs are separately 'cleaned up' by making appropriate allowances for intra- and inter-sectoral 'quality' shift changes in labour input, and for inter-sectoral 'quality' shift changes in capital input. Lack of data precludes the estimation of the intra-sectoral 'quality' shift change in capital input.

These adjustments to labour and capital inputs are made on the assumption that differences in the rates of remuneration reflect differences in the 'qualities' of the factors concerned.

In Table 3.9 a summary is given of the results of measuring, adjusting and combining factor inputs. Adjustments, it may be noticed, are made for shift changes in the 'quality' of inputs and for changes in weekly hours of work and in public and annual holidays allowed.

Within the Measured Transport industry only two sectors, air transport and road haulage contracting, have increased their demand for labour; they are, notably, also the outstanding growth sectors in terms of net output and productivity (both labour and total factor productivity). The same sectors are also the leaders in growth of capital input.

Other sectors, with the exception of sea transport, have capital inputs which are a very low positive or, in two cases, negative rates. In sea transport labour input has declined and capital input increased to an extent which is sufficient, after suitable weighting has been applied to the changes in both labour and capital, to make total, combined factor input positive. So the sea, air and road haulage sectors are increasing their usage of factors on the combined factor input calculation, and all the other sectors of the Measured Transport industry are using fewer combined factors over the period concerned.

In aggregate, the Measured Transport industry is very slightly increasing its usage of factors, on the fully adjusted basis. The rate is 0.19 per cent per annum

Table 3.9   Movements and Levels of Factor Input and Adjustment for 'Quality', 1952–62 (Exponential rates of change per annum)

| | MOVEMENTS | | | | | LEVELS IN 1962 | | |
| | LABOUR INPUT | | CAPITAL INPUT | | TOTAL FACTOR INPUT | LABOUR | CAPITAL | CAPITAL INTENSITY |
	Labour Input Adjusted for Hours and 'Quality', ΔLI	Adjustment for Hours & 'Quality', $\Delta LQ_s + \Delta SLU/H$	Capital Input unadjusted, ΔK	Capital Intensity, Δ(K/L)	Combined Labour (ΔLI) and Capital (ΔK) Input, ΔTFI	Standard Labour Unit Hours, SLU/H (Millions)	Gross, at 1958 Replacement cost (£'s M.), K.	Gross, at 1958 Replacement cost per person in employment (£'s), K/L.
1. Railways	−1.77	0.09	0.05	1.92	−1.32	973	5,485	12,466
2. Road Passenger Transport	−1.25	0.06	−0.60	0.71	−1.02	676	405	1,382
3. Road Haulage Contracting	1.39	0.69	5.19	4.49	2.79	566	457	2,059
4. Sea Transport	−0.65	−0.03	1.55	2.17	0.34	438	2,570	16,474
5. Port and Inland Water Transport	−1.66	−0.38	−0.74	0.54	−1.54	330	1,040	7,123
6. Air Transport	4.56	−0.26	11.20	6.37	7.27	94	475	10,106
7. MEASURED TRANSPORT	−0.81	0.13	0.80	1.74	−0.28	3,077	10,432	8,006
8. MEASURED TRANSPORT additionally adjusted for the inter-sectoral 'quality' shift change in factor inputs	−0.69		1.91	2.85	0.19			
9. Postal Services and Telecommunications	0.72	−0.40	4.10	2.98	1.42	774	2,065	5,111
10. Miscellaneous Transport Services and Storage	5.41	0.42	...	...	...	165	...	...
11. TOTAL ORGANISED TRANSPORT AND COMMUNICATION	−0.33	−0.02	...	...	...	4,016	...	...
12. TOTAL ORGANISED TRANSPORT AND COMMUNICATION, additionally adjusted for inter-sectoral 'quality'	−0.15							

Table 3.10.   Movements in Labour Input per Person Employed,

1952–1958 and 1958–1962

(Exponential rates of change per annum)

	1952–1958	1958–1962
Railways	0.41	−0.39
Road Passenger Transport	0.26	−0.28
Road Haulage Contracting	1.01	0.20
Sea Transport	0.28	−0.47
Port and Inland Water Transport	−0.03	−0.91
Air Transport	−0.90	0.67
MEASURED TRANSPORT	0.40	−0.27
MEASURED TRANSPORT additionally adjusted for the inter-sectoral 'quality' shift change	0.49	−0.11
Postal Services and Telecommunications	−0.26	−0.61
Miscellaneous Transport Services and Storage	0.70	0.03
TOTAL ORGANISED TRANSPORT AND COMMUNICATION	0.25	−0.46
TOTAL ORGANISED TRANSPORT AND COMMUNICATION additionally adjusted for the inter-sectoral 'quality' shift change	0.40	−0.23

and this is the net, weighted result of a 0.7 per cent per annum decline in adjusted labour input and a 1.9 per cent per annum increase in adjusted capital input.

Some further light is shed on the movements in labour 'quality', hours of work and holidays by considering labour input (in terms of standardised labour unit hours) per person in employment. These movements are shown in Table 3.10 for two sub-periods of the whole period.

A general conclusion which may be drawn from this table is that on average each person in employment contributed an increasing amount of standardised labour input [which takes account of both 'quality' and quantity (hours of work per annum)] in the first period (1952–58), and a declining amount in the second period (1958–62). The principal exception is air transport which moved against this trend in both periods.

No comparison of this rate with the rate of change of total factor input in all service industries in the United Kingdom is possible within the compass of this

Paper, because the work involved in calculating the various shift changes over such a large field was considered to be too great; but if unadjusted, 'crude' labour input (manpower in work) alone is considered it is shown that the Measured Transport industry reduced its demand for labour at an annual rate of −0.94 per cent in the period 1952–62, compared with the rate of increase of 1.46 per cent per annum for all civilian service industries, excluding Measured Transport.

It may therefore be concluded that, with the exception of a small but rapidly growing sector of miscellaneous transport services and storage, the organised transport industry (that is, all transport except private cars and 'C' licenced road goods vehicles) slightly reduced its demand for labour over a period when the total number in civil employment was rising by 0.90 per cent per annum, and when other service industries considered as a whole were increasing their demands at an annual rate considerably faster than this.

Postal services and telecommunications increased their demand for factors at a greater rate than the Measured Transport industry as a whole. This is true in respect of both labour and capital, and particularly capital where the annual rate of increase of input was 4.1 per cent.

In terms of the level of labour and capital factor inputs, the position in 1962 is shown in Table 3.9. Although the railways had the highest rate of decline of labour input, the level of this input still accounted for nearly a third of the total for the Measured Transport industry in 1962. In terms of capital, where the rate of input into the railways was negligible, the railways still dominated the industry with 52.6 per cent of the total capital employed.

Capital intensity in Measured Transport was relatively very high. At £8,006 per person in employment in 1962 it compares with £3,252 in all civilian service industries, excluding private dwellings, and only £2,791 in the goods industries.[1]

A distinction is made between those sectors where an increase in capital intensity has occurred *predominantly* because of a decrease in the number of persons in employment and where the K/L ratio has increased chiefly because of an increase in capital input. The position is summarised below.

    A.   Sectors where a decline in labour input has been predominant in $\Delta(K/L)$ in the period 1952–1962

        Railways
        Road Passenger Transport
        Port and Inland Water Transport

    B.   Sectors where an increase in capital input has been predominant in $\Delta(K/L)$ in the period 1952–1962

        Road Haulage Contracting
        Sea Transport
        Air Transport
        Postal Services and Telecommunications

---

[1] Fixed assets only; stocks and work in progress excluded in all cases.

The implication for the effectiveness of contributions from capital intensity changes is that the B sectors are likely to be more effective in this respect than the A sectors. The production function does not recognise this distinction, so it is made now rather than later.

One conclusion to the analysis of factor requirements per unit of output is that the Measured Transport industry over the period 1952 to 1962 has been labour and capital saving, on an unadjusted basis. This is so for the industry as a whole to the extent of −2.46 per cent per annum for labour requirements and −0.85 per cent for capital.

Road haulage contracting, port and inland water transport and air transport are decreasing their requirements for *both* labour and capital per unit of output. Sea transport is labour saving, but has tended to substitute capital for labour. Postal services and telecommunications are labour saving but capital using per unit of output.

The two sectors which are labour and, more heavily, capital using, are railways and road passenger transport. They are so mainly because output is declining considerably faster than either factor input. These results suggest that capital is less easily adjusted to downward changes in demand and output than is labour.

The final results of the study of total requirements per unit of output are shown in summary form in Table 3.11.

Table 3.11.   Summary of Movements in Total Factor Requirements per Unit of Output, 1952 to 1962

(Exponential rates of change per annum)

Railways	0.64
Road Passenger Transport	1.25
Road Haulage Contracting	−4.46
Sea Transport	−0.92
Port and Inland Water Transport	−3.79
Air Transport	−5.47
MEASURED TRANSPORT	
1. Unadjusted	−1.93
2. Adjusted for inter-sectoral 'quality' shifts in both labour and capital	−1.46
Postal Services and Telecommunications	−1.68

The most striking result which appears in this table is that both the railways and road passenger transport required, on average, *more* combined factor inputs in 1962 than they did in 1952 in order to produce each unit of output. The implications of this result for productivity movements are clear enough, since of course the productivity ratio (output per unit of total factor input) is the inverse of the ratio of total factor requirements per unit of output.

Methodological Note on Inter-sectoral 'Quality' Shifts in Factor Inputs in Measured Transport

If it is assumed that higher remuneration of a factor input in some sectors of the transport industry than in others reflects higher 'quality' and productivity of that factor in those sectors, then an index of Total Factor Input (TFI) for Measured Transport as a whole may be constructed which is adjusted for 'quality' differences. By comparing this measure with one unadjusted for 'quality' differences of this sort it is possible to obtain an index of this 'inter-sectoral quality shift' in Measured Transport.

This adjustment has been attempted with the method outlined below. The key to the symbols used is given on the following page.

General notes on method

The calculation of the indices built up here is based on the 'chaining' of year-to-year movements, as measured by exponential rates of change equivalent for year-to-year movements to taking the natural logarithms (logs to base e) of the year-to-year ratios.

Because of the extent of available information, the weighting system used here is based on the detailed figures of reward to labour and capital which are available for 1954, 1958 and 1963. The figures for 1954 are used as the base for 1952–56, 1958 figures for 1956–60 and 1963 figures for 1960–65. The subscript b, referring to base years, should be interpreted in this way throughout the note.

Labour input

The adjusted labour input for Measured Transport is given by

$$\log_e\left(\frac{\mathrm{LI}'_{i,n}}{\mathrm{LI}'_{i,(n-1)}}\right) = \sum_s \frac{W_{s,b}\,\mathrm{LI}_{s,b}}{W_{i,b}\,\mathrm{LI}_{i,b}}\,\log_e\left(\frac{\mathrm{LI}_{s,n}}{\mathrm{LI}_{s,(n-1)}}\right)$$

$$= \sum_s \frac{\mathrm{Y_L}_{s,b}}{\mathrm{Y_L}_{i,b}}\,\log_e\left(\frac{\mathrm{LI}_{s,n}}{\mathrm{LI}_{s,(n-1)}}\right)$$

Capital input

The adjusted capital input for Measured Transport is given by

$$\log_e\left(\frac{\mathrm{K}'_{i,n}}{\mathrm{K}'_{i,(n-1)}}\right) = \sum_s \frac{r_{s,b}\,\mathrm{K}_{s,b}}{r_{i,b}\,\mathrm{K}_{i,b}}\,\log_e\left(\frac{\mathrm{K}_{s,n}}{\mathrm{K}_{s,(n-1)}}\right)$$

$$= \sum_s \frac{\mathrm{Y_K}_{s,b}}{\mathrm{Y_K}_{i,b}}\,\log_e\left(\frac{\mathrm{K}_{s,n}}{\mathrm{K}_{s,(n-1)}}\right)$$

Total factor input

For each sector the total factor input has been defined in the following way,

$$\log_e\left(\frac{TFI_{s,n}}{TFI_{s,(n-1)}}\right) = \log_e\left(\frac{LI_{s,n}}{LI_{s,(n-1)}}\right) + a_{s,b}\,\log_e\left(\frac{K_{s,n}/L_{s,n}}{K_{s,(n-1)}/L_{s,(n-1)}}\right)$$

In Measured Transport we define total factor input in the following ways,

(i) Unadjusted for inter-sectoral 'quality' shift,

$$\log_e\left(\frac{TFI_{i,n}}{TFI_{i,(n-1)}}\right) = \log_e\left(\frac{LI_{i,n}}{LI_{i,(n-1)}}\right) + a_{i,b}\,\log_e\left(\frac{K_{i,n}/L_{i,n}}{K_{i,(n-1)}/L_{i,(n-1)}}\right)$$

(ii) Adjusted for inter-sectoral 'quality' shift,

$$\log_e\left(\frac{TFI'_{i,n}}{TFI'_{i,(n-1)}}\right) = \log_e\left(\frac{LI'_{i,n}}{LI'_{i,(n-1)}}\right) + a_{i,b}\cdot\log_e\left(\frac{K'_{i,n}/L_{i,n}}{K'_{i,(n-1)}/L_{i,(n-1)}}\right)$$

Inter-sectoral 'quality' shifts in factor inputs

Index numbers of these 'quality' shifts are obtained for Measured Transport thus:

$$LIQ_{i,n} = \frac{LI'_{i,n}}{LI_{i,n}}$$

$$KQ_{i,n} = \frac{K'_{i,n}}{K_{i,n}}$$

$$TFQ_{i,n} = \frac{TFI'_{i,n}}{TFI_{i,n}}$$

The following relationship exists between these 'quality' shifts, as a direct result of the use of the above definitions.

$$\log_e\left(\frac{TFQ_{i,n}}{TFQ_{i,(n-1)}}\right) = \log_e\left(\frac{LIQ_{i,n}}{LIQ_{i,(n-1)}}\right) + a_{i,b}\,\log_e\left(\frac{KQ_{i,n}}{KQ_{i,(n-1)}}\right)$$

Results for Measured Transport

The results of applying these methods to labour, capital and total factor inputs are given in Table 3.8. Exponential rates of change for periods and sub-periods can be derived in the usual way from the calculated indices.

Total organised transport and communication (TOTC)

An analagous procedure has been followed for the labour input in TOTC to determine exponential rates of change of labour input (adjusted for inter-sectoral 'quality' shift) and for the inter-sectoral 'quality' shift in the labour input itself.

KEY TO SYMBOLS

	SECTORS OF MEASURED TRANSPORT	MEASURED TRANSPORT INDUSTRY		
		Unadjusted	Adjusted	Inter-sectoral 'quality' shift
		[for inter-sectoral 'quality' shift]		
LABOUR INPUT				
Crude manpower, number, year n	$L_{s,n}$	$L_{i,n}$		
Standardised labour unit (SLU) hours, year n	$LI_{s,n}$	$LI_{i,n}$	$LI'_{i,n}$	$LIQ_{i,n}$
CAPITAL INPUT				
Gross capital stock (at constant prices), year n	$K_{s,n}$	$K_{i,n}$	$K'_{i,n}$	$KQ_{i,n}$
TOTAL FACTOR INPUT in year n	$TFI_{s,n}$	$TFI_{i,n}$	$TFI'_{i,n}$	$TFQ_{i,n}$
FACTOR REMUNERATION[a] AND FACTOR SHARES				
Average wage rate (£ per SLU hour) in base year (b)	$W_{s,b}$	$W_{i,b}$		
Total remuneration[a] of labour input (£) in base year (b)	$Y_{L_{s,b}}$	$Y_{L_{i,b}}$		
Rate of return[a] on capital in base year (b)	$R_{s,b}$	$R_{i,b}$		
Total remuneration[a] of capital input (£) in base year (b)	$Y_{K_{s,b}}$	$Y_{K_{i,b}}$		
Share of capital in net output[a] in base year (b)	$\alpha_{s,b}$	$\alpha_{i,b}$		

[a] Factor remuneration and net output are here measured on a 'full factor cost' basis, i.e. including subsidies.

4 Productivity

The objective in this Chapter is to present the results of productivity measurement. An interpretation and explanation of these results is reserved to Chapters 5 and 6; but the results of measurement, in some cases measurement by more than one method, lead directly to certain conclusions in terms of relationships between output and productivity movements and of the ranking of sectors by productivity performance. Productivity movements are shown both in terms of output per man hour (standardised) and per unit of total factor input. Productivity levels are considered only in terms of output per unit of total factor input.

Methods of measurement are explained first and are followed by an examination of productivity movements. Then comparative productivity levels are considered and the two measures are combined and shown graphically (Figure 8). The measure of productivity levels in each sector of the Measured Transport industry and in postal services and telecommunications is shown both unadjusted and adjusted for differences in the 'quality' of the labour employed.[1]

A.   Methods of Measurement

Attention has already been drawn[2] to the limitations of the traditional measure of output per person employed. It has been shown by others[3] that such a measure bears no relation to the efficiency of labour. It relates output to one type of factor input chosen arbitrarily from among several. Later in this Paper a production function is applied to the measure of movement in output per unit of labour input in order to interpret the movement in terms of the contribution to it of movement in capital intensity and other factors. In this present chapter the productivity movements in the transport sectors are shown in this traditional form first (Table 4.1, Panel A) and are followed by a measure which is more complete and meaningful in that it brings into account the input of both labour and capital in order to reach a productivity measure of output per unit of combined, labour and capital, factor input (Table 4.1, Panel B).

---

[1] On the assumption that all labour quality differences are reflected in the differences between sectors in average hourly earnings per standardised labour unit input.

[2] Chapter 1, pages 17 and 18.

[3] Salter and Kendrick, op. cit.

Table 4.1. Movements in Labour Productivity and Total Factor Productivity   United Kingdom SIC 1958

Exponential rates of change per annum

	A. Output (unadjusted) per Standardised Labour Unit Hour, (ΔP_{LI}) (at 1958 prices)				B. Output (unadjusted) per Unit of Total Factor Input, (ΔATOKE) (at 1958 prices)			
	1952–62	1952–58	1958–62	1962–65 (Provisional)[a]	1952–62	1952–58	1958–62	1962–65 (Provisional)[a]
Railways	−0.16	−0.69	0.64	5.40	−0.64	−0.93	−0.20	4.03
Road Passenger Transport	−1.05	−1.48	−0.37	−3.84	−1.25	−2.42	0.50	−4.63
Road Haulage Contracting	5.87	6.75	4.56	3.43	4.46	5.43	2.99	2.62
Sea Transport	1.88	0.82	3.46	7.95	0.92	0.20	2.01	5.17
Port and Inland Water Transport	3.92	2.85	5.55	4.06	3.79	2.92	5.11	3.69
Air Transport	8.02	9.15	6.33	13.38	5.47	5.21	5.87	13.41
MEASURED TRANSPORT								
1. Unadjusted	2.46	1.90	3.31	5.01	1.93	1.46	2.62	4.19
2. Adjusted[b]	2.34	1.81	3.15	5.06	1.46	0.92	2.26	3.85
Postal Services & Telecommunications	2.38	2.17	2.69	4.24	1.68	1.42	2.06	3.61

a The figures given for the period 1962 to 1965 must be regarded as provisional. One main reason is that there has been no road goods survey results published since those relating to 1962. The output indicator for road haulage contracting for 1962 to 1965 in terms of ton miles is officially stated to be an extrapolation, and may be subject to revision when the results of the 1967/68 survey are available. (Cf. Highway Statistics, 1967, Table 47, footnote, Ministry of Transport, London).

b For 'aggregation bias' in labour input, Panel A, and in both labour and capital inputs in Panel B.

There are several methods of combining movements in labour and in capital input in order to arrive at movements in total factor input. Two such methods are considered here and one is chosen. The first may be summarised in the following expression:[1]

$$\frac{TFI_t}{TFI_b} = (1 - a) \frac{LI_t}{LI_b} + a \frac{K_t}{K_b}$$ (1)

where TFI is total factor input, a and $(1 - a)$ are the shares of capital and labour respectively in the base year b; LI is labour input in terms of standardised manhours; K is capital stock input; and subscript, t indicates the time period in relation to the base year (indicated by subscript, b).

The second method may be summarised in the following form:

$$\frac{T\hat{F}I_n}{T\hat{F}I_{n-1}} = \frac{LI_t}{LI_b} + a \frac{(K/L)_t}{(K/L)_b}$$ (2)

where, in addition to the terms already explained for the first method, K/L is capital stock intensity in terms of capital per person in employment.

These functions are applied to the data in the following way.

The period under examination, 1952 to 1965, is first divided into three sub-periods, 1952–56, 1956–60 and 1960–65. Values for a and $(1 - a)$ are available for the Census of Production years 1954, 1958 and 1963, and applied respectively to each of the sub-periods distinguished.[2] Total factor productivity movement is calculated in exponential terms, and movements in the sub-periods are spliced together, a process made possible by the overlapping of these periods.

The actual functions used weight year-on-year exponential movements of the factor by the share of that factor in output (gross value added + subsidies)[3] in the base years for each sub-period. The functions are as follows:

$$\log_e \left(\frac{TFI_n}{TFI_{n-1}} \right) = (1 - a_n) \log_e \left(\frac{LI_n}{LI_{n-1}} \right) + a_n \log_e \left(\frac{K_n}{K_{n-1}} \right)$$ (3)

$$\log_e \left(\frac{T\hat{F}I_n}{T\hat{F}I_{n-1}} \right) = \log_e \left(\frac{LI_n}{LI_{n-1}} \right) + a_n \log_e \left(\frac{(K/L)_n}{(K/L)_{n-1}} \right)$$ (4)

where n refers to the number of years.

These functions give values for TFI_n / TFI_{n-1} and $T\hat{F}I_n / T\hat{F}I_{n-1}$ which are then chained to give alternative indexes of total factor input for each sector of the

---

1 In basic form the same as that employed by R.C.O. Matthews, op. cit., and by others.

2 For data underlying a values see Statistical Appendix, Section D, Table D2.

3 Referred to also as the 'full factor cost' measure of net output.

113

Measured Transport industry and for postal services and telecommunications. For the Measured Transport industry as a whole total factor input is measured by the methods described above, using first the unadjusted labour and capital input data and, second, data adjusted for the sectoral 'quality' shifts (aggregation biases) which are described in Chapter 3 and in the methodological note to that chapter. This gives two 'chained' indexes for total factor input into Measured Transport, one of which is adjusted and the other unadjusted.[1]

Productivity movements are then calculated by dividing the index of net output (base 1952 = 100) by the chosen index of total factor input (base 1952 = 100). This gives an index of output per unit of total factor input. In broad terms this is called the 'residual', because it is the gain (or loss) in output which is achieved after account has been taken of the contributions made to output by the factors of labour and capital as such.

Exponential rates of change, by sector and industry, for output, total factor input and output per unit of total factor input (the 'residual') are shown in Table 4.2.

B.   A Digression on the 'Residual'

A short digression seems necessary at this point in order to relate to one another the two methods, described above, of measuring output per unit of combined factor input (the 'residual'). The first method, involving functions (1) and (3) in the preceding section, measures capital intensity per standardised unit of labour input whereas the second method,[2] shown earlier by functions (2) and (4), measures capital intensity per manyear of labour input. Apart from this difference the theoretical concepts and the assumptions are the same for both functions. For the purpose of demonstrating that the two functions do have the same meaning, it is assumed that capital intensity is measured by one of the two methods, say K/LI.

The productivity function derived directly from the production function described in Chapter 1 is:

$$\Delta P_{LI} = \alpha(\Delta K - \Delta LI) + \Delta ATOKE$$

and the Kendrick/Matthews-type function for output per unit of combined factor input is:

$$\Delta P_{TFI} = \Delta R$$

where P_{LI} is output per unit of labour input.

α is the share of capital in total factor income.

LI is labour input adjusted for hours, holidays and the intra-sectoral 'quality'

---

1 See Statistical Appendix, Section D, Table D1.

2 Described in Chapter 1, page 28, where the underlying assumptions and theoretical context of this type of production function is also given.

Exponential rates of change per annum

	Output, (ΔY) (value at 1958 prices)				Total Factor Inputs,[a] (ΔTFI)				Output per Total Factor Input (ΔATOKE)			
	1952–62	1952–58	1958–62	1962–65 (Provisional)[b]	1952–62	1952–58	1958–62	1962–65 (Provisional)[b]	1952–62	1952–58	1958–62	1962–65 (Provisional)[b]
Railways	-1.93	-1.62	-2.39	-0.18	-1.32	-0.71	-2.21	-4.22	-0.64	-0.93	-0.20	4.03
Road Passenger Transport	-2.30	-2.84	-1.49	-3.74	-1.02	-0.41	-1.93	0.90	-1.25	-2.42	0.50	-4.63
Road Haulage Contracting	7.26	7.43	6.99	6.90	2.79	1.98	3.99	4.28	4.46	5.43	2.99	2.62
Sea Transport	1.23	1.20	1.29	1.47	0.34	1.02	-0.68	-3.69	0.92	0.20	2.01	5.17
Port & Inland Water Transport	2.26	2.00	2.67	1.92	-1.54	-0.92	-2.47	-1.76	3.79	2.92	5.11	3.69
Air Transport	12.58	11.86	13.67	16.65	7.27	6.85	7.89	3.26	5.47	5.21	5.87	13.41
MEASURED TRANSPORT 1. Unadjusted[c]	{1.65	1.39	2.04	3.08	-0.28	-0.07	-0.58	-1.12	1.93	1.46	2.62	4.19
2. Adjusted[c]			2.04	3.08	0.19	0.46	-0.23	-0.77	1.46	0.92	2.26	3.85
Postal Services & Telecommunications	3.10	2.32	4.27	6.28	1.42	0.90	2.20	2.68	1.68	1.42	2.06	3.61

[a] For the method used to combine labour and capital inputs see Chapter 4, Section A. Annual indices of combined factor inputs are given in the Statistical Appendix Section D, Table D.1.

[b] See footnote (a) to Table 4.1.

[c] Figures in the higher row are unadjusted and, in the lower row, adjusted, for the inter-sectoral 'quality' shifts in factor inputs, see the Methodological Note to Chapter 3.

shift change for sectors, and also the inter-sectoral 'quality' shift change in the case of the Measured Transport industry.

K is capital stock gross, new at 1958 replacement cost.

ATOKE is applied technical and organisational knowledge and external factors, a residual term equal to total factor productivity.

P_{TFI} is output per unit of total factor input.

R is the 'residual' in the Kendrick/Matthews sense, and is necessarily equal to output per unit of total, combined factor input.

Δ is the percentage exponential rate of change per annum of the variable concerned.

Both methods involve a residual term which represents, in each case, the contribution to output movements made by influences other than changes in the input of labour and capital as such. It is necessary to show that the two residual terms, reached by different methods, are equal to one another, thus implying equality under each method of the contributions to output movements of movements in the input of factors. It has been shown that:

$$\Delta \text{ATOKE} = \Delta P_{LI} - a(\Delta K - \Delta LI) \tag{1}$$

and
$$\Delta R = \Delta P_{TFI} \tag{2}$$

If $\Delta \text{ATOKE} = \Delta R$

then
$$\Delta P_{TFI} = \Delta P_{LI} - a(\Delta K - \Delta LI) \tag{3}$$

and
$$\Delta Y - \Delta \text{TFI} = \Delta Y - \Delta LI - a(\Delta K - \Delta LI) \tag{4}$$

Substituting $[(1 - a) \Delta LI + a\Delta K]$ for ΔTFI in equation (4), we get:

$$- [(1 - a) \Delta LI + a\Delta K] = - \Delta LI - a(\Delta K - \Delta LI)$$

and
$$- \Delta LI + a\Delta LI - a\Delta K = - \Delta LI - a\Delta K + a\Delta LI,$$

therefore $\Delta \text{ATOKE} = \Delta R$.

If the assumption about the measure of capital services is now removed and in equation (1) $(\Delta K - \Delta L)$ is substituted for $(\Delta K - \Delta LI)$, we get:

$$\Delta \text{ATOKE} = \Delta Y - \Delta LI - a(\Delta K - \Delta L)$$

and
$$\Delta R = \Delta Y - [(1 - a) \Delta LI + a\Delta K]$$

therefore
$$\Delta \text{ATOKE} = \Delta R - a(\Delta LI - \Delta L) \tag{5}$$

The meaning of equation (5) is that if labour input per person employed $(\Delta LI - \Delta L)$ declines, as it does for example in the railways in the period 1958–1962 by 0.39 per cent per annum, then ΔATOKE is higher than ΔR over this period by $0.39a$; and the contribution of movements in capital intensity to output movements are greater by $0.39a$ where the Kendrick/Matthews function is applied to the same data. But greater capital intensity due to a decline in hours of work or to negative movements in intra-sectoral labour 'quality' are most unlikely to result in an increase in capital's contribution to output. Capital 'deepening' brought about in this way may be counter productive in transport operations and is due, basically, to the relatively very great indivisibility and specificity of capital in relation to labour. To put the point another way. If we assume that capital stock is a constant, then the input of capital services is reduced by a reduction in labour's working hours and vice versa because of the change in the degree of utilisation of the associated capital equipment. As it is intended later in this Paper to study in some detail the levels and movements in capacity utilisation and to compare the latter with movements in total factor productivity, it is necessary to notice that ΔATOKE will include the effects of these, quite small, movements in the input of capital services, and ΔR will exclude them. For these reasons it seems right to adopt ΔATOKE as our measure of total factor productivity, recognising that it is a 'residual' term.

The next question to ask about ΔATOKE, now that it has been distinguished from ΔR, is: How far does ΔATOKE represent a measure of technical progress in some form (i.e. the contribution to labour productivity movement which stems from concurrent movement in applied technical and organisational knowledge), and how far are other, extraneous factors included in this residual term?

An answer is attempted in the following terms. Under the general heading of aggregation bias the factor inputs into the sectors concerned in this research have been 'cleaned up' to a considerable extent. This 'cleaning up' process is described in Chapter 3, in the associated Methodological Note and in Section B of the Statistical Appendix. Included there is a detailed description of the method of calculating the following bias or 'quality' shift factors which have been calculated or, where necessary, estimated and an appropriate allowance made for them in the measures of labour and capital input. In brief, the shift changes calculated or estimated are as follows.

1. Intra-sectoral labour 'quality' shift. This allows for the changes over time in the age and sex composition of the labour force *within* each sector.

2. Inter-sectoral labour 'quality' shift. This allows for the quality differences of labour input *between* sectors of the Measured Transport industry.

3. Inter-sectoral capital 'quality' shift. This makes the same type of allowance for capital 'quality' as that for labour under paragraph 2.

In addition, the measures of total factor input, of output and of productivity per unit of labour input and per unit of total factor input have been improved by the construction of a 'chained' index of year-on-year changes in the variables concerned.

Because data are lacking it is not possible to calculate or even estimate the 'shift' component in the input of capital into each sector. To do this would require a 'vintage' model of the capital stock in each sector. This could be done by making a separate valuation of each year's addition to the capital stock and devising a weight which is specific to each addition, with higher weights for the more recent and, presumably, more productive additions. This shift factor is therefore, by default of data, thrown in with our residual terms ATOKE. Nevertheless, as a result of the elimination of the various aggregation biases which have been described, these measures are less of an assortment of various shifts in factor inputs and are much more concentrated upon:

1. What Solow has called 'slowdowns and speed-ups', that in our terms is movements in capacity utilisation, which is a part of ATOKE.[1]

2. True shifts in the production function itself, representing the effects on output movement of movement in 'applied technical and organisational knowledge'.

3. Movements in 'external factors'. These can be important generally and perhaps particularly in transport operations. They include such factors as the legal obligation to provide transport services in certain areas regardless of the level of demand and of the financial (or economic) viability of doing so; the licencing system which restricts the expansion of capacity in road haulage contracting; and, possibly more significant, the economies of scale which are gained (or lost) as output moves up or down steadily and to a significant degree for longer than a short period.

Some undetected biases in input and output measures will inevitably remain, and the only place for their dynamic effects to show up will be in the residual term, ATOKE.

C.   Productivity Movements

The exponential rates of productivity movement by sector and by industry are shown in terms of output per unit of labour input as well as of output per unit of combined (labour and capital) factor input in Table 4.1. The measure of net output is unadjusted for aggregation bias. Such adjustments as can be made on the basis of the research described in Chapter 2 are applied in the interpretative analysis which is given in Chapter 5.

One of the more general conclusions which may be drawn from the analysis in Table 4.1 is the fairly obvious one that when both labour and capital are brought into the productivity ratio then the movement of the ratio is generally less rapid in an upwards direction, and more rapid in a downwards direction, than it is for labour productivity alone. This is true unless the K/L ratio of capital intensity is concurrently stationary or moving in a negative direction, as it is in road passenger transport in 1958–62, in port and inland water transport in 1952–58 and surprisingly, in air transport in 1962–65.[2] For similar reasons, where K/L movements are only very slightly positive then the movements shown in panel B do not differ very greatly from those in panel A. So where capital input is rising

---

1   Capacity utilisation is examined in Chapter 6.

2   This comparison may be made by an inspection of panels A and B of Table 4.1 and of the sectoral movements of K/L in Table 3.6 and the Statistical Appendix Section C. Table C.1.

relatively to labour input, total factor productivity movement will be less positive (or more negative) than labour productivity movement, and vice versa.

The total factor productivity movement (ΔATOKE) of the Measured Transport industry accelerated over the period 1952 to 1962. The rate of increase 1.93 per cent per annum, unadjusted, was high in comparison with the rate for service industries as a whole,[1] and close to the rate for manufacturers. All sectors in the analysis except road haulage contracting, where the rate of increase was lower in the 1958–62 period, contributed to the later improvement, and although productivity in the railways continued to decline, it did so at a slower rate than in the first sub-period. The dispersion of sectoral rates about the mean was appreciably less in the period from 1958 to 1962 than it was in the earlier period, 1952–58.[2]

For the Measured Transport industry the effects of aggregation biases in labour input were small and virtually constant throughout the whole period, but inter-sectoral aggregation bias in capital input was relatively much greater, but its effect declined markedly in the 1958–62 period compared with 1952–58.

On a provisional basis (for reasons given in a footnote to Table 4.1) total factor productivity increased from 1962 to 1965. During this period a marked improvement occurred in the Measured Transport industry where the adjusted rate rose to 3.85 per cent per annum (2.26 in 1958–62). It is particularly interesting to notice that the railways contributed to this improvement, due largely to the Beeching cuts in factor input (see Table 4.2) after 1962 while output continued to fall, but much less rapidly. Sea and air transport contributed markedly higher rates of total factor productivity change in this most recent period, but road passenger transport produced a large negative rate and became the only declining sector; road haulage contracting and ports had lower rates than in the immediately preceding period.

D.   Relationships between Measured Transport Output, Total Factor Productivity and Gross Domestic Product

In Figure 6 are shown the movements in gross domestic product (at constant, 1958 factor cost), in the volume of output of Measured Transport and in total factor productivity in Measured Transport over the period 1952–65.

One directly observable conclusion to this analysis of movements of total factor productivity is the close relationship between movements in total factor productivity and output in Measured Transport, and between movements in output in Measured Transport and movements in gross domestic product.

---

[1] As measured by Matthews, op. cit., for the rather different but largely overlapping period, 1948–1962, he finds annual average cumulative percentage rates of change in the 'residual' of 0.7 for 'services and distribution' and 1.7 for manufacturing.

[2] Dispersion 3.22 for 1952–58; 2.54 for 1958–62.

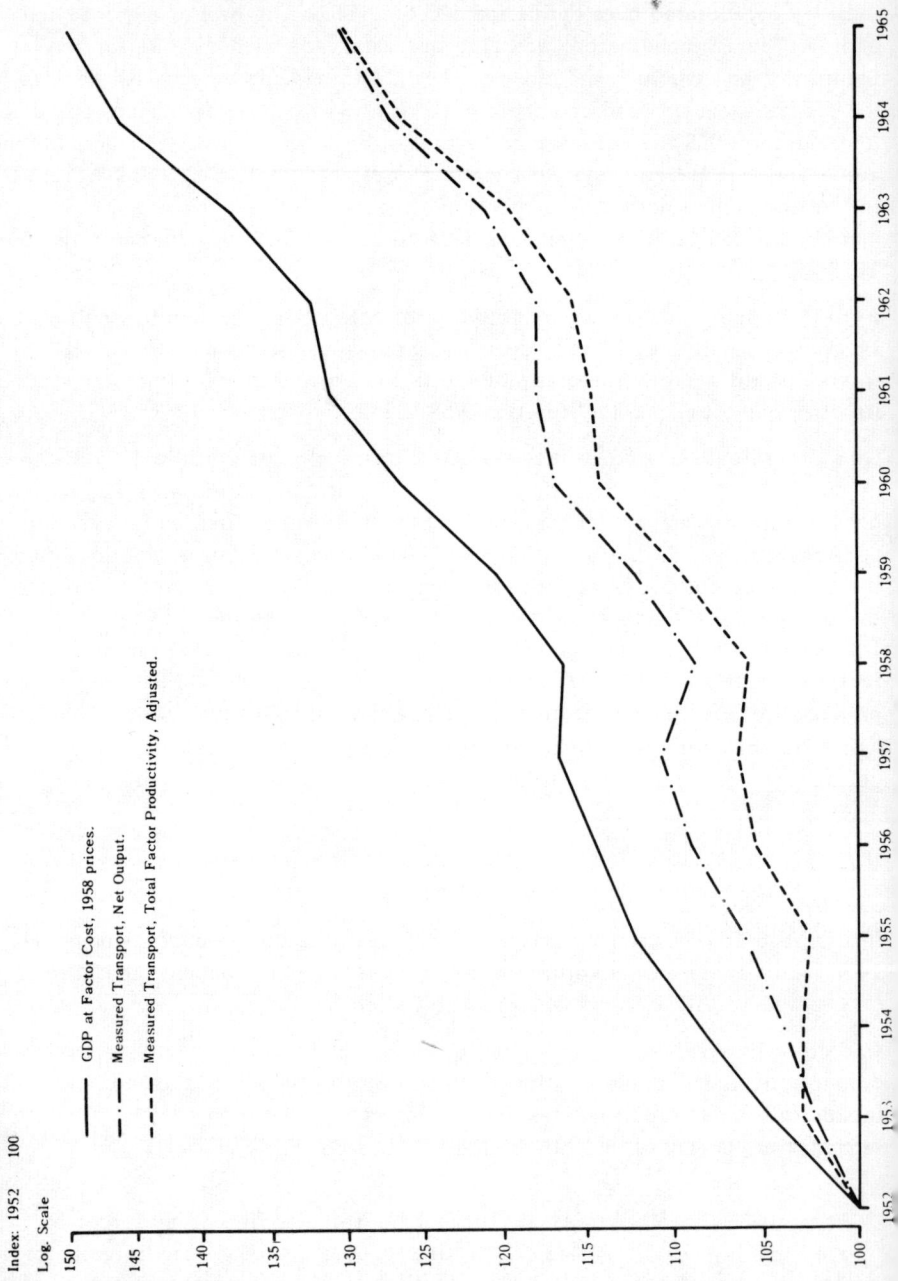

Figure 6. Trends in Gross Domestic Product and in Output and Total Factor Productivity (Adjusted) in Measured Transport, 1952–1965

Index: 1952   100

Log. Scale

———— GDP at Factor Cost, 1958 prices.

—·—· Measured Transport, Net Output.

– – – – Measured Transport, Total Factor Productivity, Adjusted.

120

Table 4.3.   Year-on-Year Movements in Gross Domestic Product and in Output
and Total Factor Productivity in Measured Transport, 1953–65.

	1 ΔGDP	2 ΔMT Output	3 ΔMT Total Factor Productivity
1953	4.7	2.2	2.9
54	3.5	1.7	0
55	3.4	2.0	−0.3
56	2.0	2.7	2.7
57	1.9	1.6	1.0
58	−0.2	−1.7	−0.6
59	3.4	3.0	3.5
60	5.1	4.2	4.4
61	3.6	1.0	0.4
62	0.9	0	0.9
63	4.2	2.2	3.2
64	5.8	5.3	5.4
65	2.6	2.5	3.1

The relationship between output and productivity is examined further in Chapter 6
but it is shown clearly in Figure 6 that in Measured Transport, while output
increased at a faster rate than productivity in the period 1954–57, it was
productivity that was rising faster from 1962–65. The tendency for all three
variables to move together over time is also clearly shown in the graph.[1]

To investigate the association between the variables further, the variations from
trend were calculated by taking year-on-year movements of all three series, and
these are shown in Table 4.3. The correlation coefficients were then calculated
together with the regression equations to estimate the form of the relationship
(and the closeness of fit) between the variables.

The results obtained were as shown in Table 4.4. The first regression equation
indicates that an increase in GDP of 1 per cent per annum above its average
annual movement has been associated with an above average increase of 0.86 per
cent in Measured Transport output. The regression of productivity change (Y) on
output change (X) in Measured Transport indicates that a one per cent movement
above its average in MT output has been associated with a 0.93 per cent movement
in total factor productivity above its average.

It is perhaps not surprising that with the near 'one for one' relationship between
changes in MT output and productivity, the amount of change in MT productivity

---

1 Gross domestic product is clearly rising at a faster rate than output in
Measured Transport and this can be explained partly by the omission
of non-marketed transport services from Measured Transport.

Table 4.4.

Relationship (Year-on-year changes in each variable, 1952–65)	Correlation coefficient, R^2	Regression equation and standard error of the b term
1. ΔGDP (X) and ΔMT Output (Y)	0.700	$Y = -0.66 + 0.86\,X$ (S.E. $= 0.170$)
2. ΔMT Output (X) and ΔMT Productivity (Y)	0.842	$Y = 0.14 + 0.93\,X$ (S.E. $= 0.179$)
3. ΔGDP (X) and ΔMT Productivity (Y)	0.661	$Y = -0.32 + 0.75\,X$ (S.E. $= 0.257$)

Table 4.5.　Productivity Levels in terms of Output per unit of Combined Factor Input, 1954, 1958 and 1963

(Pence per Standardised Labour unit hour equivalent, at current prices)

	1954		1958		1963	
	Unadjusted	Adjusted[a]	Unadjusted	Adjusted[a]	Unadjusted	Adjusted[a]
	d.	d.	d.	d.	d.	d.
Railways	31.9	33.1	35.5	36.5	47.3	48.0
Road Passenger Transport	57.6	64.8	75.1	83.5	101.3	117.8
Road Haulage Contracting	77.0	69.8	91.4	86.2	136.1	119.3
Sea Transport	57.6	57.8	71.8	70.6	102.7	97.4
Port and Inland Water Transport	50.2	44.4	61.7	58.6	89.0	86.2
Air Transport	97.2	66.0	110.2	81.1	152.6	120.2
Postal Services & Telecommunications[b]	61.4	50.2	93.4	71.5	115.9	97.4

a For inter-sectoral labour 'quality' differences.

b Factors are combined using Measured Transport weights.

above its average associated with a 1 per cent change above its average of GDP has not been very different (at 0.75 per cent) from that between GDP and MT output changes (0.86 per cent).

122

E.   Comparative Productivity Levels

Inter-sectoral comparisons of absolute productivity levels in terms of the conventional measure of output per unit of labour input would be made meaningless by the different capital intensity levels of sectors. These problems may be surmounted by aggregating both labour and capital inputs in terms of 'standard labour unit hour equivalents'. The method of doing this has been explained in Chapter 1 (pages 30 and 31).

The results of applying this method to the Measured Transport industry and the six sectors of it which have been distinguished are shown in Table 4.5.[1] Absolute levels of output per unit of combined factor input are given. The combined input units are standard labour unit hour equivalents, and output is in *current* value terms.

For the railways the measure of net output is 'full factor cost'; by this is meant total factor rewards including subsidies and 'subsidy equivalents'.[2] The gross rate of return to capital is calculated on the same basis. In all other sectors output has been measured on the basis of total factor rewards including depreciation.

The adjustments to the total factor productivity levels (shown in Table 4.5) are made on the assumption that labour quality differences are reflected in the differences between sectors in earnings per hour. The effect is to adjust productivity upwards in those sectors where the rate of earnings is below the Measured Transport industry average and to adjust productivity downwards where the earnings rate is above this average and where labour input is accordingly judged to be correspondingly greater. The downward adjustment to productivity in air transport is very marked for this reason, but in other sectors the effect of these adjustments is much less.[3]

The relative importance of these inter-sectoral adjustments to productivity levels in 1954, 1958 and 1963 may be seen in graphical form by comparing closely sections A and B of Figure 7. The effect of the adjustment to levels is to reduce the dispersion of sectoral levels about the level for Measured Transport when account is taken of the greater weight which should be attached to labour of higher quality as measured by higher remuneration. Intra-sectoral aggregation bias has been considered earlier[4] and, in the case of labour, the adjustments made are incorporated in the sectoral levels shown in both sections of this Figure.

---

1   A sequential analysis of the calculation of total factor productivity levels is shown in Table 4.9 in the appendix to this Chapter.

2   These are Government loans to meet current deficits rather than direct subsidies.

3   It would not be right to make *further* allowances for the differences which occur in the remuneration of capital between sectors, as this has already been done in the process of combining factor inputs.

4   Chapter 3, Section A.

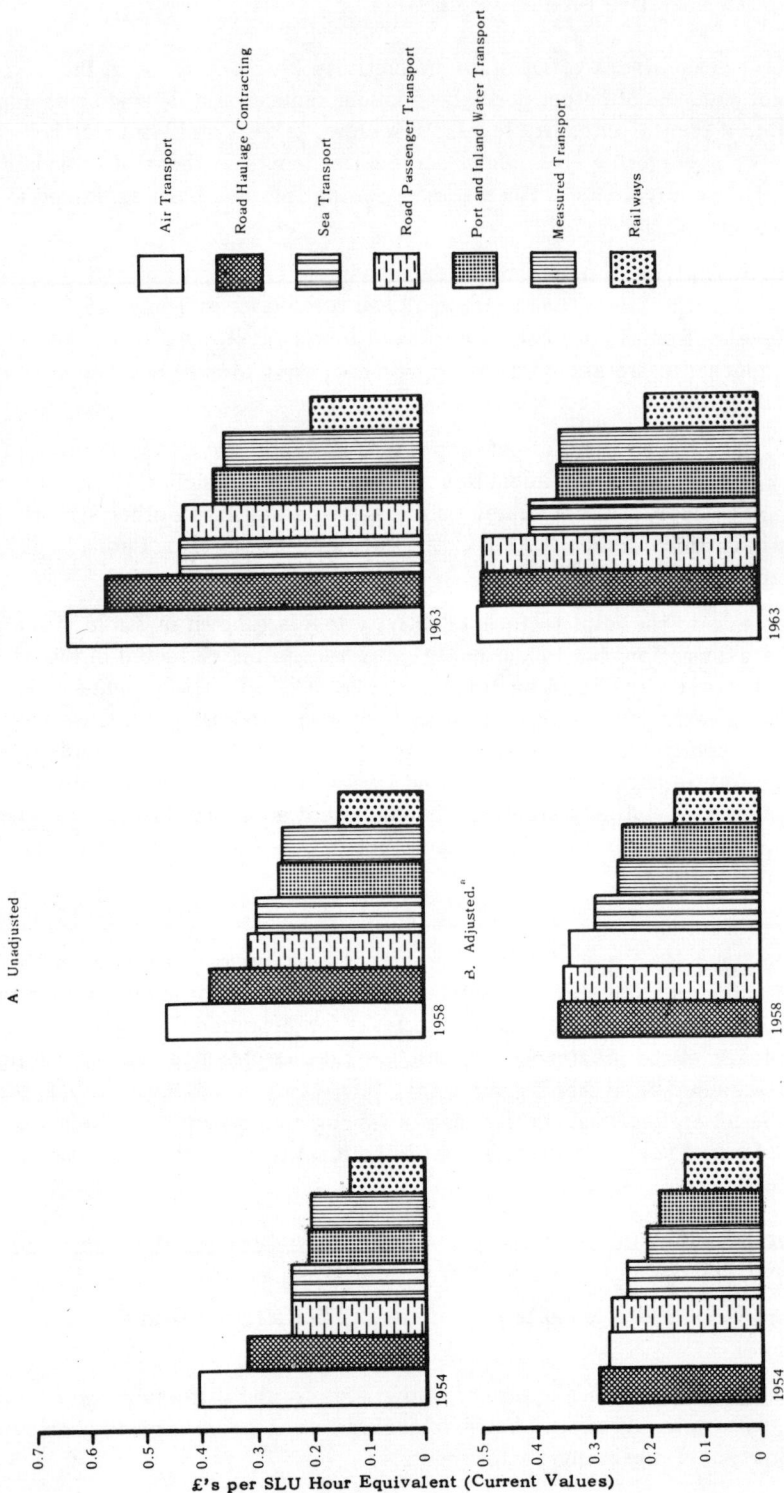

Figure 7. Comparative Productivity Levels in Measured Transport. Net Output per unit of Combined Factor Input, 1954, 1958 and 1963 at current prices.

A. Unadjusted

B. Adjusted.ª

Air Transport

Road Haulage Contracting

Sea Transport

Road Passenger Transport

Port and Inland Water Transport

Measured Transport

Railways

£'s per SLU Hour Equivalent (Current Values)

ª Adjusted for 'qualitative' inter-sectoral differences in labour input as measured by differences in average earnin₁s per hour

124

The question now arises as to what can be learned from a comparison of total factor productivity levels by sector. Perhaps the most striking feature is the consistently low position of the railways, whose bottom ranking place is established by a substantial margin in all years whether inputs are adjusted for aggregation bias or not. In view of its relatively poor total factor productivity movement, it is perhaps surprising to notice also that road passenger transport has such a relatively high ranking position in all three years.[1]

F.   Total Factor Productivity Levels, Movements and Convergence

Movements in total factor productivity, measured in terms of constant 1958 prices, are combined in Figure 8 with total factor productivity levels in 1954.

The longer period 1954–1965 is sub-divided into three sub-periods (1954–58, 1958–62 and 1962–65), and the 1954 levels, and the movements in these periods, are also given in Table 4.6.

Table 4.6.   Total Factor Productivity Level and Movement, 1954–1965

Sectors in Ranking Order of Total Factor Productivity *Level*, adjusted, 1954.	Total Factor Productivity *Level*, adjusted, 1954. (Pence per SLU hour equivalent)	Total Factor Productivity *Movement*			
		1954–58	1958–62	1962–65	1954–65
1. Road Haulage Contracting	69.8	4.95	2.99	2.62	3.60
2. Air Transport	66.0	3.28	5.87	13.41	7.04
3. Road Passenger Transport	64.8	3.09	0.50	−4.63	−2.20
4. Sea Transport	57.8	0.68	2.01	5.17	2.38
5. Port and Inland Water Transport	44.4	1.69	5.11	3.69	3.47
6. Railways	33.1	−1.00	−0.20	4.03	0.60
Postal Services and Telecommunications	50.2	0.72	2.06	3.61	1.99

[4] When 1963 is compared with 1954 in current price terms part of an explanation for this lies in the large rise in the *relative* price of net output of this sector. See Chapter 6, Table 6.12.

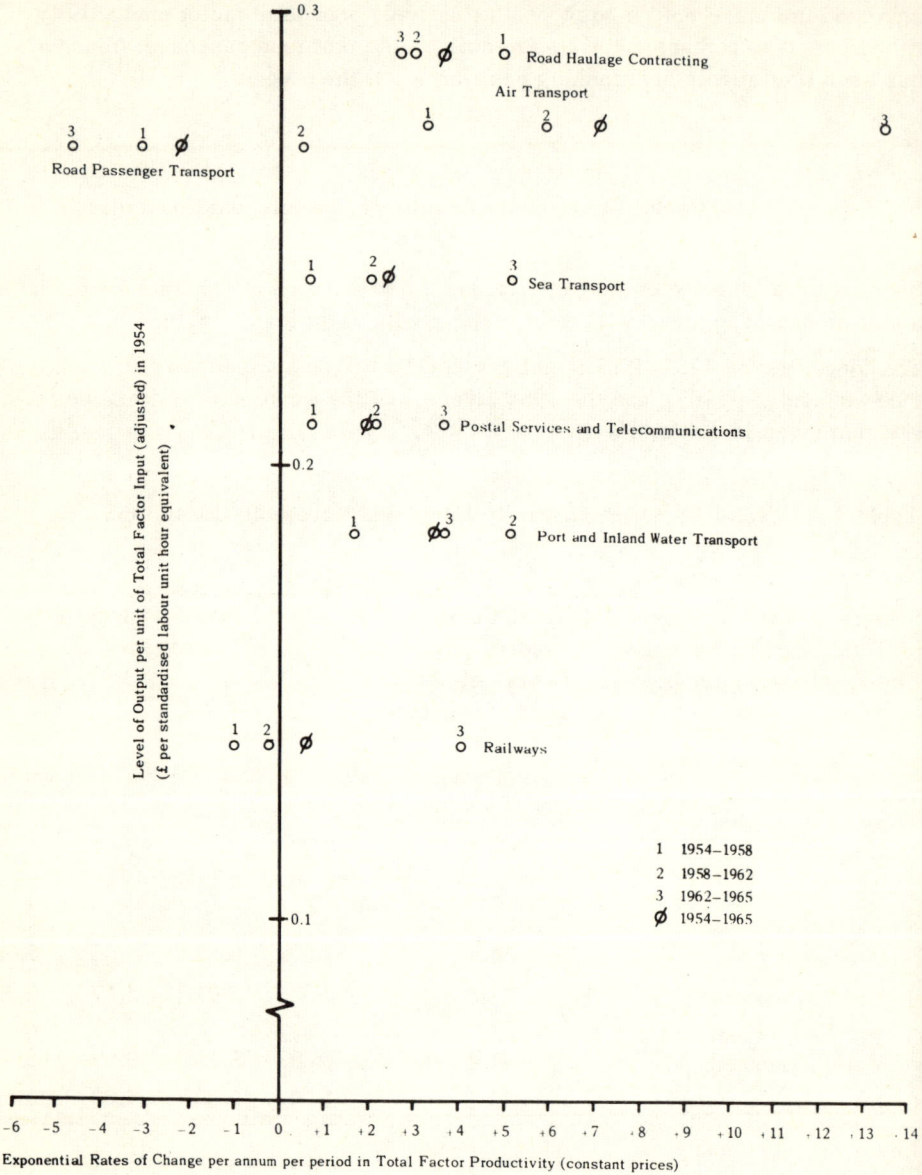

Figure 8.   Levels and Movements per Period in Total Factor Productivity in Measured Transport Sectors and in Postal Services and Telecommunications (Levels in 1954, movements 1954–1965 and sub-periods)

0.3

3 2   1
○○ ∅   ○   Road Haulage Contracting

Air Transport

3   1   1   2   3
○   ○   ∅   ○   ○   ∅   ○
Road Passenger Transport

2
○

1   2
○   ○∅   3
                       ○   Sea Transport

1   2   3
○   ∅○   ○   Postal Services and Telecommunications

0.2

1   2 3   2
○   ∅○   ○   Port and Inland Water Transport

1   2   3
○   ○   ∅   ○   Railways

1   1954–1958
2   1958–1962
3   1962–1965
∅   1954–1965

0.1

Level of Output per unit of Total Factor Input (adjusted) in 1954
(£ per standardised labour unit hour equivalent)

-6   -5   -4   -3   -2   -1   0   +1   +2   +3   +4   +5   +6   +7   +8   +9   +10   +11   +12   +13   +14

Exponential Rates of Change per annum per period in Total Factor Productivity (constant prices)

126

Implications for alterations in the 1954 ranking order of sectors by total factor productivity levels are seen in the acceleration[1] of movements over the whole 1954–65 period in air, sea and rail transport (in this last named sector the improvement occurs chiefly in 1962–65); a decelerating movement in road haulage contracting; and little change on balance in road passenger transport, which declines over the whole period, and in port and inland water transport.

Postal services and telecommunications[2] are shown separately in Table 4.6. If this sector were ranked with the transport sectors, it would rank as low as fifth (out of a total of seven) in terms of total factor productivity level in 1954. In terms of movement, total factor productivity accelerates in this sector, but not very fast (see Figure 8); it would rank lowest of the accelerating sectors in terms of rate of change of movement.

There is some tendency towards convergence in that the first and last ranking sectors, road haulage contracting and railways, are decelerating and accelerating respectively. Furthermore, in the 1962–65 period, the growth rate of total factor productivity in the railways was greater than that in road haulage contracting. However, the gap between the total factor productivity levels of these two sectors is a very wide one; it started to narrow only in 1962 and this trend was due to what will surely prove to have been no more than a large and long overdue reduction in factor inputs in the railways during Lord Beeching's chairmanship. This type of backlog reduction in factor input cannot persist to the same degree in the longer term.

Summary

The results of measuring total factor productivity in Measured Transport and Communication are shown in summary form in Table 4.7.

For the 1952–1962 period the results indicate very wide differences in total factor productivity movements within the Measured Transport industry. The movements range from –1.25 per cent per annum for road passenger transport to 5.47 per cent for air transport. An analysis of the movement of these variables by sub-periods of this period shows that all sectors except road haulage contracting have experienced an acceleration of total factor productivity gain (or a slowing of the rate of loss).

The provisional figures for total factor productivity movements in the 1962–65 period show that the acceleration continues most markedly in air transport and sea transport. There is a dramatic reversal from loss to a high rate of gain in the railways. Road haulage contracting (the figure here should be treated with reserve because of what is stated in footnote (a) to Table 4.7) and ports and

---

1 As judged from a comparison of growth rates by sub-periods of the whole period.

2 Fuller data on total factor productivity levels in this sector are given in Table 4.10 in the appendix to this Chapter.

Table 4.7. Movements and Levels of Net Output per Unit of Combined Factor Input at 1958 Prices

Sectors of Measured Transport in Ranking Order of Total Factor Productivity Movements in 1952–62	Movements (Percentages at exponential rates of change per annum)				Levels Pence per Standard Labour Unit hour equivalent 1958	
	1952–62	1952–58	1958–62	1962–65[a]	Unadjusted	Adjusted[b]
Air Transport	5.47	5.21	5.87	13.41	110.2	81.1
Road Haulage Contracting	4.46	5.43	2.99	2.62	91.4	86.2
Port and Inland Water Transport	3.79	2.92	5.11	3.69	61.7	58.6
Sea Transport	0.92	0.20	2.01	5.17	71.8	70.6
Railways	−0.64	−0.93	−0.20	4.03	35.5	36.5
Road Passenger Transport	−1.25	−2.42	0.50	−4.63	75.1	83.5
MEASURED TRANSPORT						
a. Unadjusted	1.93	1.46	2.62	4.19	60.2	...
b. Adjusted[c]	1.46	0.92	2.26	3.85	...	...
Postal Services & Telecommunications	1.68	1.42	2.06	3.61	93.4[d]	71.5[d]

a The figures given for the period 1962 to 1965 must be regarded as provisional. One main reason is that there has been no road goods survey since 1962. The output indicator for road haulage contracting for 1962 to 1965 in terms of ton miles is officially stated to be an extrapolation and 'may be subject to revision when the results of the 1967/68 survey are available'. (Cf. Highway Statistics, 1967, Table 47, footnote. Ministry of Transport, London).

b For labour 'quality'. For method see page 123 and Table 4.9, footnote b.

c For the inter-sectoral 'quality' shift change in both labour and capital inputs.

d The factors are combined using Measured Transport weights. If 'own weights' are used the unadjusted productivity level is 92.2 pence and there is no inter-sectoral shift in this case. See Chapter appendix Table 4.10.

Table 4.8.　Labour and Total Factor Productivity Movements Compared, 1952–1962. At constant 1958 prices

Measured Transport Sectors in Ranking Order of Total Factor Productivity Movement	Labour Productivity (Output per standardised labour unit hour)	Total Factor Productivity (Output per unit of total, combined factor input)
Air Transport	8.02	5.47
Road Haulage Contracting	5.87	4.46
Port and Inland Water Transport	3.92	3.79
Sea Transport	1.88	0.92
Railways	−0.16	−0.64
Road Passenger Transport	−1.05	−1.25
MEASURED TRANSPORT		
a. Unadjusted	2.46	1.93
b. Adjusted[a]	2.34	1.46
Postal Services and Telecommunications	2.38	1.68

a　See footnote (c) to Table 4.7.

inland water transport move at a slower rate than in 1958–62, the immediately preceding period, and also more slowly than in the longer period, 1952–62. Road passenger transport moves downwards much more steeply in the most recent period. Postal services and telecommunications follow quite closely the total factor productivity trend for the Measured Transport industry (after adjustment for aggregation bias), with a slowly accelerating rate of total factor productivity; but this sector compares rather poorly with the measured transport sectors. If ranked by movements with these sectors it would be in fourth place in all the periods distinguished except in the latest period (1962–65), when it would rank fifth.

Labour productivity and total factor productivity compared

This comparison is made for the period 1952–1962 in Table 4.8.

It may be seen that when account is taken, in the measurement of productivity, of movements of capital as well as labour inputs the effect is relatively very small only in port and inland water transport and in road passenger transport where, in this period, the movement of capital input is negative (Table 3.9). It might be expected that such a movement in capital input would make the total factor productivity movements more positive (or less negative) than the labour productivity movements, but in these two sectors capital input is falling more slowly than labour input. In effect therefore, capital input is rising *relatively* to labour, and this is true of every sector.

129

Relationships between movements in GDP, and in output and total factor productivity in Measured Transport

The short run cycles of the United Kingdom economy, as indicated by movements in Gross Domestic Product at factor cost and constant prices, are reflected in the movements of output in Measured Transport (see Figure 6).

Year-on-year movements in output and total factor productivity in Measured Transport correlate closely, and a similar relationship is found between GDP and total factor productivity movements in Measured Transport.

Levels, movements and convergence

The disparate *levels* of total factor productivity (in pence per standardised labour unit hour equivalent) in 1958 are considerably reduced by the adjustment for differences in factor 'quality', but even after this adjustment the railways remain the lowest ranking sector by a wide margin (see Table 4.7 and Figure 7).

When total factor productivity *movements* and *levels* are combined on the basis of 1954 levels and constant price movements 1954–65 (see Figure 8), the ranking order of levels in 1954 and the implications provided by subsequent changes in movements for alterations in this ranking order may be summarised as follows.

1. The ranking order of Measured Transport sectors by total factor productivity levels in 1954, adjusted, is as follows:

    Road Haulage Contracting

    Air Transport

    Road Passenger Transport

    Sea Transport

    Port and Inland Water Transport

    Railways

    If ranked, postal services and telecommunications would be placed after sea transport.

2. There is an acceleration of movement in total factor productivity in air, sea and rail transport [in this last named sector the improvement occurs mainly in the 1962–65 period]; a deceleration occurs in road haulage contracting; and little change of movement on balance in road passenger transport, which declines over the whole period, and in port and inland water transport.

3. Postal services and telecommunications accelerated relatively slowly over this period (1954–65) in comparison with air, sea and rail transport.

4. There is *some* tendency towards convergence in that the first and last ranking sectors by levels are decelerating and accelerating respectively, but the gap between total factor productivity levels in these two sectors is a very wide one and it began to narrow only in 1962. The date is significant. It marks the beginning of a large and long overdue reduction in factor input in the railways following a substantial and persistent fall in output. The

higher rate of total factor productivity movement in this sector in the 1962–65 period was due to this special factor which is not likely to recur to a similar degree.

Appendix to Chapter 4

The sequential development of the estimation of the level of total factor productivity in Measured Transport is given in this appendix (Table 4.9). The postal services and telecommunications sector is treated separately (Table 4.10), but the factors are combined using Measured Transport weights.

Table 4.9. Comparative Productivity Levels
Output per Unit of Combined Factor Input in Measured Transport, 1954, 1958 and 1963

United Kingdom
SIC 1958

	(1) Net output at full factor cost^a	(2) Income from employment	(3) Gross capital remuneration	(4) Standardised labour input	(5) Gross capital stock at current prices	(6) Average hourly earnings (2) ÷ (4)	(7) Rate of return on capital (3) ÷ (5)	(8) Combined factor input (unadjusted)	(9) Combined factor input^b (adjusted)	(10) Net output (Gross value Added)	(11) Net output per unit of combined factor input (unadjusted) (10) ÷ (8)	(12) Net output per unit of combined factor input (adjusted) (10) ÷ (9)	(13) Rate of return on capital (ranking)	(14) Net output per combined factor return (unadjusted) (ranking)	(15) Net output per combined factor input (adjusted) (ranking)
	£ million	£ million	£ million	mn. SLU hours	£'000,000,000	£ per SLU hour	%	mn. SLU hours	mn. SLU hours	£ million	£ per SLU hour equiv.	£ per SLU hour equiv.	(ranking)	(ranking)	(ranking)
1954															
Railways	292	227	65	1,160	4.55	0.196	1.43	2,005	1,930	267	0.133	0.138	(6)	(6)	(6)
Road Passenger Transport	193	135	58	733	0.39	0.184	14.87	805	716	193	0.240	0.270	(2)	(3-)	(3)
Road Haulage Contracting	174	115	59	494	0.26	0.233	22.69	542	597	174	0.321	0.291	(1)	(2)	(1)
Sea Transport	201	101	100	483	1.90	0.209	5.26	836	835	201	0.240	0.241	(4)	(3-)	(4)
Port and Inland Water Transport	113	92	21	370	0.92	0.249	2.28	541	610	113	0.209	0.185	(5)	(5)	(5)
Air Transport	36	21	15	59	0.16	0.355	9.37	89	131	36	0.405	0.275	(3)	(1)	(2)
TOTAL MEASURED TRANSPORT	1,009	691	318	3,299	8.18	0.209 w_i^b	3.89 r_i^b	4,817		984	0.204				
1958															
Railways	380	288	92	1,098	5.33	0.262	1.73	1,850	1,805	274	0.148	0.152	(6)	(6)	(6)
Road Passenger Transport	242	170	70	707	0.47	0.243	14.89	774	695	242	0.313	0.348	(2)	(3)	(2)
Road Haulage Contracting	214	150	64	514	0.34	0.292	18.82	562	597	214	0.381	0.359	(1)	(2)	(1)
Sea Transport	245	135	110	478	2.41	0.282	4.56	818	833	245	0.299	0.294	(4)	(4)	(4)
Port and Inland Water Transport	133	109	24	370	1.04	0.295	2.31	517	546	133	0.257	0.244	(5)	(5)	(5)
Air Transport	55	31	24	70	0.35	0.440	6.86	120	163	55	0.459	0.338	(3)	(1)	(3)
TOTAL MEASURED TRANSPORT	1,269	885	384	3,237	9.94	0.273 w_i^b	3.86 r_i^b	4,641		1,163	0.251				
1963															
Railways	456	348	108	923	5.88	0.377	1.84	1,632	1,613	322	0.197	0.200	(6)	(6)	(6)
Road Passenger Transport	310	223	87	683	0.43	0.327	20.23	734	632	310	0.422	0.491	(2)	(4)	(3)
Road Haulage Contracting	329	233	96	580	0.47	0.402	20.43	636	662	329	0.567	0.497	(1)	(2)	(2)
Sea Transport	311	168	143	398	2.73	0.442	5.24	727	765	311	0.428	0.406	(4)	(3)	(4)
Port and Inland Water Transport	170	131	39	324	1.11	0.404	3.51	458	474	170	0.371	0.359	(5)	(5)	(5)
Air Transport	97	50	47	89	0.53	0.563	8.87	153	194	97	0.636	0.501	(3)	(1)	(1)
TOTAL MEASURED TRANSPORT	1,673	1,153	517	2,996	11.15	0.385 w_i^b	4.64 r_i^b	4,340		1,539	~0.354				

a Includes subsidies and 'subsidy equivalents' (subsidy loans), in railways.

b Combined factor input figures are undadjusted (in Col.(8)), and (in Col.(9)) adjusted for intersectoral quality differences thus:-

$$(8) = (4) + \frac{r_i}{w_i} \times (5)$$

$$(9) = \frac{((6) \times (4)) + r_i \times (5)}{w_i} = \frac{w_i (4) + r_i \times (5)}{w_i}$$

r_i = rate of return in Measured Transport; w_i = average hourly earnings in Measured Transport.

Table 4.10. Productivity Level in Postal Services and Telecommunications. Output per Unit of Combined Factor Input, 1954, 1958 and 1963.   United Kingdom SIC 1958

(1) Net Output at Full Factor Cost	(2) Income from Employment	(3) Gross Capital Remuneration	(4) Standardised Labour Input	(5) Gross Capital Stock Current Prices	(6) Average Hourly Earnings (2)÷(4)	(7) Rate of Return on Capital (3)÷(5)	(8)(i) Combined Factor Input (Measured Transport Weights) Unadjusted[a]	(8)(ii) Adjusted[a]	(9) Net Output (Gross Value added)	(10)(i) Net Output per Unit of Combined Factor Input (Measured Transport Weights) Unadjusted	(10)(ii) Adjusted
£ million	£ million	£ million	mn SLU hours	£'000 million	£ per SLU hour	%	mn SLU hours equiv.	mn SLU hours equiv.	£ million	£ per SLU hour equiv.	£ per SLU hour equiv.
244	195	49	716	1.27	0.272	3.86	952	1169	244	0.256	0.209
377	279	98	727	1.72	0.384	6.08	970	1265	377	0.389	0.298
520	385	135	797	2.32	0.483	5.82	1077	1280	520	0.483	0.406

(Years labelled for rows: 1954, 1958, 1963)

a   The weighting of capital and labour inputs is as follows for cols. 8 (i) and (ii)

$$ \text{(i)} \quad 8(i) = (4) + \frac{r_i}{w_i} \times (5) \qquad \text{(ii)} \quad 8(ii) = \frac{(6) \times (4)}{w_i} + \frac{r_i}{w_i} \times (5) $$

where r_i is rate of return in Measured Transport, w_i is average hourly earnings in Measured Transport

Values of r_i, w_i

	r_i (%)	w_i (£ per SLU hour)
1954	3.89	0.209
1958	3.86	0.273
1963	4.64	0.385

5 An Interpretation of Productivity Movements

The principal aim in this Chapter is to interpret the productivity movements which have been measured in Chapters 2, 3 and 4. The measurement of movements and levels of outputs, inputs and productivity is an exercise of use and interest in itself in a field such as transport and communication which has not previously been the subject of much attention in this sense, but inevitably such a process leads on to the asking of further questions of the following type. What are the causes which underlie these productivity movements? An answer in two stages may be sought to a question drawn in these broad terms. At the first stage an 'interpretative' answer may be attempted in terms which state that a given actual movement in productivity is due to certain contributory movements in the input of the various, related factors of production and to changes in the 'quality' (as defined) of these factors. This is a process of segregating the different contributory causes of an actual movement in productivity. It may also be seen as a process of 'decomposing' a movement in productivity into its constituent parts. But it is a limited process, limited to saying that movements in output per man (or manhour) are due to the changing 'quality' of the related labour input and to changes in the amount of capital each man (or woman) has to work with.

To say that outputs per unit of labour input change because other factor inputs change is a useful but rather limited exercise. It is limited for two reasons. The first is that only a part of a movement in productivity can be interpreted in terms of movements in factor inputs. We are left with a sometimes large residual term to which it would be useful to attach meaning. The second reason is that such a process of segregation or 'decomposition' throws only a limited amount of light on the more basic determinants of productivity change. There are deeper and more fundamental causes which lie behind both the productivity movements themselves and what may be seen as their reflections in terms of movements in the quantity and 'quality' of factor inputs. So behind and beyond these interpretative causes lie what we have named the explanatory factors. In the present state of knowledge in this branch of economics these factors cannot positively be identified and studied. The best that we think possible is to attempt to test a number of explanatory hypotheses, and to probe for the more fundamental causes in this way. Correspondingly, in this Chapter we attempt a 'decomposition' exercise on productivity movements, and in Chapter 6 we test the hypotheses which are set out in Chapter 1.

Methods of interpretation

It was explained in the first Chapter[1] that productivity ratios of various 'partial' kinds and the movements in such ratios gave little information, in either absolute or comparative terms, about the productive efficiency of the activity subjected to such measurement. The conclusion was reached that the production function underlies all really meaningful analysis of productivity movements.

Accordingly a production function has been used to interpret our sectoral and industry measures of labour productivity. The methods of application and the assumptions involved are fully discussed in the introductory chapter.[2] In sum, the function is used to separate the contributions to changes in productivity of changes in capital per person employed (more commonly referred to in this Paper as changes in capital intensity) from the contributions arising from all other sources, including applied technical and organisational knowledge and external factors; it may be written as follows :[3]

$$\frac{dy \cdot LI}{dli \cdot Y} = \alpha \left(\frac{dk}{K} - \frac{dl}{L} \right) + \frac{datoke}{ATOKE}$$

or, in the more applicable and practical form in terms of exponential, continuously compounding rates of change[4] per period :

$$\Delta \left(\frac{Y}{LI} \right) = (\Delta K - \Delta L) + \Delta ATOKE$$

and

$$\Delta ATOKE = \Delta \left(\frac{Y}{LI} \right) - \alpha (\Delta K - \Delta L)$$

This function is applied in the interpretative analysis which follows and which is set out in Table 5.1 and 5.2. It may be seen from these tables that the analysis is sequential, starting with a calculation of movements, by industry and sector, in 'crude' labour productivity (that is, movements in output per person employed per year). It is particularly important to notice that the production function is not applied to these data, but is introduced later in the sequence at Row 7 in Table 5.1 and Row 6 in Table 5.2. The reason for this is that some proportion of the movement in crude labour productivity is interpreted in terms of aggregation bias

---

See pages 17 and 18.

Chapter 1, section B, pages 28 to 31.

Where Y, K and L are net output, capital stock (gross, in place, at constant replacement cost) and manpower in work. LI is labour input in terms of standardised labour unit hours per year, α is the average share of capital in total factor rewards over the period concerned. ATOKE represents the net residual factors including technical change, which in turn embraces completed improvements to capital, labour and organisation, and the effects of external factors.

Signified in the expression which follows by the prefix Δ.

Table 5.1. An Interpretative Analysis of Movements in   United Kingdom
Labour Productivity in Measured Transport,   SIC 1958
1952–1962, 1952–1958 and 1958–1962

Exponential rate of change per year	MEASURED TRANSPORT		
	1952–62	1952–58	1958–6
1. Output, ΔY	1.65	1.39	2.04
2. Employment, ΔL	−0.94	−0.91	−1.00
3. Productivity unadjusted, ΔP_L (output per head per year). (Row 1 − Row 2)	2.59	2.30	3.04
of which due to movements in:			
4. Intra-sectoral Labour Quality, ΔLQ_s	0.04	0.08	−
5. Inter-sectoral Labour Quality, ΔLQ_i	0.12	0.09	0.1
6. Hours of Work and Holidays, $\Delta SLU/H$ (average hours worked per standard labour unit per year)	0.09	0.32	−0.2
7. Productivity adjusted,[a] ΔP_{LI} (output per standardised manhour). P_{LI} (Row 3 − Row 4 − Row 5 − Row 6)	2.34	1.81	3.15
of which due to movements in:			
8. Capital Intensity, $\Delta (K/L)$	0.53	0.44	0.6
9. Capital Quality, ΔKQ_i (the inter-sectoral quality shift)	0.35	0.45	0.2
10. Applied Technical and Organisational Knowledge and External Factors, $\Delta ATOKE$ (Row 7 − Row 8 − Row 9)	1.46	0.92	2.2

a For movements in weekly hours worked, public and annual holidays allowed, and the intra-sectoral labour 'quality' shift.

in both the *intra*-sectoral and *inter*-sectoral senses. In addition, other adjustment to 'crude' labour productivity arise from the need to refine labour input in another sense which involves bringing into account movements in average weekly hours of work and in public and annual holidays allowed.

If the aggregation biases are not separately distinguished and removed from movements in the productivity ratio before the production function is applied, the they will appear as a part of the shift in the production function, that is, as an element in $\Delta ATOKE$ in our expression. So the 'cleaning up' process which is carried out on the inputs[1] is a contribution towards making the shift of the production function more accurately representative of changes in 'applied technic and organisational knowledge and external factors' than it would otherwise be.

1 Described in full in Chapter 3 and in the methodological note to Chapter 3.

One further interpretative process is attempted before the production function is applied; that is the attempt to improve the accuracy of the output measure by a process of differentiation and relative price weighting.[1] Significant allowances of this type are available from our own research for only one sector, road haulage contracting, but it should be remembered that in other sectors the official output series is far from being a completely undifferentiated measure[2] as, in unadjusted form, it is in road haulage contracting. The allowance which should be made to correct for aggregation bias in the output measure in road haulage contracting in the period 1958 to 1962 is not very large. The estimated magnitude of it is shown in Table 5.2 at Row 5a. The implications of it for 'downstream' stages in the interpretative analysis for this sector and period are shown by the figures given in this table in brackets.

A.   An Interpretative Analysis

Movements in labour productivity are set out on Tables 5.1 (the Measured Transport industry) and 5.2 (the six measured transport sectors and postal services and telecommunications). The interpretative analysis to which these movements are subjected is in two main parts as follows:

1. Crude, unadjusted labour productivity movements are adjusted for intra- and, for the industry, inter-sectoral 'quality' shift changes, and for changes in average weekly hours of work and in public and annual holidays allowed.

2. A production function is then fitted to the adjusted labour productivity data and the results are shown in three ways.

    (a) The annual exponential rate of change in adjusted labour productivity is divided into that part which is due to a concurrent movement in capital intensity (K/L), and that part which is due to concurrent movement in other factors which are termed 'applied technical and organisational knowledge and external factors'. (ATOKE). (Tables 5.1 and 5.2).

    (b) As an alternative, labour productivity is shown in money terms of pence (at 1958 values) per unit of standardised labour input. This amount for the industry and for each sector is attributed as due in part to $\Delta(K/L)$ and in part to ΔATOKE. (Tables 5.3 and 5.4).

    (c) The production functions are illustrated (Figure 9), for sectors only. They are drawn twice, incorporating the (constant level) techniques of 1952 and, separately, those of 1962. The shift of function over the 1952–62 period, representing ΔATOKE, is thereby distinguished from movements along the function which represent the effect of $\Delta(K/L)$.

---

1 As described in Chapter 2.

2 See Chapter 1, section A(1) and appendix note to Chapter 1, section (b) (i).

Table 5.2 An Interpretative Analysis of Movements in Labour Productivity in the Sectors of Measured Transport and in Postal Services and Telecommunications, 1952–1962, 1952–1958 and 1958–1962   United Kingdom   SIC 1958

Exponential rate of change per year Δ	RAILWAYS			ROAD PASSENGER TRANSPORT			ROAD HAULAGE CONTRACTING			SEA TRANSPORT		
	1952–62	1952–58	1958–62	1952–62	1952–58	1958–62	1952–62	1952–58	1958–62	1952–62	1952–58	1958–62
1. Output, ΔY	−1.93	−1.62	−2.39	−2.30	−2.84	−1.49	7.26	7.43	6.99	1.23	1.20	1.29
2. Employment, ΔL	−1.86	−1.34	−2.64	−1.31	−1.62	−0.84	0.70	−0.33	2.23	−0.62	0.10	−1.70
3. Productivity unadjusted, ΔP_L (output per head per year) (Row 1 − Row 2) of which due to movements in:	−0.07	−0.28	−0.25	−0.99	−1.22	−0.65	6.56	7.76	4.76	1.85	1.10	2.99
4. Intra-sectoral Labour 'Quality', ΔLQ_x	0.08	0.14	−0.01	0.01	0.01	−0.02	0.03	0.08	−0.04	−0.04	0.01	−0.09
5. Hours of work and Holidays, ΔSLU/H (average hours worked per standard labour unit per year)	0.01	0.27	−0.38	0.05	0.25	−0.26	0.66	0.93	0.24	0.01	0.27	−0.38
5a. (Aggregation Bias in the Output Measure, ΔYB)									(0.32)			
6. Productivity adjusted,[a] ΔP_{LI} (output per standardised manhour per year) ΔP_{LI} (Row 3 − Row 4 − Row 5) of which due to movements in:	−0.16	−0.69	0.64	−1.05	−1.48	−0.37	5.87	6.75	4.56 (4.24)	1.88	0.82	3.46
7[b]. Capital Intensity, Δ(K/L)	0.46	0.22	0.81	0.24	0.94	−0.82	1.40	1.30	1.55	0.98	0.64	1.50
8[a]. Applied Technical and Organisational Knowledge and External Factors (net), Δ ATOKE	−0.64	−0.93	−0.20	−1.25	−2.42	0.50	4.46	5.43	2.99 (2.67)	0.92	0.20	2.01

Exponential rate of change per year Δ	PORT AND INLAND WATER TRANSPORT			AIR TRANSPORT			POSTAL SERVICES AND TELECOMMUNICATIONS		
	1952–62	1952–58	1958–62	1952–62	1952–58	1958–62	1952–62	1952–58	1958–62
1. Output, ΔY	2.26	2.00	2.67	12.58	11.86	13.67	3.10	2.32	4.27
2. Employment, ΔL	−1.28	−0.82	−1.97	4.82	3.61	6.67	1.12	0.41	2.19
3. Productivity unadjusted, ΔP_L (output per head per year) (Row 1 − Row 2) of which due to movements in:	3.54	2.82	4.64	7.76	8.25	7.00	1.98	1.91	2.08
4. Intra-sectoral Labour Quality, ΔLQ_x	0.10	0.08	0.12	0.37	0.50	0.13	−0.03	0.25	−0.45
5. Hours of work and Holidays, ΔSLU/H (average hours worked per standard labour unit per year)	−0.48	−0.11	−1.03	−0.63	−1.40	0.54	−0.37	−0.51	−0.16
6. Productivity adjusted,[a] ΔP_{LI} (output per standardised manhour) ΔP_{LI} (Row 3 − Row 4 − Row 5) of which due to movements in:	3.92	2.85	5.55	8.02	9.15	6.33	2.38	2.17	2.69
7[b]. Capital Intensity, Δ(K/L)	0.12	−0.08	0.43	2.71	4.13	0.57	0.70	0.75	0.62
8[a]. Applied Technical and Organisational Knowledge and External Factors (net), Δ ATOKE	3.79	2.92	5.11	5.47	5.21	5.87	1.68	1.42	2.06

a For movements in weekly hours worked, public and annual holidays allowed and the intra-sectoral labour quality shift; and for aggregation bias in the output measure in road haulage contracting in 1958–62 only.

1.   Adjustments to labour productivity movements

The Measured Transport industry

The allowances which account for the differences between the adjusted and unadjusted measures of labour productivity change are made before the production function is applied to the data. In the Measured Transport industry (Table 5.1) there are three allowances, all adjustments to 'crude' labour input, and therefore to the trend in the unadjusted, labour productivity ratio. Two of the three are aggregation biases: the *intra-* and *inter-*sectoral shifts in the 'quality' (as defined) of labour input. The third is the allowance for changes in average weekly hours of work and for public and annual holidays allowed. In Measured Transport in the whole period studied (1952–62) the direction of all these allowances is the same, the movement being towards an increase in labour input, so making the rate of change in output per unit of labour input lower than movements in output per manyear unadjusted. The analysis by sub-periods shows that the two labour 'quality' factors considered together change little over time, but the national movement towards shorter hours of work and longer holidays is reflected in this industry after 1958.[1]

The sectors

In the various sectors (Table 5.2) only the intra-sectoral labour 'quality' shift change (row 4), and changes in average weekly hours of work and in public and annual holidays allowed (row 5) are relevant.

Labour 'quality' changes are positive in the 1952–62 period in all the measured transport sectors except sea transport, where there is a very small negative change. In postal services and telecommunications there is also a small negative change. Only in air transport is the positive change in labour 'quality' large (0.37 per cent per annum) in relation to labour 'quality' changes in other sectors, but it is not large in relation to movement in labour productivity in this sector. The effect of the 'quality' change declines over the 1952–62 period in all sectors except port and inland water transport. The effect upon labour productivity movement of any increase in labour 'quality' is to make adjusted labour productivity movement lower than crude, unadjusted productivity movement, but the effect is not great in any sector.

Change in hours of work per person employed per year (this measure combines changes in average weekly hours of work with changes in public and annual holidays allowed) were rather more important than changes in labour 'quality' in most sectors in the 1952–62 period. The greatest change, a positive one, occurred in road haulage contracting, but the rate of increase was lower during the second part of the 1952–62 period. A fairly general tendency was for hours of work per manyear to increase less rapidly, or to decline, in the 1958–62 period. This occurs in all sectors except air transport and postal services and

---

1   The turnround from increasing to decreasing hours of work per annum actually comes in 1956. See Statistical Appendix, section B, Table B.3.

telecommunications. The effect of a decline in manhours worked per year is of course to make the movement in adjusted labour productivity greater than the cruder measure of this variable.

2. Fitting a production function

Having removed from the scene certain aggregation biases in crude factor input measures, and having made adjustments for changes in the quantity of labour services which are not shown by changes in the quantity of manpower in employment, we are now in a position to segregate and interpret the more refined labour productivity movements by the process of fitting a production function.

The object of this treatment is to enable a breakdown to be made of any given change in adjusted labour productivity in terms of the proportion of such change which is due to the concurrent change in the input of capital services per man (as measured in this case by a change in the amount of capital in place per person employed). The results of this process are shown in terms of annual exponential (continuously compounding) rates of change in Table 5.1, rows 7, 8, 9 and 10 and Table 5.2, rows 6, 7 and 8.

An alternative way of presenting the analysis is shown in Tables 5.3 and 5.4. Here labour productivity gain is expressed in terms of pence (at constant 1958 value) per standardised labour unit hour. The advantage of this alternative method is that it shows actual gain (or loss) in relation to the level of labour productivity in the initial base year for each period.

Further illustration of the results of applying this interpretative technique is provided on Figure 9 where the production function for each sector is plotted. In order to ensure that movements *along* the production function are not mixed up with *shifts* in the function when it is depicted over time, q (that is output per standardised labour unit hour) plotted on the vertical axis in each case is adjusted for technical change and becomes q/A, where A represents ATOKE.[1] On the horizontal axis we plot k (which stands for K/L, the input of capital services per employed person per annum). The graphical production functions therefore show the effect upon adjusted labour productivity of various levels of capital intensity. Also shown is the effect upon labour productivity (P_{LI}) of technical change over the period 1952 to 1962. For each sector of Measured Transport, and for postal services and telecommunications, two production functions are represented, one incorporates the techniques[2] of 1952 and the other the techniques of 1962. All functions slope upwards, at various

---

1 See Chapter 4 and Statistical Appendix section D. Table D.1, and for annual data for q, A, q/A and k see Statistical Appendix section E. Table E.1.

2 Applied techniques are measured by ATOKE, and this term includes not only technical and organisational knowledge which has been applied to the production process but also the effect of external factors.

Figure 9. Production Functions in Measured Transport and Communication at Constant (1952 and 1962) Levels of 'Applied Technical and Organisational Knowledge and External Factors' (ATOKE), 1952–1965

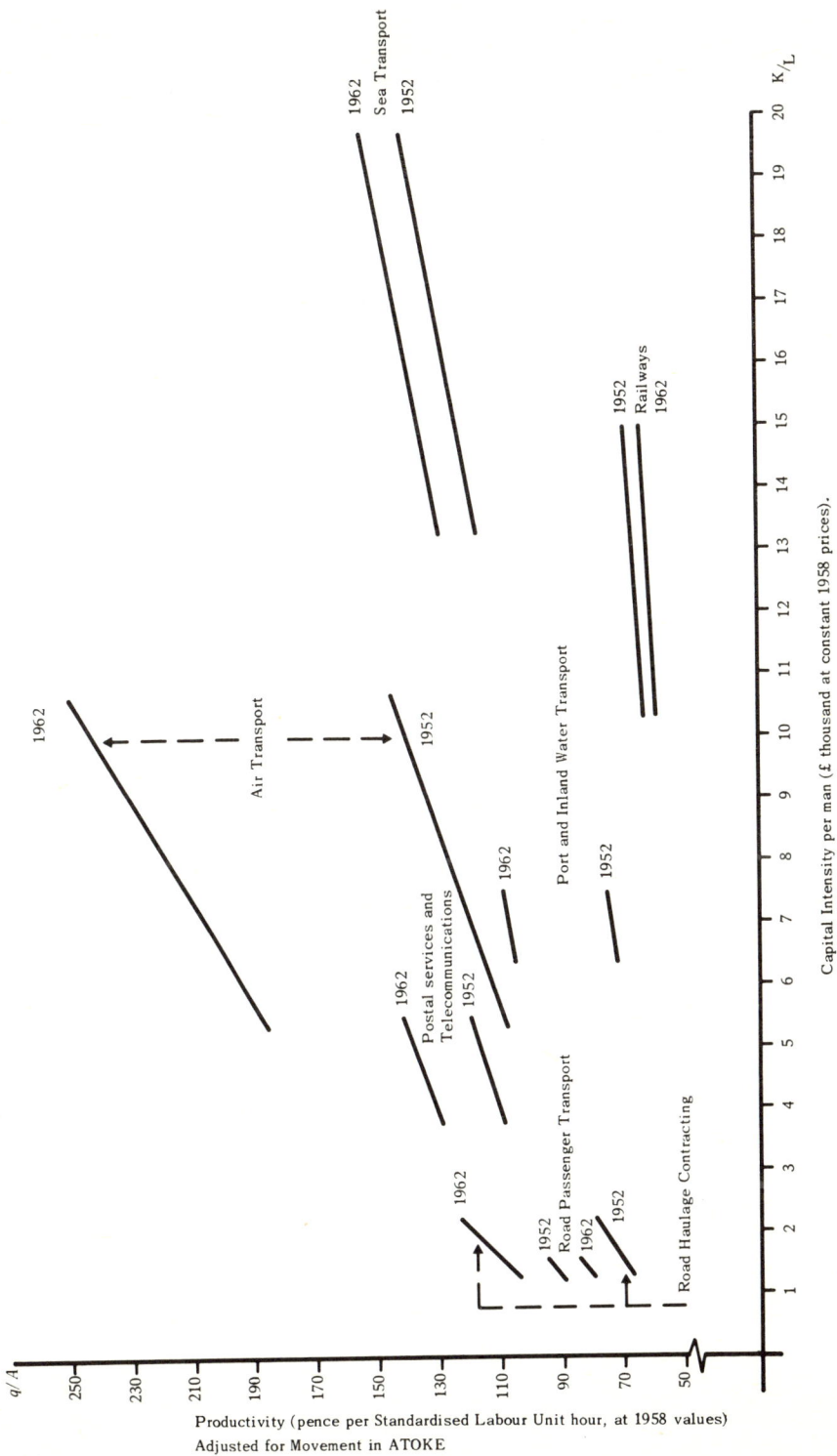

141

angles[1] and, with two very important exceptions, all are shifted upwards to various extents when the applied techniques of 1962 are substituted for those of 1952. The exceptions are the railways and road passenger transport, where the effect of changes in applied techniques and of the influence of external factors[2] (ATOKE) between 1952 and 1962 has been to shift the production function *downwards*, thereby causing a reduction in labour productivity as measured in this case by output per unit of standardised labour input.

A further point of some importance is brought out by the results shown on Figure 9. This is that there are widely different production functions within the Measured Transport industry and in postal services and telecommunications. There are great differences in levels of capital intensity and in changes in them during the 1952 to 1962 period, and the effects upon labour productivity of the application of new techniques is markedly different as between sectors.

The results of the interpretative processes, as indicated by (i) exponential rates of change of labour productivity apportioned causally as due to $\Delta (K/L)$ and ΔATOKE; (ii) labour productivity gain in constant value money terms apportioned as in (i); and, (iii) slopes and shifts in estimated production functions by industry and sector, are now brought together.

The Measured Transport industry

Over the whole period of the adjusted labour productivity gain of 2.34 per cent per annum (Table 5.1, row 7), just over a third is attributable to an increase in capital intensity after the *inter*-sectoral shift in capital 'quality' has been brought into the calculation, (the shift itself accounts for 14 per cent out of the total 37 per cent due to the change in capital intensity). The balance of 63 per cent is due to an increase in 'applied technical and organisational knowledge and external factors' (ATOKE). In constant 1958 money terms (Table 5.3) the productivity gain per standardised labour unit (SLU) hour is 20.4 pence over the whole period 1952–1962, 7.6 pence of this is due to the increase in capital per head introduced over this period (of which 2.9 pence to the positive 'quality'

---

1 The slope of the function represents the *proportional* effect on labour productivity of a given actual change in K/L. The rates of profit (α values in our terminology of the production function) are the same for both the constant 1952 and 1962 levels of ATOKE, but, where the shift is upwards, the slope of the function is steeper in the 1962 case because although the proportional gain in labour productivity is the same as it is in 1952, the starting level is higher. The slope is visibly steeper in some sectors only. Another point to explain about Figure 9 is that the first and last plotted points for each production function do not necessarily represent the first (1952) and last (1962) years of the 1952–62 period.

2 These, particularly, are likely to be of greater importance when output is declining (as it is in these two sectors) than when it is rising. See Chapter 6 where further attention is given to this point.

Table 5.3   An Interpretative Analysis in Constant Money Terms of Changes in Labour Productivity,   United Kingdom
Capital Intensity and Applied Technical and Organisational Knowledge and External Factors   SIC 1958
in Measured Transport, 1952–1962

YEARS	LEVELS 1 — Level of Real Net Output Per Standardised Labour Unit (SLU) Hour at the Start and End of Each Period, P_{LI} (Pence, 1958 values)	CHANGES 2 — Period	3 — Change in Real Net Output per SLU Hour Over Period, ΔP_{LI} (Pence, 1958 values)	4 AMOUNT OF CHANGE SHOWN IN COLUMN 3 WHICH IS DUE TO:- (a) Change in Real Capital (Unadjusted) Input Per Man Per Period, (K/L) (Pence, 1958 values)	(a) %	(b) Change in Inter-Sectoral Capital 'Quality', ΔKQ (Pence, 1958 values)	(b) %	(c) Total Change in Capital Intensity (a)+(b) (Pence, 1958 values)	(c) %	(d) Change in Applied Technical and Organisational Knowledge and External Factors, Δ ATOKE (Pence, 1958 values)	(d) %
MEASURED TRANSPORT											
1952	77.4										
		1952–62	20.4	4.7	(23)	2.9	(14)	7.6	(37)	12.8	(63)
1958	86.2										
		1952–58	8.9	2.2	(25)	2.2	(25)	4.4	(49)	4.5	(50)
		1958–62	11.5	2.5	(22)	0.7	(6)	3.2	(28)	8.3	(72)
1962	97.8										

Totals may not equal the sum of their components due to rounding.

143

shift change) and the balance of 12.8 pence to an increase in ATOKE. The input of capital per head, and particularly the 'quality' shift element, plays a relatively more important causal role in the first sub-period when productivity is growing rather slowly. When the productivity growth rate speeds up in the second period, ΔATOKE accounts for 72 per cent of it.

The sectors

The first sector subjected to a similar interpretative analysis is the *Railways*. In Table 5.2, it is shown that over the whole period a slightly negative trend in adjusted labour productivity is the *net* effect of a proportionately larger and positive contribution from changes in ATOKE. In constant, 1958 money terms productivity per SLU hour in the railways fell by 1.1 pence over the whole period; a net change of −3.9 pence due to ΔATOKE and +2.8 pence due to Δ(K/L). In the sub-periods the trends are for capital to contribute an increasing amount to productivity and for ATOKE to become less negative as regards its contribution. The net result of these trends is that the labour productivity movement becomes positive over the period 1958 to 1962. As was pointed out in Chapter 3, the increase in capital intensity comes about in this sector by a reduction of labour input rather than by any increase in the total capital stock in place (although a very slight increase in this total has occurred). This aspect of the railways' situation, coupled with the fact that the value of α (the proportion of total, gross factor rewards going to capital) is rather unreal in the railways. This is because the railways' capital is largely rewarded out of subsidies (or their equivalents) rather than from value added by the factor of production concerned and this means that the contribution to the change in productivity of change in capital intensity is not well founded in terms of marginal productivity theory. Too much reliance should not therefore be placed on this rather odd interpretation, which in graphical terms yields a relatively very low (despite a large quantity of capital per man) and relatively flat and undistinguished production function as shown on Figure 9, indicating that movements *along* the function due to increased capital intensity cause little productivity gain and, furthermore the function shifts *downwards* when the applied techniques of 1962 are substituted for those of 1952.

In *Road Passenger Transport* negative movements in adjusted labour productivity persist in all the periods included in the analysis. These movements are interpreted for the whole period in terms of a relatively very small positive contribution from changes in capital intensity which are more than offset by a considerably larger negative contribution from movements in ATOKE. The pattern is therefore the same as it is in the railways, but the movements are larger in terms of rates of change. In constant money terms the adjusted productivity movement for the whole period, −8.7 pence, is attributable very largely to a negative movement in ATOKE. The analysis by sub-periods reveals a rapidly changing situation in which the labour productivity movement is becoming less negative due to a reversal in the contribution of ATOKE from a relatively large negative (−12.8 pence in the first sub-period to +1.7 pence in the second), but this change is partly offset by a fall in total capital stock in place which is a little faster than the decline in labour input in the second sub-period. The

Capital Intensity and Applied Technical and Organisational Knowledge and External Factors   SIC 1958
in the Sectors of Measured Transport and Communication, 1952–1962

SECTORS AND YEARS	LEVELS		CHANGES			AMOUNT OF CHANGE SHOWN IN COLUMN 3 WHICH IS DUE TO:			
	1		2	3		4			
	Level of Real Output Per Standardised Labour Unit (SLU) Hour at the Start and End of Each Period, P_{Li}		PERIOD	Change in Real Output Per SLU Hour Over Period, ΔP_{Li}		(a) Change in Real Capital Input Per Man Per Period, $\Delta(K/L)$	%	(b) Change in Applied Technical and Organisational Knowledge and External Factors, Δ ATOKE	%
	(Pence, 1958 values)			(Pence, 1958 values)		(Pence, 1958 values)		(Pence, 1958 values)	
RAILWAYS									
1952	62.5		1952–62	–1.1		2.8	(–247)	–3.9	(347)
1958	59.9		1952–58	–2.6		0.8	(– 31)	–3.4	(131)
1962	61.4		1958–62	1.5		2.0	(135)	–0.5	(–35)
ROAD PASSENGER TRANSPORT									
1952	89.8		1952–62	–8.7		2.4	(– 28)	–11.1	(128)
1958	82.1		1952–58	–7.6		5.2	(– 68)	–12.8	(168)
1962	81.0		1958–62	–1.1		–2.8	(247)	1.7	(–147)
ROAD HAULAGE CONTRACTING[a]									
1952	66.8		1952–62	53.1		13.3	(25)	39.8	(75)
1958	100.0		1952–58	33.2		6.4	(19)	26.8	(81)
1962	119.9		1958–62	19.9		6.8	(34)	13.1	(66)
			[1958–62]	[18.4]		[6.8]		[11.6]	
SEA TRANSPORT									
1952	117.0		1952–62	24.6		12.4	(51)	12.1	(49)
1958	123.1		1952–58	6.0		4.6	(77)	1.4	(23)
1962	141.6		1958–62	18.5		7.8	(42)	10.7	(58)
PORT AND INLAND WATER TRANSPORT									
1952	72.8		1952–62	34.9		1.3	(4)	33.6	(96)
1958	86.3		1952–58	13.5		–0.4	(–3)	13.9	(103)
1962	107.6		1958–62	21.3		1.7	(8)	19.7	(92)
AIR TRANSPORT									
1952	107.0		1952–62	135.5		43.2	(32)	92.3	(68)
1958	187.5		1952–58	80.5		39.1	(49)	41.4	(51)
1962	242.5		1958–62	55.0		4.1	(7)	50.9	(93)
POSTAL SERVICES AND TELECOMMUNICATIONS									
1952	109.3		1952–62	29.3		8.5	(29)	20.8	(71)
1958	124.5		1952–58	15.2		5.3	(35)	9.9	(65)
1962	138.6		1958–62	14.1		3.2	(23)	10.9	(77)

a In square brackets the gain in output per SLU hour when aggregation bias in the output measure is removed.

Totals may not equal sum of their components due to rounding.

movement of capital intensity is slight over the whole period. This gives a very 'short' production function (Figure 9), which is shifted *downwards* when the techniques of 1962 are substituted for those of 1952. In other words, over the 1952–62 period the net effect of the factors included in ATOKE has outweighed the effect of the upwards slope of the function which is due to increased capital input per person employed.

Road Haulage Contracting is one of the two outstanding growth sectors of the Measured Transport industry (the other being air transport). Starting in 1952 from a labour productivity level (output per SLU hour) nearly the same as the railways in spite of a large capital intensity difference between the two sectors, (railways £10.3 thousand and road haulage contracting £1.3 thousand in 1952 both at 1958 prices), the road haulage contracting sector increased its adjusted labour productivity by 53.1 pence over the whole period (the railways –1.1 pence over the same period), equivalent to an annual rate of 5.87 per cent (exponential). Approximately a quarter (13.3 pence) of this change is attributable to an increase in the input of capital per person and three-quarters (39.8 pence) to an increase in the input of applied technical and organisational knowledge and external factors. The analysis by sub-periods shows first that the influence of changes in capital input is increasing relative to the influence of movements in ATOKE; in the period 1958 to 1962 a third of the rather lower rate of 4.56 per cent per annum productivity gain is attributable to capital and the balance to ATOKE. This analysis is on the basis of an unadjusted output measure; but it was shown in Chapter 2 that due to the assumption of homogeneity in the output indicator for this sector an aggregation bias exists which on our estimation causes indicated output to be 0.32 per cent per annum higher in this period than true output. If a correction is made for this aggregation bias (as it is in the figures shown in brackets in Table 5.2), then the adjusted labour productivity movement is lower for this reason. The contribution of increased capital intensity to movements in productivity are not altered by the correction made for this bias, but the residual term, representing ATOKE, is lower for this reason.[1] The relative positions of these two contributors to labour productivity change now become Δ(K/L) 37 per cent and ΔATOKE 63 per cent. The approximate result in money terms is shown by the figures in brackets in Table 5.4. The production function adjusted for technical change (Figure 9) shifts up substantially when constant 1962 techniques are applied.

Sea Transport is the most capital intensive of all included in this Paper; in 1962 each person employed worked with £16.5 thousand of capital (£13.3 thousand in 1952, both figures gross at constant 1958 replacement cost). This fact goes some way towards explaining why output per SLU hour in this sector in 1952 was higher than in any other. For the same reason, among others, capital has a larger than average share in total factor rewards in this sector. This constitutes one reason for the greater than average contribution of movements in capital per person

---

[1] Thus emphasising the point made earlier (p. 136) that undetected aggregation biases in either output measures or in factor inputs will appear in the residual term (ATOKE).

employed to movements in labour productivity. In the whole period the positive movement in adjusted productivity was at the annual rate of 1.88 per cent; just over a half of this movement is attributable to increased capital intensity, and the remainder to changes in ATOKE. In constant money terms the labour productivity gain (increase in output per SLU hour) of 24.6 pence is divided as due to increased capital intensity, 12.4 pence, and to increased ATOKE 12.1 pence. The analysis by sub-periods shows that the contribution from capital intensity was even more important, accounting for over three-quarters of the concurrent productivity change in the first sub-period, but the proportion falls to less than a half in the 1958–62 period. It may be noticed that this is the only sector in which in the 1952–62 period *movements along* the production function contribute more to concurrent increases in productivity than do *shifts* in the function.

Capital intensity in *Port and Inland Water Transport*, (£7,100 in 1962 at 1958 replacement cost), is about average for the Measured Transport industry,[1] but in this sector the value for α (the capital coefficient in the production function) is relatively low, and the average rate of increase in capital intensity is also very low (0.54 per cent per annum) over the whole period 1952 to 1962. These conditions add together to produce a very small contribution from increases in capital intensity towards the labour productivity increase. In money terms for the whole period capital contributes only 1.3 pence out of a total productivity change of 34.9 pence. The analysis by sub-periods shows that capital's contribution moves in a slightly negative direction in the first period. The productivity gain is at a considerably higher rate in the second sub-period, with 92 per cent of it attributable to increases in the input of ATOKE. The production function at constant levels of technical change (Figure 9) shows the labour productivity implications of changes in capital intensity in *both* directions by relatively small percentages.

The labour productivity levels in 1958 and 1962 and the rate of change of labour productivity (output per SLU hour) in all periods are all greater in *Air Transport* than in any other sector studied here. In terms of capital intensity it approaches the levels found in the railways in 1958 and 1962, but remains well behind the much higher levels found in sea transport (Table 3.6 and Figure 5, Chapter 3). Over the whole period, of the 8.02 per cent per annum rate of increase in adjusted productivity approximately one third is attributable to the increased input of capital per person employed and about two-thirds to an increase in ATOKE. An analysis by sub-periods indicates that the movement along the production function was a very much less important contributor to labour productivity gain in the period 1958 to 1962, and the contribution to this gain from shifts in the production function measured by changes in ATOKE, was correspondingly greater than in the earlier sub-period. Capital intensity nearly doubles over the whole period and the value of output per SLU hour at constant 1952 and 1962 levels of ATOKE rises steeply due to this cause and also because α values are relatively high. The effect of applying more recent (1962) techniques is also a powerful influence

---

1 See Figure 5 in Chapter 3.

upon labour productivity change and this effect is represented by a shift in the production function (Figure 9).

Postal Services and Telecommunications have been included in this analysis for the purpose of comparisons between this sector, the various sectors of the Measured Transport industry and the whole of this industry. The sector's annual rate of increase in output per SLU hour over the whole period (2.38 per cent) is very nearly the same as the rate for the Measured Transport industry, although an analysis by sub-sectors shows that it is much more stable than Measured Transport, with a gradually accelerating tendency. One third of the productivity gain in this sector over the whole period is attributable to increased capital intensity, compared with rather more than one third (37 per cent) in Measured Transport, and the balance to an increased input of ATOKE. An analysis by sub-periods shows rather more importance, in proportional terms, attaching to movements in the ATOKE group of factors in the more recent sub-period, 1958 to 1962; in Measured Transport a similar tendency is evident (Tables 5.1 and 5.3). The capital intensity of this sector is at a level rather below that in the Measured Transport industry, but the sectoral level is rising faster than that of the industry if the industry's figures are unadjusted for the inter-sectoral 'quality' shift change. The sectoral production function at constant 1952 and 1962 levels of ATOKE is shown in Figure 9.

3. The contribution of increased capital intensity to productivity gain

Where there has been positive labour productivity gain, it is now possible to rank the transport sectors by the proportion of such gain which is attributable to a change in capital intensity, that is, a movement along the production function.

The railways and road passenger transport are disqualified from placing in this comparison because their labour productivity gains over the period concerned were negative. In both these sectors capital intensity did increase and its effect was positive in the sense that labour productivity decline would have been greater without this effect, but this positive K/L effect was outweighed by a negative movement in 'applied technical and organisational knowledge and external factors' (ATOKE). It may be seen (Table 5.4) that the K/L effect for railways was +2.8 pence (labour productivity loss −1.1 pence), and for road passenger transport the K/L effect was +2.4 pence (labour productivity loss −8.7 pence). There is, however, some artificiality involved in this particular exercise in respect of these two sectors because the increase in K/L which does occur is brought about *predominantly* because labour input fell; and total capital input also fell in road passenger transport.

One conclusion which may be drawn from this comparison (Table 5.5) is that, with the notable exception of sea transport, capital deepening (increasing capital intensity) is considerably less important as a contributor to labour productivity gain than all other contributory factors considered together. Further, it is shown that where capital deepening is relatively more important in this rôle over the whole period its effect is declining and where it is of relatively small importance its effect is increasing. The corollary is that, with the exception of

148

Table 5.5.   Approximate proportion of Labour Productivity Gain attributable to
Capital Intensity change, 1952–1962

	(In brackets whether this proportion was rising (R) or falling (F) over the period)[a]	
Sea Transport	51	(F)
Air Transport	32	(F)
Postal Services and Telecommunications	29	(F)
Road Haulage Contracting	25	(R)
Port and Inland Water Transport	4	(R)

a As judged by examining the proportions for the sub-periods, 1952–58 and 1958–62.

sea transport, an increase (or decrease) in 'applied technical and organisational knowledge and external factors' (ΔATOKE), represented by a shift upwards (or downwards) of the production function, is the chief contributor to labour productivity gain (or loss), and that where the proportion of total gain due to this factor is low it is increasing and where it is high it is decreasing.

The interpretative process ends here. An attempt to find deeper, explanatory reasons for the productivity movements which have occurred in these sectors of public transport and communication is described in the next chapter.

Summary

The philosophy behind the interpretative treatment adopted is to seek an answer in two stages to the question: What are the causes of the labour productivity movements which have been measured in this Paper?

An interpretative answer is attempted in terms which postulate that a given actual movement in labour productivity is due to certain contributory movements in the input of the various, related factors of production and to changes in the 'quality' (as defined) of these factors. This is a process of segregating the various contributory causes of a given movement in productivity. It may also be seen as a process of 'decomposing' a movement in labour productivity into its constituent parts. The process is necessarily a limited one, first because only a part of a movement in labour productivity can be interpreted in terms of movements in factor inputs and changes in their 'quality'; a sometimes large residual term is left, and it would be useful to attach meaning to this term. Second, the segregation or 'decomposition' process throws only a limited amount of light on the more basic determinants of productivity change. It is clear that there exist deeper and more fundamental causes which lie behind both the productivity movements themselves and what may be seen as their reflections in terms of movements in the quantity and 'quality' of factor inputs. In this chapter we dealt with the more

Table 5.6.   An Interpretative Analysis of Productivity Gain (or Loss), 1952–1962
(In brackets the corresponding movements measured in exponential rates of change per annum)[a]

| | 1. Labour Productivity Gain in constant money terms 1952–62, output per SLU hour.[b] (Pence at 1958 values), ΔP_{LI} | 2. Amount of Gain (or Loss) in Col. 1 which is due to: | |
		A. Movement in Real Capital Input per person employed (Pence at 1958 values), $\Delta(K/L)$	B. Movement in the Input of 'Applied Technical and Organisational Knowledge and External Factors'. (Pence at 1958 values), ΔATOKE
Railways	−1.1 (−0.16)	2.8 (0.46)	−3.9 (−0.64)
Road Passenger Transport	−8.7 (−1.05)	2.4 (0.24)	−11.1 (−1.25)
Road Haulage Contracting	53.1 (5.87)	13.3 (1.40)	39.8 (4.46)
Sea Transport	24.6 (1.88)	12.4 (0.98)	12.1 (0.92)
Port and Inland Water Transport	34.9 (3.92)	1.3 (0.12)	33.6 (3.79)
Air Transport	135.5 (8.02)	43.2 (2.71)	92.3 (5.47)
MEASURED TRANSPORT			
a. Unadjusted	.21.6 (2.46)	4.7 (0.53)	16.9 (1.93)
b. Adjusted[c]	20.4 (2.34)	7.6 (0.88)	12.8 (1.46)
Postal Services and Telecommunications	29.3 (2.38)	8.5 (0.70)	20.8 (1.68)

a Cols. 2A and 2B do not in all cases add to Col. 1 due to rounding.

b Standardised labour unit hour.

For the inter-sectoral labour and capital 'quality' shift changes.

superficial interpretative causes and in Chapter 6 we attempt to probe for the deeper explanatory causes.

The results of the interpretative analysis are summarised in Table 5.6.

The labour productivity gain in constant money and exponential growth rate terms (shown in Col. 1 of Table 5.6) has been calculated after adjustments have been made for hours and 'quality' of labour input for each sector (this latter is the *intra*-sectoral 'quality' shift change). In the case of the Measured Transport industry the 'adjusted' figures are, in addition, net of both the labour and capital *inter*-sectoral 'quality' shift changes. These processes of adjustment are carried out in order to 'clean up' the factor inputs before a production function is applied. The reason for doing this is that we are then better able to segregate the contributions to adjusted labour productivity gain into that due to capital intensity change and that due to movement in 'applied technical and organisational knowledge and external factors'. This last term is then more nearly identifiable as such and is less adulterated by 'quality' shifts, which may alternatively be termed aggregation bias, in the factor inputs.

The greatest sectoral 'quality' shift change occurs in air transport. Here the age and sex structure of the work force has changed over this period in a way which has led to an increase in labour 'quality'. If the labour factor input in this sector had not been pre-adjusted (as it has been in Col. 1 of Table 5.6) then this shift change would have been thrown into the residual term, ΔATOKE, making it 5.84 instead of 5.47 per cent per annum.

Inter-sectorally the greatest 'quality' shift change is in capital input. Here the disparate rates of capital input into sectors and the different productivities of capital (as measured by their gross rates of return) have led to a 'quality' shift change of +0.34 per cent per annum. The pre-adjustment of the capital input into the Measured Transport industry by this figure has prevented this movement being wrongly added to the movement over the same period of ΔATOKE of 1.46 per cent per annum after adjustment.

The results of interpreting adjusted labour productivity gain (or loss) in quantitative rather than qualitative terms are given both in absolute terms as constant value money amounts, and in terms of exponential rates of change per annum (Table 5.6). The results are perhaps more striking when they are expressed in absolute terms of money (at constant values) gain or loss per standardised labour unit hour rather than as percentage rates of increase or decrease over time.

In both the railways and road passenger transport the constant value output per hour of standardised labour input fell over the period 1952 to 1962; and this despite a positive contribution to adjusted labour productivity in each case from the input of capital per person employed. The positive contribution from this 'deepening' of capital was in both cases outweighed by a greater negative contribution from movements in ATOKE, and where output has declined over a fairly long period (as it has in these two sectors) the 'external' factors in ATOKE are likely to have been particularly influential.

In all the other sectors of the Measured Transport industry, in the industry itself and in postal services and telecommunications the labour productivity gain was positive and, with one exception, the greater part of the gain was found to be due to technical change, ΔATOKE, and the lesser part to increased capital intensity, $\Delta(K/L)$. The exception is sea transport where $\Delta(K/L)$ is a slightly more important contributor to productivity gain than is ΔATOKE.

One way of illustrating these results is to plot each production function at constant 1952 and 1962 levels of ATOKE (Figure 9). Movements along the production function represent labour productivity gain which is due exclusively to movements in capital intensity. Shifts in the whole function, in either direction, represent a change in applied techniques and in the influence of external factors (ATOKE). In every sector the production function *slopes upwards*, indicating that increased capital per person employed leads to labour productivity gain. The production functions for the railways and for road passenger transport *shift downwards* when the techniques of 1962 are substituted in the production function for those of 1952; in all other sectors the production function *shifts upwards*.

There is no typical production function in transport. The functions shown in Figure 9 are widely distributed in terms of capital intensity levels and movements and also in respect of the labour productivity levels and movements due to movements in capital intensity and the degree of labour productivity gain or loss due to changes in applied techniques and the influence of external factors.

The approximate proportional importance of the contribution made by movements in capital intensity to labour productivity gain is measurable. In other words we are able to answer the question: What is the relative importance in each sector of movements along the production function in comparison with shifts in the function It is also possible to say whether the shifts are becoming more or less important.

The results show that with the exception of one sector (sea transport) the effect of increasing capital per man accounted for less than half, and in some sectors much less than half (Table 5.5) of the labour productivity gain in the 1952–62 period. In sea transport, increased capital intensity accounted for 51 per cent of total labour productivity gain over the same period. In railways and road passenger transport labour productivity gains over this period were negative. In both these sectors capital intensity did increase and it may reasonably be concluded that their labour productivity losses would have been even greater without this positive contribution from capital. But there is some artificiality in these particular cases because the increase in K/L comes about *predominantly* because labour input fell, and in road passenger transport total capital input also fell.

A general conclusion which may be drawn from the interpretative analysis is that with the notable exception of sea transport, capital 'deepening', that is, increased capital intensity represented by a movement along the production function, was considerably less important as a contributor to labour productivity gain than all other contributory factors considered together. Further, it is shown that when capital deepening was relatively more important in this rôle over the whole period it was declining and where it was of relatively little importance it was increasing (Table 5.5). The corollary is that, with the exception of sea transport, an increase (or decrease) in applied technical and organisational knowledge and external factors (ΔATOKE), represented by a shift upwards (or downwards) of the production function, was the chief contributor to labour productivity gain (or loss) and that where the proportion of a total gain due to this factor was low it was increasing and where it was high it was decreasing.

L

6   An Explanatory Analysis

In the preceding chapter an interpretative analysis was made of movements in labour productivity, distinction being drawn between the amount of each specified movement in labour productivity which is due to a concurrent movement in the amount of financial capital per labour unit and the amount which is due to concurrent movement in the input of technical and organisational knowledge and the influence of external factors (Δ ATOKE). This ATOKE group of factors was found in six out of the seven sectors examined to account for at least fifty per cent, and in many cases more, of the labour productivity gain (or loss) occurring over the period 1952 to 1962.

The measure of capital in this previous exercise is a financial one and its contribution to labour productivity gain is in financial terms.[1] Physical additions to the existing stock of capital are reflected in this financial measure and expirations, on the basis of an average length of life, are also reflected. However, early retirements from the stock of capital in use which are due to obsolescence or to redundancy following a large and sustained decline in the demand for the services of the stock are not reflected in this financial measure, nor should they be if the physical capital in which the financial capital has been invested are very specific to their use. Such specificity will mean that the stock of unexpired services which such physical capital represents is not recoverable, and the financial capital such units represent is 'sunk' in the sectors concerned. In this sense therefore a physical measure of *capacity* will not be an alternative to a financial measure of *capital*, but a comparative study of the levels and movements of physical capacity in relation to movements in output will throw some light on the efficiency with which physical resources are employed. There are two elements in physical resource utilisation which are of particular interest. The first is the part played by the input of organisational knowledge and methods involved in matching physical capacity to output under dynamic conditions. The second is the influence of external factors upon output and physical capacity. Such external factors will include institutional restraints upon cutting back underutilised transport services when demand for them falls heavily and permanently,[2] and the restraint exercised by a licensing system upon the

---

1 A description of the concepts involved in gross capital stock are given in a technical note in the Statistical Appendix, Section C. The method of estimating the contribution of changes in capital intensity to output is explained in Chapter 1, pages 28–31.

2 Often in the form of statutory instruments requiring the provision of passenger and freight transport services so long as any demand for them exists.

expansion of capacity in the face of strongly rising demand for the transport services concerned. Also included will be the effects of substantial and sustained falls in demand and output which, even if they could have been foreseen, are so great that sufficient adjustments to capacity in a downwards direction could not have been made simply by deciding not to add to capacity or not to replace fully depreciated, life expired capital stock.

In the first section of this chapter the levels and movements in physical capacity, output and capacity utilisation are examined. This exercise is followed by a measure of the movement of the 'productivity of total capacity' in terms of output per unit of physical capacity. An allowance is made in this measure for the concurrent change in the contribution to movement in capacity productivity which arises from movement in the amount of labour per unit of capacity, in other words the allowance is for change in the labour intensity of capacity.[1] The formulation of this measure is as follows:

$$\Delta PTC = \Delta\left(\frac{Y}{C}\right) - (1 - \alpha)(\Delta LI - \Delta C)$$

where PTC is the productivity of total capacity

      Y is output as measured

      C is physical capacity as measured

    $1-\alpha$ is the share of labour in total factor rewards

     LI is labour input in terms of standardised labour unit hours

    Δ as a prefix is exponential rate of change per annum.

The assumptions underlying the measure used here of the contribution to capacity productivity movement of movement in labour per unit of capacity are the same as those described earlier.[2]

The results of applying this function are compared in the first section of this chapter with total factor (labour and financial capital) productivity movement in those sectors for which movement in the productivity of total capacity can be estimated.

In the second section four hypotheses are tested. They are concerned with postulated relationships between a number of variables. They have been designed to throw light upon factors which underlie productivity movements and which follow from such movements. The hypotheses are as follows:

A.   That movements in output and labour productivity correlate significantly (across sectors of the Measured Transport industry[3] in a positive sense.

---

[1] See Chapter 1, page 32 for an explanation of this concept.

[2] See Chapter 1, page 28.

[3] The correlations are of this nature throughout this chapter.

B. That movements in labour productivity and net price correlate significantly in a negative sense.

C. That movement in output and technical change (applied technical and organisational knowledge and external factors) correlate significantly in a positive sense.

D. That movement in capital stock input and technical change (as defined under C) correlate significantly in a positive sense.

A. An Alternative Measure of Productive Efficiency

1. The measurement of capacity and capacity utilisation in rail and road transport

The purpose of this sub-section is to make a comparative analysis of measures of physical capacity and of output. From these measures are calculated comparative levels and movements of capacity utilisation and movements in output per unit of total capacity (physical capacity and labour combined).

First it is necessary to state what we mean by physical capacity and physical capacity utilisation. We are concerned with more than the load factor. In road passenger transport, for example, this measure would be the proportion of total passenger miles of total seat miles, or the seat occupancy rate. This factor is not separately estimated. We are concerned with the output obtained from the physical service production units, buses in the above example, which operators deem it necessary to maintain to the official standards [1] and to make available for service. The volume of basic capacity in this sense will necessarily include a margin of capacity to cover normal out of service maintenance time.

It is particularly important to notice that movement in basic physical capacity in the sense just described is only a part of the movement in potential output. A movement in potential output (e.g. capacity ton miles of rail freight transport service) will include movement in physical capacity (tonnage of rail freight carrying capacity available for service), movement in applied technical knowledge (e.g. increased speed due to the use of diesel in the place of steam locomotives), and movement in applied organisational knowledge which could take many forms: examples are changes in freight handling, turn-round time, union-management relations and the incidence of strikes. Output per unit of potential would therefore be a measure of the average load factor, which would not be expected to change greatly over time. Of greater interest, for the reasons given earlier, is the movement of physical capacity in relation to concurrent movement in output, with an allowance for the contribution to output of movement in the amount of labour input per unit of capacity employed.

---

[1] These standards for public passenger transport vehicles in both rail and road service are of course particularly high.

In some sectors of the Measured Transport industry a difficulty arises about the measure of physical capacity. The specification 'available for service' may not coincide with the existing stock of carrying capacity. Where, as for example in the railways, output has fallen fast and where the carrying capacity, rail wagons, are very specific to their designed uses, then it is questionable whether in these circumstances such assets truly represent active physical capacity. Reductions in such capacity are sometimes delayed because the physical assets have no alternative uses, after a time it is realised that it is not worthwhile to maintain and repair a stock of wagons which is too large in relation to the demand for their services. A part of the stock is not used at all and quite abruptly is scrapped. Such scrapping decisions will give a rather spurious boost to productive efficiency measured in terms of output per unit of physical capacity with allowance for change in labour per unit of capacity. In the case of the railways a measure of physical capacity which is more accurately representative of the movement of total capacity is employed. This is an average of the rate of change of carrying capacity and of track miles for rail freight transport, and of seating capacity and track miles for rail passenger transport.

In the series of tables which follow, a comparative analysis is made of physical capacity, output and capacity utilisation in both rail and road, freight and passenger transport in Great Britain in 1952, 1958 and 1962.[1] The analysis which is in two parts, first freight and then passenger transport, is in terms of shares and of movements of the variables concerned.

The coverage of the freight statistics is rail and road (both marketed and private) which in 1962 accounted for 95.8 per cent of total inland freight tonnage transported and 81.3 per cent of total inland ton mileage performed (in 1952 these proportions were 95.7 and 81.6 respectively). The remainder, excluded from the analysis because of lack of data, includes the freight services performed by coastal shipping, air transport, inland waterways and pipelines.

In passenger transport, rail and road services provided 98.9 per cent of the total passenger mileage performed by public, *marketed* transport services in 1962 (99.9 per cent in 1952); air transport providing the very small but expanding share which is omitted. When total inland passenger transport is considered the passenger mileage performed by private passenger cars is included and then the share of public, marketed rail and road passenger transport in the total is only 38.4 per cent in 1962 (66.1 per cent in 1952). No very reliable statistics are available of the occupancy of passenger cars, and the changes in this ratio over time; therefore private cars have been omitted from this part of the analysis as they have from most earlier analyses[2] for similar reasons.

---

1 Annual series for many of these variables for the period 1952–1966 are given in the Statistical Appendix. Section F. Because the last road goods survey, for which results are available, was in 1962/63, any statistics after this date must be regarded as provisional.

2 Except in Chapter 2 where they are included in the analysis of output.

Table 6.1. Rail[a] and road goods transport

A. Capacity and output

	1 Number of vehicles (000's) (at mid-year)			2 Carrying capacity of vehicles (000 tons) (at mid-year)			3 Tonnage forwarded (million tons)			4 Ton mileage performed (000 m)			5 Value of Gross Output[b] (£s M. 1958 prices)		
	1952	1958	1962	1952	1958	1962	1952	1958	1962	1952	1958	1962	1952	1958	1962
Rail	1,108	1,048	895	14,708	15,414	13,773	285	243	228	22.4	18.4	16.1	315	259	227
Total Road of which	917	1,209	1,414	2,335	2,935	3,458	847	1,061	1,248	18.8	25.2	33.6	657	840	1,123
Contractual	162	173	190	841	998	1,200	341	448	510	8.4	13.1	17.3	193	300	396
Non-Contractual	755	1,036	1,224	1,494	1,937	2,258	506	613	738	10.4	12.1	16.3	464	540	727
Total Rail and Road	2,025	2,257	2,309	17,043	18,349	17,231	1,132	1,304	1,476	41.2	43.6	49.7	972	1,099	1,350

PERCENTAGES

B. Rail and road shares

	1952	1958	1962	1952	1958	1962	1952	1958	1962	1952	1958	1962	1952	1958	1962
Rail	54.7	46.4	38.8	86.3	84.0	80.0	25.2	18.6	15.4	54.4	42.2	32.4	32.4	23.6	16.8
Road	45.3	53.6	61.2	13.7	16.0	20.0	74.8	81.4	84.6	45.6	57.8	67.6	67.6	76.4	83.2

C. Contractual and non-contractual shares in total rail and road

	1952	1958	1962	1952	1958	1962	1952	1958	1962	1952	1958	1962	1952	1958	1962
Contractual[c]	62.7	54.1	47.0	91.2	89.4	86.9	55.3	53.0	50.0	74.8	72.2	67.2	52.3	50.9	46.1
Non-Contractual[d]	37.3	45.9	53.0	8.8	10.6	13.1	44.7	47.0	50.0	25.2	27.8	32.8	47.7	49.1	53.9

D. Contractual and non-contractual shares in road only

	1952	1958	1962	1952	1958	1962	1952	1958	1962	1952	1958	1962	1952	1958	1962
Contractual	17.7	14.3	13.4	36.0	34.0	34.7	40.3	42.2	40.9	44.7	52.0	51.5	29.4	35.7	35.3
Non-Contractual	82.3	85.7	86.6	64.0	66.0	65.3	59.7	57.8	59.1	55.3	48.0	48.5	70.6	64.3	64.7

a British Railways only

b Ton miles by mode valued at cost to user at 1958 prices.

c Rail and 'A' + 'B' + BTC licensed road goods transport.

d 'C' licensed road goods transport.

Shares and trends in output, capacity, capacity utilisation and the productivity of total capacity

Freight transport

In Table 6.1 are shown the absolute levels and shares of rail and road freight transport services in total rail/road capacity[1] and output. It was pointed out in the previous section that the rail and road modes of freight transport together account for a very high proportion (95.8 per cent) of the total tonnage of inland goods movements. It may be seen from Table 6.1 Col. 2, Section B that the total carrying capacity of rail transport in 1962 was 80.0 per cent of the rail/road total, although the rail share had declined from 86.3 per cent in 1952. With such a large, even dominant, share in total capacity it might be expected that rail freight transport services would carry at least half the total rail/road freight traffic. But, as shown in Section B of Table 6.1, this is far from what in fact happened. In 1962 the rail services carried only 15.4 per cent of the tonnage forwarded via rail and road, performed only 32.4 per cent of the ton-miles, and accounted for only 16.8 per cent of the gross output of rail/road freight services valued at 1958 prices. To maintain and to have available for operation approximately 80 per cent of total capacity and to use it to gain only 16.8 per cent of the total market for freight transport services in value terms is a performance to notice and to explore in further detail. Perhaps the first question to ask within the context of this chapter is: Given that the demand for rail freight transport services declined sharply between 1952 and 1962, how

Table 6.2. Indices of carrying capacity, output and capacity utilisation in rail and road freight transport, 1952–1962

(1952 = 100)

	Rail[a]	Total Road	Contractual Road	Non-Contractual Road
Carrying Capacity 1962 (1952 = 100)	93.6	148.1	142.7	151.2
Output 1962 (1952 = 100)	71.9	178.7	206.0	156.7
Carrying Capacity Utilisation 1962 (1952 = 100)	76.8	120.7	144.3	103.7

a When capacity is measured in terms of track miles, the index of capacity for 1962 (1952 = 100) is 94.6, and that of capacity utilisation (ton miles per track mile) is 76.0. The base for the utilisation index is 433 ton miles per track mile in 1952 and 329 in 1962. After 1962 British Railways cut down both track miles and wagons drastically. (See Figure 10).

1 For a description of the method and process of estimating tonnage of carrying capacity (from statistics of unladen weight) in road freight transport see Statistical Appendix, Section F.

successful have the railway management been in adjusting capacity downwards in order to match the decline in demand for rail services? The answer is clearly apparent from the information given in Table 6.2. This table shows that between 1952 and 1962 rail freight capacity has declined by only six per cent in the face of a decline of 28 per cent in the demand for the services provided by this capacity, and the capacity utilisation ratio has consequently declined steeply by approximately 23 per cent.

Road freight transport experienced an increasing demand for its services over the same period, 1952–62, but capacity increased at a much slower rate than output. In road haulage contracting capacity utilisation increased by as much as 44 per cent. In non-contractual road freight transport the gain in capacity utilisation was much less at just under 4 per cent.

Contractual and non-contractual shares in total rail and road freight transport are shown in Section C of Table 6.1. In terms of ton mileage performed the non-contractual services (which are road services only) remain at a level which is well below that of the contractual side (rail and contractual road haulage), but the trend over the period 1952–1962 is for the gap to narrow appreciably: the non-contractual services accounting for a quarter of total ton miles performed in 1952 and nearly a third in 1962. Since non-contractual freight transport services are more expensive per ton mile, their share in the total gross output of all rail and road freight services is higher than their share in total ton mileage, and by 1962 their share in value terms had grown to exceed the share of the contractual services.

The growing relative importance of the non-contractual services disappears when road freight transport services are considered on their own (Section D, Table 6.1), and the offsetting effect of the absolute and relative decline of the rail freight services is excluded. In terms of tonnage forwarded there is a marked stability in the shares of each of the two types of road freight transport, but in terms of ton mileage performed and value of gross output the non-contractual services became relatively less important between 1952 and 1958, but between 1958 and 1962 there is stability in the relative shares in terms of both ton miles and value of output.

A clear conclusion which may be drawn from the analysis of levels of capacity utilisation (Table 6.3) is the comparatively very low level of utilisation of, first, rail in relation to road freight transport as a whole in terms of tonnage forwarded, ton mileage performed and gross value of output (in constant prices) per capacity ton available for employment and, second, the substantially lower level of capacity utilisation of non-contractual road freight transport services compared with contractual road freight services in terms of ton mileage performed, but less markedly in tonnage forwarded and in value of gross output per capacity ton available for employment. In fact in 1952 the value comparison was in favour of the non-contractual services.

Perhaps the most outstanding single comparative statistic of capacity utilisation levels is that of output, in ton miles, per capacity ton in rail and in contractual road freight transport in 1962. This shows capacity utilisation in contractual road freight transport to be 12.3 times as great as that in rail freight transport.

An alternative measure of capacity utilisation in terms of ton mileage per vehicle available for employment is vitiated by the differences in average vehicle carrying capacities between the modes of freight transport, and these are shown in Col. 4 of Table 6.3. The increasing average carrying capacity of contractual road freight vehicles matches the increases in ton mileage per vehicle and in average haul, but an increase in the average carrying capacity of rail freight vehicles is a movement counter to the declining ton mileage of work performed per vehicle which is, in part, explained in terms of the decline in average haul.

In ton mileage terms the increase in the share of road freight transport, and the corresponding decline in the share of rail freight transport (Table 6.1 B, Col. 4), has been of substantial proportions over the period 1952 to 1962. This shift in the pattern of demand for road freight transport services would lead to the expectation that the average length of haul of rail and of road services (Table 6.3, Col. 6) would reflect this shift movement. Although the average haul of rail freight services has declined and that of road freight services has increased, the extent of the change is less than might be expected in the light of the shift in the demand pattern.[1]

Capacity and output movements for rail and road freight transport are shown in relative terms on a common base in Figure 10. The contrast between these divergent movements is striking in its implications for movements in capacity utilisation. It has already been noticed[2] that the relative capacity utilisation levels, implied here by the use of a common base of 100 in 1952, are also very different for each freight transport mode. In 1952 the level of rail freight transport utilisation in terms of ton miles per capacity ton was only 15 per cent of that of contractual road freight utilisation.

Movements in output, capacity, capacity utilisation, the productivity of total capacity and the difference between the rail and road rates of change in these variables are shown in Table 6.4. The difference between movements of output and capacity, and therefore of capacity utilisation, within each mode in the period 1952—62 was 3.67 per cent per annum in road haulage contracting and −2.70 per cent per annum in rail freight transport. When this period is divided into two sub-periods, 1952—58 and 1958—62, it is seen that road output increased quite steadily throughout the whole period with some slight falling off in the rate of growth in the second sub-period. In rail, the decline in output was much the same in both sub-periods. In road, the capacity utilisation movement accelerated

---

[1] An explanation of this is suggested in the Ministry of Transport's Survey of Road Goods Transport, 1962, Final Results Part I, p. 7—10. The main point is that the 'rapid growth of road (freight) transport in recent years appears to arise more from growth in activities which depend on the services of road transport than from actual switches of traffic from rail to road'.

[2] See page 159.

Table 6.3. Rail[a] and Road Goods Transport, 1952, 1958 and 1962
Capacity Utilisation and Average Haul

	1 Tonnage forwarded per capacity ton			2 Ton mileage performed per capacity ton			3 Value of Gross Output per capacity ton (£s. 1958 prices)			4 Average carrying capacity of vehicles (tons)			5 Ton mileage of work performed per vehicle (000)			6 Average Haul (miles)		
	1952	1958	1962	1952	1958	1962	1952	1958	1962	1952	1958	1962	1952	1958	1962	1952	1958	1962
Rail	19	16	17	1,523	1,194	1,169	21	17	16	13.27	14.71	15.39	20.2	17.6	18.0	78.6	75.7	70.6
Total Road	363	361	361	8,051	8,586	9,717	281	286	325	2.55	2.43	2.45	20.5	20.8	23.8	22.2	23.8	26.9
Contractual Road	405	449	425	9,988	13,126	14,417	229	301	330	5.19	5.77	6.32	51.9	75.7	91.1	24.6	29.2	33.9
Non-Contractual Road	339	316	327	6,961	6,247	7,219	311	279	322	1.98	1.87	1.84	13.8	11.7	13.3	20.6	19.7	22.1
Total Rail and Road	66	71	86	2,417	2,376	2,884	57	60	78	8.42	8.13	7.46	20.3	19.3	21.5	36.4	33.4	33.7

a British Railways only.

Index: 1952 = 100

Road Haulage Contracting

—— Output[a]

----- Carrying Capacity[b]

Rail Freight

—— Output

----- Carrying Capacity

—·— Track Miles

Index

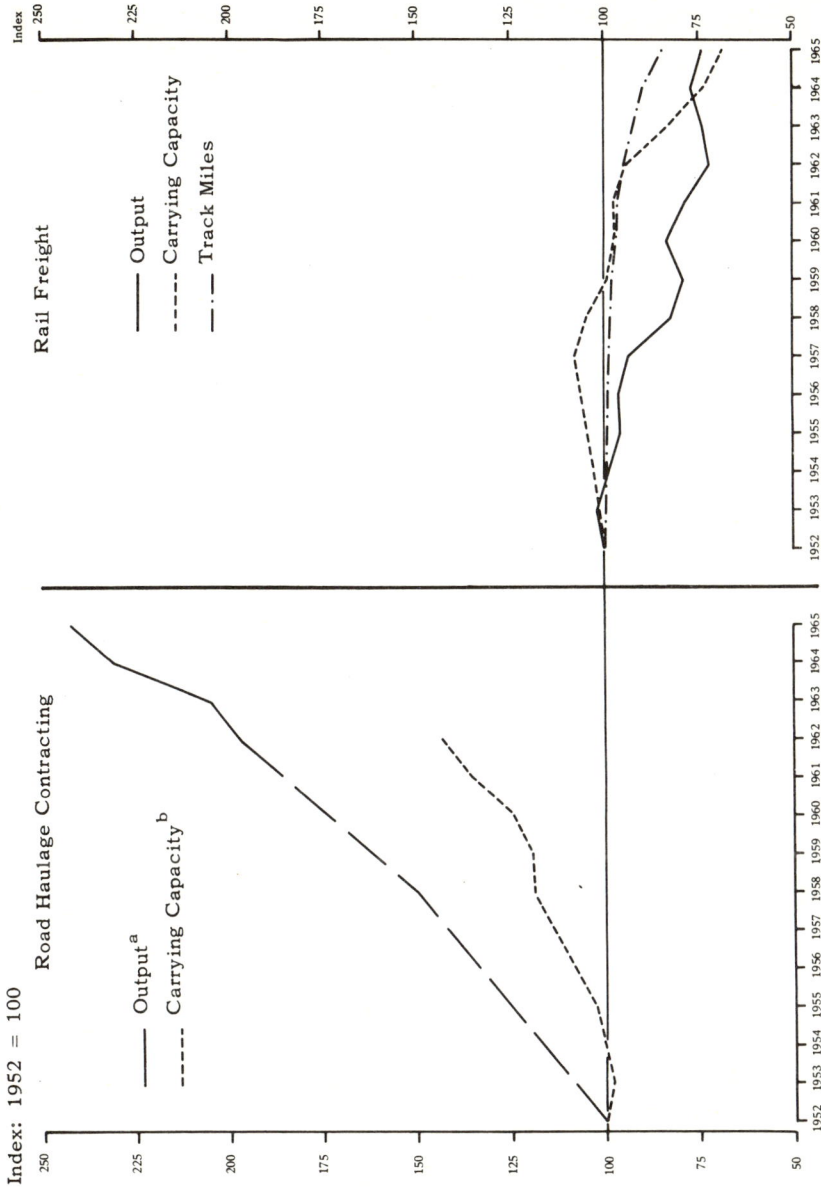

a Figures not available for the years between 1952 and 1958 and between 1958 and 1962

b Figures not available after 1962

163

Table 6.4. Absolute and Relative Movements in Output, Capacity, Capacity Utilisation and Productivity of Total Capacity in Rail[a] and Contractual Road Freight Transport, 1952–1962 (with sub-periods) and 1962–1965

Great Britain

(Exponential rates of change per annum)

	1952–62			1952–58			1958–62			1962–65 (provisional)		
	Road	Rail	Difference (Road-Rail)	Road	Rail	Difference (Road-Rail)	Road	Rail	Difference (Road-Rail)	Road	Rail	Difference (Road-Rail)
1. Output, ΔY	7.23	−3.30	10.53	7.41	−3.28	10.69	6.96	−3.34	10.30	6.9	0.8	6.1
2. Capacity,[b] ΔC	3.56	−0.60	4.16	2.85	0.27	2.58	4.61	−1.91	6.52	(4.6)[d]	−7.1	(11.7)
3. Capacity Utilisation, ΔCU[c]	3.67	−2.70	6.37	4.55	−3.55	8.10	2.34	−1.43	3.77	(2.3)	7.9	−5.6
4. Productivity of Total Capacity, ΔPTC	5.17	−1.80	6.97	6.03	−2.63	8.66	3.88	−0.58	4.46	(2.8)	6.8	4.0

a British Railways only.

b Capacity for road = carrying capacity. Capacity for rail = an unweighted average of the rates of change of carrying capacity and track miles.

c Row 1 − Row 2 = Row 3, since $\Delta Y - \Delta C = \Delta CU$; observable small discrepancies are due to rounding.

d Extrapolated.

164

ver the whole period, and in rail (where the measure is an average of rates of change in carrying capacity and in track miles), capacity actually increased (due to an increase in carrying capacity) in the first period (1952–58) in the face of a concurrent steep decline in output. Thereafter, from 1958 up to 1962, capacity was cut back, but only just over half as fast as output fell.

A question which seems to arise naturally here is: What are the chief factors which explain the differences in the movements of output and capacity, given that the movement of output is determined by the market? An answer is suggested under four heads.

. *Speed*

In the terminology developed and used in this Paper, speed will be included with applied technical knowledge, a part of ATOKE. In *rail*, diesel engines have replaced steam in the period covered. It is clear that an increase in average speed will be an explanatory factor contributing positively to capacity utilisation movement. We have measurability of average speeds for rail only. There was an increase in the average speed of freight trains over the period 1952–62. The extent by which speed increased should logically go towards explaining how *greater* output has been obtained from each unit of capacity. As capacity utilisation has been declining in this mode, it is clear that other factors have outweighed the effect of increased average speed.[1] In road haulage contracting

---

Since capacity has been measured by an average of the rates of change of tonnage of carrying capacity and of track miles, it would not be wholly meaningful to add changes in speed to this measure of capacity in order to reach a measure of the movement of *potential* capacity, which must not be confused with potential output (see p. 156). But if we measure capacity solely by tonnage carrying capacity (and bear in mind the limitations of this measure, see page 157), then we get:

Rail Freight Movements in:	1952–62	1952–58	1958–62	1962–65 (provisional)
. Carrying Capacity, ΔCC	−0.66	0.78	−2.81	−10.4
. Average speed,[a] ΔAS	1.33	1.39	1.24	2.9
. Potential carrying capacity, ΔPCC. (Row 1 + Row 2)	0.67	2.17	−1.57	− 7.5
. Output, ΔY	−3.30	−3.28	−3.34	0.8
. Carrying Capacity Utilisation, ΔCCU. (Row 4 − Row 1)	−2.64	−4.06	−0.53	11.2
. Potential Carrying Capacity Utilisation, ΔPCCU. (Row 4 − Row 3)	−3.97	−5.45	−1.77	8.3

a Source: British Transport Commission and British Railways Board annual reports.

average speeds have also probably risen but precise data are lacking. It is known only that the speed limit for heavy vehicles (over 3 tons unladen weight) was raised from 20 to 30 miles per hour in May 1957. This limit was raised further to 40 miles per hour (for all goods vehicles) in July 1961. It is not known to what extent the old, and new, limits were adhered to and the effect they had upon average speeds; nor can estimates be made of the effects of increasing traffic congestion between 1952 and 1965 on average speeds in road haulage contracting. If average speeds have increased then this factor contributes to the increased capacity utilisation which has occurred and explains a part of that movement.

2. *Institutional constraints*

Included among these, and possibly the most important, is the licensing system for contractual road haulage vehicles (they are all either 'A' or 'B' licensed vehicles), and the obligation upon the railways (until the Transport Act of 1962) to continue to provide services even though underutilised and unrewarding in financial terms. Although not measurable in specific terms, these constraints on the adjustment of road haulage capacity upwards and rail freight capacity downwards should be noticed as probable elements in movements of rail and road freight capacity utilisation.

In the period 1952–62, the relative movement in output (Road-Rail) was 10.53 per cent per annum (Table 6.4), while the corresponding relative movement in capacity was less than half this at 4.16 per cent, making the movement in relative capacity utilisation 6.37 per cent per annum. This relative capacity differential movement was much higher (6.52 per cent) in the second sub-period (1958–62) than it was in the first (2.58 per cent in 1952–58). As the output differential movement was about the same (10 per cent) in both sub-periods, the capacity utilisation differential rate fell, from 8.10 to 3.77 per cent between the two sub-periods. After 1962 the output differential rate fell to 8.4, the capacity differential rate rose above this to an estimate of 11.7, and this moved the capacity utilisation differential rate in favour of rail to an estimated extent of −3.3 per cent per annum. This reflects the 'Beeching era' on the railways and the removal of the institutional constraint upon cutting back rail freight services and capacity, thus influencing capacity utilisation movement.

Footnote 1 cont. from page 165.

Not until the 'Beeching era', which effectively started in 1962, did actual tonnage carrying capacity decline sufficiently to bring it down by 1965 to about the same relationship to output as had existed in 1952. Over this thirteen year period as a whole (1952–65) output declined by 2.36 per cent per annum and tonnage carrying capacity by 2.90 per cent per annum. By implication carrying capacity utilisation barely changed, but the average speed of freight trains increased by 1.70 per cent per annum over the same period, so the utilisation of potential carrying capacity declined by 1.16 per cent per annum for this reason.

3. Applied organisational knowledge

Although in some respects constrained by the legal instruments just referred to, applied organisational knowledge is likely to be an influential factor in the rate of output per unit of physical capacity. Not only is this factor applied to the task of matching capacity to demand under dynamic conditions, involving forecasts of future demand, but it is also concerned with the many management tasks involved in making better use of existing physical capacity and of the labour associated with it. It would therefore include the ability to avoid, or reduce the length of strikes.

The organisational problem of matching capacity to demand is enormously different in the expanding case from what it is in the contracting case, and there are also differences in this respect between road and rail. In contractual road haulage, a part of the capital employed (roads) is an externality not provided by the industry. An expansion of demand for road freight transport services can normally be met by the industry in the short run by an increase in capacity utilisation brought about by any or all of the following factors: an increase in load factor, an increase in the labour associated with physical capacity in the form of longer hours for drivers and mates,[1] or of additional labour. These processes involve no great organisational effort. In the longer term, capacity may be expanded subject to the licensing constraints. In contrast, enormous organisation problems arise when capacity becomes excessive in relation to demand over what turns out to be the long term, but when looked at from the viewpoint of the decision makers at an earlier moment in time may not have been so obviously recognisable as such. When, as in the railways, demand and output are declining, capacity utilisation must also decline unless capacity is reduced at least as fast as output, and this must involve major management decisions. When, on the other hand, output is rising, capacity utilisation will increase almost automatically and in default of major management action, at least in the short term.

These factors may be grouped under the title of applied organisational knowledge and they will be influential in movement in capacity utilisation.

4. Scale economies

There is a well known relationship between movements in output and productivity. This relationship is explored further, in respect of all the main modes of public transport in the United Kingdom, in the second half of this chapter. Capacity utilisation movement, used here in the wider sense than mere change in load factor, is a measure of productivity change. Economies of scale are much more likely to be achieved when output is rising consistently, as it is in road haulage contracting and, correspondingly, such economies are likely to be lost when

---

1 In recent years the hours of work of drivers have become so long as to constitute a safety problem which has engaged the attention of the authorities. Data on the average weekly hours worked by a sample of employees in this sector are given in the Statistical Appendix. Table B3.

when output declines consistently over quite a long period, as it does in rail freight transport. One basic reason for this is that in transport operations generally, and particularly in rail transport, overhead or fixed costs comprise a very large proportion of total costs.

*   *   *

These four factors, and others which have not been identified, will have influence upon the movement of capacity in relation to the movement of output in road and rail freight transport. Quantification of the influence of each factor is not attainable, except for that of changes in the average speed of freight trains. In rail freight transport in the periods concerned output has usually fallen faster than capacity; as average speeds have increased the difference between changes in capacity plus changes in average speed on the one hand and changes in output on the other hand will be greater than the difference between changes in capacity and in output. The inclusion of speed therefore 'explains' this latter difference in a rather perverse way by making the difference greater, but it is clearly an influential factor in capacity utilisation movement.

So far no account has been taken of the use of more, or less, labour per unit of capacity as output changes over time. The measure of the movement of capacity utilisation (Row 3 of Table 6.4) takes no account of the contribution to changes in capacity utilisation which arise from changes in the labour intensity of capacity. To reach a measure of the movement of productivity of total capacity it is necessary to estimate the contribution to the movement of capacity utilisation which comes from the concurrent movement in the labour intensity of each unit of capacity. The method of making this calculation has been explained in an earlier section of this chapter (page 155). Movements in the productivity of total capacity are shown in Row 4 of Table 6.4, and the contribution to these movements which came from changes in the labour intensity of capacity was as shown in Table 6.5.[1]

Table 6.5   Amount of movement in the productivity of total capacity due to movement in the labour intensity of capacity. (Exponential rates of change per annum)

Period	Road	Rail	Difference (Road-Rail)
1952–62	1.50	0.90	0.60
1952–58	1.48	0.92	0.56
1958–62	1.54	0.85	0.69
1962–65p	(0.5)	–1.1	(1.6)

p provisional.

In road freight transport in all these periods there was a reduction in the labour intensity of capacity. The effect of this is to make output per unit of combined

---

1 This is Row 4 – Row 3 of Table 6.4.

capacity and labour input[1] greater than movement in capacity utilisation. The same is true of rail freight transport, except for the 1962–65 period when capacity fell faster than labour input thus inducing a lower rate of increase in productivity of total capacity than in capacity utilisation. The contribution of labour input change to capacity productivity change was considerably greater in the road than in the rail mode and it may be seen that this differential change in favour of road increased over the period 1952–65.

The relative movements of the productivity of total capacity, as shown by calculations and estimations for the three periods 1952–58, 1958–62 and, in provisional terms, 1962–65, indicate that the railways which start from a large relative disparity improved their relative position until, in the most recent period, it is shown that the estimated differential has moved over in their favour. The immediate reason for this relative improvement of the railways' position is that their absolute performance in these physical terms has improved; a negative movement has become a positive one, while the movement in road haulage contracting has been at a slower rate in more recent years.

These movements in the productivity of total capacity are compared with movements in total factor productivity after public passenger transport has been considered.

Shares and trends in output, capacity, capacity utilisation and productivity of total capacity

Public passenger transport

The coverage of the analysis of passenger transport excludes private cars because this type of transport could not be included in the Measured Transport industry for the reasons already given,[2] but it is included in terms of gross output in the analysis given in Chapter 2. Air passenger transport is included in the Measured Transport industry but is excluded here because it is a tiny fraction of total public inland passenger transport.

The absolute levels and shares of public rail and road passenger transport in capacity and output are shown in Table 6.6, and the trends in Figure 11 and in Table 6.7 (with further detail in the Statistical Appendix Table F.2.) As has been indicated earlier (Chapter 2, Table 2.13), private cars have taken a large

---

1 The contribution of labour input movement to capacity productivity movement is of course accounted after an allowance has been made for the *extra* labour required to man *additional* units of capacity. In other words account is taken only of labour input which is labour 'deepening' and not of that proportion of labour input which is 'widening'.

2 See page 157 and Chapter 1, p. 21. Also given there are estimates showing the importance of private passenger car transport as a proportion of total passenger miles.

Table 6.6.   Public Rail and Road Passenger Transport

Great Britain

A.   Capacity and output

	1 Number of Vehicles			2 Seating Capacity of Vehicles ('000s)			3 Passenger Journeys millions			4 Passenger Miles '000 million			5 Value of Gross Output £m. at 1958 prices		
	1952	1958	1962	1952	1958	1962	1952	1958	1962	1952	1958	1962	1952	1958	1962
Rail[a]	41,984	41,915	35,728	2,491	2,446	2,078	1,017	1,090	965	20.5	22.2	19.7	127.3	138.0	122.3
Road[b]	82,815	78,491	77,930	3,750	3,700	3,800	16,336	13,840	13,030	50.1	43.4	42.4	344.4	297.8	291.5
Total Rail and Road	124,799	120,406	113,658	6,241	6,146	5,878	17,353	14,930	13,995	70.6	65.6	62.1	471.7	435.8	413.8

B.   Rail and road shares

PERCENTAGES

	1952	1958	1962	1952	1958	1962	1952	1958	1962	1952	1958	1962	1952	1958	1962
Rail	33.6	34.8	31.4	39.9	39.8	35.4	5.9	7.3	6.9	29.0	33.8	31.7	27.0	31.7	29.6
Road	66.4	65.2	68.6	60.1	60.2	64.6	94.1	92.7	93.1	71.0	66.2	68.3	73.0	68.3	70.4

a   British Railways only.

b   All public road passenger transport services.

Table 6.7.   Public Rail and Road Passenger Transport

Great Britain

Capacity utilisation and average journey length

	1 Average Seating Capacity of Vehicles (Number of seats)			2 Passenger Journeys per capacity seating unit			3 Passenger Miles per vehicle ('000s)			4 Passenger Miles per capacity seating unit			5 Value of Gross Output per capacity seating unit (£s. at 1958 prices)			6 Average Length of Passenger Journeys (miles)		
	1952	1958	1962	1952	1958	1962	1952	1958	1962	1952	1958	1962	1952	1958	1962	1952	1958	1962
Rail	59	58	58	408	446	464	488	530	551	8,230	9,076	9,480	51.1	56.4	58.9	20.2	20.4	20.4
Road	45	47	49	4,356	3,741	3,429	605	553	544	13,360	11,730	11,158	91.8	80.5	76.7	3.07	3.14	3.25

Figure 11. Output and Capacity in Road and Rail Passenger Transport, 1952–1965

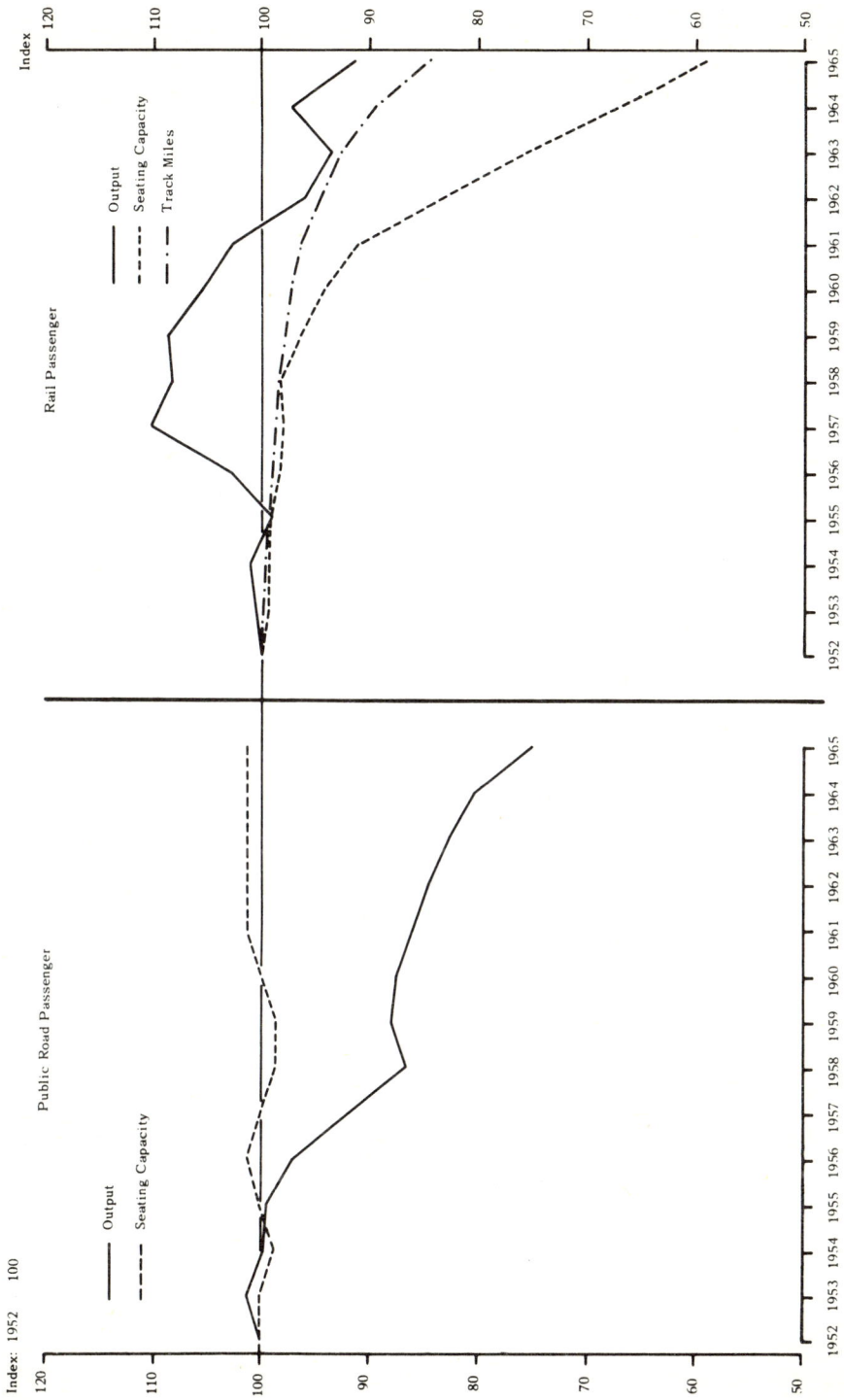

and expanding share of the total passenger transport market in the period covered here. The public passenger transport share of the total market is thus a declining one. In terms of all the measures of both capacity and output the share of rail rose between 1952 and 1958 and declined between 1958 and 1962, with the exception of seating capacity where the relative position of the two modes was virtually unchanged between 1952 and 1958.

When capacity is measured by seating capacity, and this is the best available measure which is common to both rail and road, we do not get as we do in freight transport one mode possessing a dominant, 80 per cent share of capacity and a tiny, 17 per cent share of the total value of the market for the services produced by that capacity. In total public rail and road passenger transport rail had a 35 per cent share of capacity in 1962 and a 32 per cent share of output as measured by total passenger miles and 30 per cent as measured by value of gross output (receipts). Thus the absolute levels of capacity utilisation in public road passenger transport (Table 6.7) were not so widely different as between the two modes in public passenger transport as they were in public freight transport. Furthermore, there was a narrowing of the gap between rail and road in terms of output per unit of capacity (measured by seats available) between 1952 and 1962. Over this period, capacity utilisation increased in rail and decreased in road passenger transport. Again this is the opposite of the results of the freight transport analysis conducted in similar terms.

Capacity [1] and output movements in rail and road passenger transport are shown in related terms on a common base in Figure 11. Over the whole of the period 1952–65 there was a decline in output in both modes, although in the early sub-period (1952–58) there was a rise in the output of rail passenger transport services. There is however a significant difference between modes in the movement of capacity. In road, capacity rose slightly in the face of a substantial decline in the demand for public road passenger services. In rail, capacity, as measured by seats available, fell much faster; as measured by track miles it fell less rapidly but nevertheless faster than output.

A qualification and analysis of these movements in output and capacity by sub-periods, with the implications for capacity utilisation and for the productivity of total capacity is given in Table 6.8. For the 1952–62 period capacity utilisation within each mode increased in rail (+ 0.78 per cent per annum) and declined in road (– 1.80 per cent per annum). An analysis of these movements by sub-periods indicates some closing of this difference between the two modes. The movement of capacity utilisation in rail became negative in the 1958–62 period, and in road the movement in the same ratio declined less steeply than in

---

[1] For reasons given earlier (p. 157) two measures of rail passenger capacity, seating capacity and track miles, are shown separately here. In Table 6.8 the movement of capacity is in each case an average of the movement of these two measures.

172

Table 6.8. Absolute and Relative Movements in Output, Capacity, Capacity Utilisation and Productivity of Total Capacity in Rail[a] and Road Passenger Transport, 1952–1962 (with Sub-periods) and 1962–1965

Great Britain

(Exponential rates of change per annum)

	1952–62			1952–58			1958–62			1962–65 (provisional)		
	Road	Rail	Difference (Road-Rail)	Road	Rail	Difference (Road-Rail)	Road	Rail	Difference (Road-Rail)	Road	Rail	Difference (Road-Rail)
1. Output, ΔY	-1.67	-0.40	-1.27	-2.39	1.33	-3.72	-0.59	-2.99	2.40	-4.00	-1.74	-2.26
2. Capacity, [b] ΔC	0.13	-1.18	1.31	-0.23	-0.27	0.04	0.67	-2.55	3.22	0	-7.56	7.56
3. Capacity Utilisation, ΔCU [c]	-1.80	0.78	-2.58	-2.16	1.60	-3.76	-1.26	-0.44	-0.82	-4.00	5.82	-9.82
4. Productivity of Total Capacity, ΔPTC.	-0.82	1.23	-2.05	-1.36	2.11	-3.47	0.02	-0.08	0.10	-4.11	4.39	-8.50

a British Railways only.

b Capacity for road = passenger seating capacity. Capacity for rail = an unweighted average of the rates of change of passenger seating capacity and track miles.

c Row 1 – Row 2 = Row 3, since $\Delta Y - \Delta C = \Delta CU$.

173

the preceding period (1952–58); so the gap closed and the movement of relative capacity utilisation (road–rail) became less negative and less in favour of rail.

An attempt to identify the chief factors governing these differences in movements in output and capacity in these two public passenger transport modes is given below. As in the similar examination carried out for freight transport, four factors are considered.

1.   Speed

In *rail*, the average speed of passenger trains has increased over the period of the analysis due to the introduction of diesel engines and possibly due to other factors besides. Changes in average speed will be reflected in movements in capacity utilisation (ΔCU) and in applied technical and organisational knowledge and external factors ($\Delta ATOKE$). In the rail mode increased average speed has contributed to the increase which has occurred in ΔCU, enabling more output to be produced per unit of capacity.[1] The results of the analysis given in the last footnote show that the increase in average speed which occurred in the 1952–62 period is likely to have contributed a substantial part of the explanation of the difference between the movements over the same period of output and capacity in rail passenger transport.

In *road* no precise data are available on changes in the average speed of public road passenger transport vehicles. It is known only that the speed limit for buses

---

[1] An exercise similar to that undertaken for rail freight transport (see p. 165 n) may be carried out for rail passenger transport. If we measure capacity solely by seating capacity, and for this purpose it would not be wholly meaningful to measure it otherwise, we get the following estimations of movements in potential seating capacity utilisation which we can compare with movements in seating capacity utilisation:

| | | | | (Exponential rates of change per annum) |
Rail Passenger Movements in:	1952–62	1952–58	1958–62	1962–65 (provisional)
1. Seating capacity, ΔSC	−1.81	−0.30	−4.08	−11.3
2. Average speed,[a] ΔAS	2.27	1.40	3.60	3.8
3. Potential capacity, ΔPC (Row 1 + Row 2)	0.46	1.10	−0.48	− 7.5
4. Output, ΔY	−0.40	1.33	−2.99	− 1.7
5. Seating Capacity Utilisation, ΔSCU (Row 4 − Row 1)	1.41	1.63	1.09	9.6
6. Potential seating capacity utilisation, $\Delta PSCU$ (Row 4 − Row 3)	−0.86	0.23	−2.51	5.8

[a]   Source: British Transport Commission and British Railways Board Annual Reports.

and coaches was raised from 30 to 40 miles per hour in July 1961.[1] It is not known to what extent the old, and new, limits were adhered to and the effect they may have had on average speeds. Nor can estimates be made of the effects of increasing urban traffic congestion between 1952 and 1965 on average speeds in public road passenger transport. However, it is known that in 1958 40.4 per cent of total public road passenger transport output (and 37.8 per cent in 1962) was produced by urban stage bus services, and other bus services do of course undertake a part of their stages in urban areas where congestion is heavier than it is in rural areas. If average speeds have in fact fallen, then this would in part explain why seating capacity has not fallen (it has in fact risen slightly) in the face of a sustained and substantial decline in demand and output.

2. Institutional constraints

Statutory obligations to provide transport services have existed in both road and rail modes in this period, and in some cases they still exist. When demand for the services concerned falls off, capacity is still needed to meet the obligation to provide a service, albeit a curtailed one, and so the negative movement of capacity tends to lag the negative movement of output. The effects of these restraints are not measurable in precise terms, but they may be important elements in movements in rail and road passenger capacity utilisation. In the period 1952—62, the relative output movement (Road—Rail)[2] was —1.27 per cent per annum; relative capacity movement, 1.31; making relative capacity utilisation —2.58. This is a bad result for road passenger services and would probably be worse if average speed changes could be taken into account in both modes. Within this longer period, the analysis shows that the relative capacity utilisation movement improves for road, not because road improved in absolute terms, but because capacity utilisation in rail declined in absolute terms. With the coming of the Beeching period (1962—65) the relative and absolute results for rail greatly improved, but the opposite occurred in road passenger transport where no move has yet been made to correct the lag in movement in capacity on movement in output.

Footnote 1 cont. from p. 174

As in the case of rail freight transport the re-organisation, which started in 1962, brought about a fall in seating capacity which was much more rapid than the reductions made in earlier periods; but in the case of rail passenger transport, unlike the rail freight case, seating capacity fell faster than output in all periods and much faster than output in the period 1962—65. The consequence for seating capacity utilisation was a sharp increase. The increased average speed of passenger trains is clearly an important influence upon *potential* seating capacity utilisation, which rises slightly in the 1952—58 period, falls by 2.51 per cent per annum in 1958—62, and rises sharply in 1962—65 but only just over half as fast as seating capacity utilisation.

1 The limit was raised further to 50 m.p.h. in August 1966.

2 See Table 6.8.

3. Applied organisational knowledge

The ability of management to match capacity to the demand for its services under dynamic conditions is clearly one aspect of applied organisational knowledge. It is subject to statutory restraints and this has been noticed. The chief problem is one of divisibility. There must be a minimum frequency below which a road or rail passenger transport service is not marketable. Load factors will fall for this reason as demand falls, and also in the case where complete services are continued only because of the statutory requirements. Strike avoidance, or minimisation, and the application of organisational knowledge in other respects (e.g. terminal and loading arrangements and fare collection) will enter as factors influential in movements of capacity in relation to output.

4. Scale economies

Throughout most of the period analysed, output of both road and rail public passenger transport services has been falling. There are clearly scale economies in the use of depot and permanent way facilities in these transport sectors as well as in the capacity utilisation flexibilities which transport equipment offers and which have often been pointed out by economists in terms of falling marginal costs of operation as output rises. When the system is put into reverse, as it is when demand and output fall, economies of scale are bound to be lost and long run marginal costs will rise. In terms of capacity utilisation a decline will occur unless capacity is reduced at least as fast.

* * *

Although quantification of these four factors is attainable only in the case of the average speed of passenger trains, it is clear that they will all influence the movement of capacity utilisation in road and rail passenger transport. The inclusion of the factor of average speed in rail passenger transport more than accounts for the gain in seating capacity utilisation in the 1952–62 period.[1] In the more recent 1962–65 period, when seating capacity was being reduced very fast under the railways 'reshaping programme', the speed factor accounted for about 40 per cent of the total gain in seating capacity utilisation.

We have yet to bring into account in public road and rail passenger transport the effect upon capacity utilisation movements of the use of more, or less, labour per unit of capacity as output changes over time. As for freight transport, the measure used is the productivity of *total* capacity. The methods of estimating movements in this measure have been given earlier.[2]

For the 1952–62 period the result of estimating the effect of changes in labour intensity upon movements in the productivity of *total* capacity is as shown in Table 6.9.[3]

---

1 See p. 174 n.

2 See p. 155.

3 This is row 4 – row 3 of Table 6.8.

Table 6.9.   Amount of Movement in the Productivity of Total Capacity due to
Movement in the Labour Intensity of Capacity

(Exponential rates of change per annum)

Period	Road	Rail	Difference (Road–Rail)
1952–62	0.98	0.45	0.53
1952–58	0.80	0.51	0.29
1958–62	1.28	0.36	0.92
1962–65[p]	−0.11	−1.43	1.32

p provisional

The labour intensity change was more important in road than in rail in all periods.[1]
It contributed positively to the movement of productivity of total capacity in all
periods except 1962–65, when capacity fell very fast in the railways, and labour
not so fast.

The relative movements of the productivity of total capacity over all the periods
distinguished in Table 6.8 indicate that the railways have improved their relative
position over road passenger transport, with a short period of setback in 1958–62.
Road passenger transport suffered declining productivity of total capacity in the
1952–62 period, and acceleration of this downwards movement in 1962–65.

2.   A comparative view of movements in productivity of total capacity and in
total factor productivity

Two separate methods have been described and applied to the best available data
in order to measure 'combined input' productivity. The first method was to
combine factor inputs of labour and capital in the same proportion as their factor
rewards bore to each other, and the second was to adjust output per unit of
capacity by the contribution made to it by changes in the amount of labour per
unit of capacity. The results of both sets of calculations are given in Table 6.10.

This comparative view shows that the two measures of 'combined output'
productivity give broadly similar results. This in itself is a useful check on the
results given in the previous chapter where a financial measure of capital was
employed.

In addition, we learn from the physical capacity method of productivity
measurement that in rail, where separate estimates are made (and they are
estimates involving the assumption of a common rate of labour input for the
freight and passenger sides of the railways), the performance of the freight side
appears to be a good deal worse than that of the passenger side.

---

[1] As noted in Table 6.8, labour input into rail passenger is assumed to move
with labour input to the railways as a whole.

Table 6.10. Movements in Total Factor Productivity and in the Productivity of Total Capacity, 1952–62 and 1962–65

(Exponential rates of change per annum)

Movements in:	1952–62	1952–58	1958–62	1962–65[p]
1. Railways				
a. Total Factor Productivity,[a] ΔTFP	−0.58	−0.81	−0.26	4.0
b. Productivity of Total Capacity[b], ΔPTC				
(i) Freight	−1.80	−2.63	−0.58	6.8
(ii) Passenger	1.23	2.11	−0.08	4.4
2. Road Passenger Transport[c]				
a. ΔTFP	−1.28	−2.41	0.45	−4.6
b. ΔPTC	−0.82	−1.36	0.02	−4.1
3. Road Haulage Contracting				
a. ΔTFP	4.47	5.45	3.02	2.6
b. ΔPTC	5.17	6.03	3.88	2.8

p provisional

a Equivalent to ΔATOKE, movement in applied technical and organisational knowledge and external factors.

b Of British Railways only.

c Some small part of the difference between a. and b. here will be due to differences in output measurement. In a. a weighted and in b. an unweighted measure of passenger miles is used.

The explanatory value of the comparative analysis of rail freight and passenger transport may usefully be pressed one stage further. In Table 6.11, movement in carrying (and seating) capacity utilisation (i.e. crude capacity productivity) is analysed in terms of the contributions to such movement which come from movements in (a) Labour intensity of capacity, (b) Average speed and, (c) Other factors.

'Other factors' are clearly important, and particularly so in rail freight transport. What are they? By a process of elimination they are likely to include organisational knowledge, institutional constraints and loss of economies of scale as demand and output declined. These influences upon productivity movement have already been pointed out; unfortunately the process of quantification of their respective influences can go no further for the present.

178

Table 6.11. A Comparative Analysis of Movements in Capacity Utilisation in Rail Freight and Passenger Transport Showing Contributions from Movements in the Labour Intensity of Capacity and from Average Speed, 1952–62

| | (Exponential rates of change per annum) | |
Movement in:	Freight	Passenger
Carrying/seating Capacity Utilisation, ΔCCU/SCU	−2.64	1.41
of which due to:		
a. Movement in labour intensity of carrying/ seating capacity, ΔLICC/LISC	−0.90	−0.45
b. Movement in average speed of freight trains/passenger trains, ΔAS	1.33	2.27
c. Movement in other factors, ΔOF	−3.07	−0.41

B.   The Test of Hypotheses

The process, followed in the last chapter, of interpreting movements in output per unit of labour input in terms of the contributions made separately by movements in the input of capital (measured per head of the labour force) and of applied technical and organisational knowledge and external factors was essentially analytical in the intensive sense. The sectoral, and industry, trends in labour productivity were interpreted in terms of movements in the inputs involved and of how effective such inputs were in contributing to output. The influence which movements in such variables as output, labour productivity and price might have upon each other was not examined. Now a more extensive comparative study is attempted, in order first to test certain relationships of productivity movements which have been shown by others[1] to be generally established over different periods and in respect of a wide range of industrial activity in the United Kingdom and the United States. The second objective is to study from another viewpoint the several relationships between movement in output and labour productivity on the one hand and movements in labour input, capital stock, capital intensity and technical change on the other; and also the inter-relations between this last-named group.

One method by which relationships between variables may be judged is by an inspection of movements by sector with the sectors arranged in ranking order. The variables concerned in the test of hypotheses A, B, C, and D, stated at the beginning of this chapter, are set out in Table 6.12. They are in ranking order of output movements in the period 1954–1963.

The ranking order of sectors is the same for movements in output (ΔY), output

W.E.G. Salter and J.W. Kendrick, op. cit.

Table 6.12. Movements in Output, Labour Productivity, Total Factor Productivity, Net Price, Labour Input, Capital Stock and Capital Intensity, 1954–1963

(Exponential rates of change per annum)

Sectors in Ranking Order of Output Movements	Unexceptional Ranking				Exceptional Ranking		
	1	2	3	4	5	6	7
	Output (unadjusted), ΔY	Labour Productivity, ΔPLI	Total Factor Productivity as measured by $\Delta ATOKE$ [a]	Net Price ΔNP	Labour Input, ΔLI	Gross Capital Stock, ΔK	Capital Intensity, $\Delta \frac{K}{L}$
1. Air Transport	12.63	8.14	5.91	−1.6	4.49	10.53	5.16
2. Road Haulage Contracting	6.78	5.00	3.57	0.3	1.78	5.97	4.66
3. Port and Inland Water Transport	2.08	3.55	3.39	2.5	−1.47	−0.47	0.64
4. Sea Transport	1.35	3.51	1.95	3.5	−2.16	1.35	3.29
5. Railways	−2.08	0.42	−0.23	4.2	−2.54	0.21	2.75
6. Road Passenger Transport	−2.53	−1.74	−1.57	7.8	−0.79	−1.26	−0.64
MEASURED TRANSPORT							
Unadjusted	1.43	2.50	2.10	3.5	−1.07	0.89	1.90
Adjusted [b]	...	2.37	1.66	...	−0.94	1.91	2.93

a ATOKE, applied technical and organisational knowledge and external factors, represents total factor productivity.

b For inter-sectoral 'quality' shift changes in labour, capital and combined factor inputs as appropriate.

er unit of labour input (ΔP_{LI}), total factor productivity (as measured by ΔATOKE), net price (ΔNP) (in *inverse* ranking order), and this has been called unexceptional ranking. The ranking order of sectors is exceptional for movements in labour input (ΔLI), gross capital stock (ΔK), and for capital intensity Δ(K/L).

Another method of examining relationships between variables is to study product moment coefficients of correlation in respect of their movement. This is the method chiefly employed in the analysis which follows.

. Output, labour productivity and net price movements

The product moment coefficient of correlation in respect of movements in output, labour productivity, total factor productivity (represented by 'applied technical and organisational knowledge and external factors', ATOKE) and net price[1] are shown (with other coefficients of correlation in respect of other movements which are discussed later) in Table 6.13.

One of the more striking results is the high correlation between movements in output and in output per unit of labour input, the coefficient for the whole period (1954 to 1963) is 0.95, 0.98 in 1954—58, and 0.85 in 1958—63. It should be borne in mind that with six sectors, and therefore six observations, the significance of coefficients of correlation at the 5 per cent level is limited to coefficient values in excess of 0.81. This result is in line with those shown in Salter's work and in Reddaway's addendum to it. The coefficients for the same relationship in 28 British manufacturing industries are 0.81 in 1924—50 and 0.69 in 1954 to 1963 (the same period, it may be noticed, as has been studied in respect of the sectors of the Measured Transport industry but with a greater number of industry sectors the significance level for the coefficients is lower). It is therefore possible to conclude that the service industry of public, measurable transport exhibits the same characteristics with respect to movements in output and labour productivity as manufacturing industries.

. is perhaps worth re-stating at this point the widely, but not universally, accepted explanation of this relationship and then to examine the other relationships which are associated with it.

s output rises greater opportunities become available both to realise economies of scale and to apply the latest techniques, whether they involve new capital equipment or only the scope for the application of improved managerial and organisational skills. The economies of scale and the application of improved techniques of both general types make possible increases in labour productivity as output rises, and the contrary should output decline. The productivity gains lead in turn to lower relative prices and thence, given an elastic demand, to the

---

Net price refers to the value of net output at current prices per unit of volume of output. It is a measure of the charges made by a sector for the transport service which it produces and sells to customers. It is the price which is implicit in the measures of output and productivity which are made in this study.

Table 6.13.   Product Moment Coefficient of Correlation [a] in Respect of Movements in Output per Head and Other Quantities in Six Measured Transport Sectors in the United Kingdom, 1954–1963, 1954–1958, 1954–1963 and 1958–1963

	Output, (ΔY)	Output per Standard Labour Unit Hours, (ΔP_{LI})	Net Price, (ΔNP)	Labour Input, Standard Labour Unit Hours, (ΔLI)	Capital Stock, (ΔK)	Capital Intensity, ($\Delta K/L$)	Technical Change (ΔATOKE)
Output, (ΔY)							
1954–63	—	.95	−.93	.92	.96	.77	.93
1954–58	—	.98	−.85	.94	.88	.85	.86
1958–63	—	.85	−.96	.86	.87	.14	.88
Output per Standard Labour Unit Hour, (ΔP_{LI})							
1954–63	.95	—	−.97	.74	.87	.80	.99
1954–58	.98	—	−.91	.87	.80	.78	.93
1958–63	.85	—	−.96	.47	.70	.36	.97
Net Price, (ΔNP)							
1954–63	−.93	−.97	—	−.74	−.88	−.85	−.96
1954–58	−.85	−.91	—	−.65	−.59	−.60	−.93
1958–63	−.96	−.96	—	−.70	−.81	−.25	−.97
Labour Input, Standard Labour Unit Hours, (ΔLI)							
1954–63	.92	.74	−.74	—	.93	.61	.72
1954–58	.94	.87	−.65	—	.96	.90	.65
1958–63	.86	.47	−.70	—	.79	−.11	.55
Capital Stock, (ΔK)							
1954–63	.96	.87	−.88	.93	—	.86	.81
1954–58	.88	.80	−.59	.96	—	.98	.53
1958–63	.87	.70	−.81	.79	—	.52	.64
Capital Intensity, ($\Delta K/L$)							
1954–63	.77	.80	−.85	.61	.86	—	.71
1954–58	.85	.78	−.60	.90	.98	—	.51
1958–63	.14	.36	−.25	−.11	.52	—	.15
Technical Change, (ΔATOKE)							
1954–63	.93	.99	−.96	.72	.81	.71	—
1954–58	.86	.93	−.93	.65	.53	.51	—
1958–63	.88	.97	−.97	.55	.64	.15	—

a   *Note on 'Significance'.* Where, as in these cases, the coefficients of correlation (r) are each calculated on the basis of six observations, the value of r must be greater than 0.81 in order to be 'significant' at the 5% level, and greater than 0.73 at the 10% level. Coefficients underlined represent correlations which are 'significant' at the 5% level.

feedback effect of higher output at a second round. Therefore, having found a significant positive correlation between output and labour productivity we should expect to find associated with this result a significant *negative* correlation between net price movements and both output and labour productivity movements. This corroborative evidence we do find (see Table 6.13). The negative coefficients for the whole period are -0.93 for output (ΔY) and net price (ΔNP) and -0.97 for labour productivity and net price, and for the sub-periods the coefficients are significant in every case. For comparison, Salter-Reddaway find for 1954–63 coefficients of -0.63 for output and net price and -0.73 for labour productivity and net price movements.

At this point we may notice that hypotheses A and B set out at the beginning of this chapter have been validated by the results of this research.[1]

2. Output, technical change and capital input movements

Hypothesis C states 'that movement in output (ΔY) and in technical change (used here as an abbreviation for ΔATOKE) correlate significantly in a positive sense'. This is a natural development of the Verdoorn, Salter, Kendrick thesis[2] on the close relationship between output and labour productivity. What we explore now is the relationship between output and the 'residual factors', named 'applied technical and organisational knowledge and external factors' (ATOKE), which also represents total factor productivity.[3] It was shown in the previous chapter (see particularly Tables 5.3 and 5.4) that ΔATOKE accounted for more than half the productivity gain, or loss, in all sectors of the Measured Transport except sea transport (where the proportion of total productivity gain due to increased capital per man was 51 per cent over the whole period examined there, 1952–1962). In some sectors the proportion due to ΔATOKE is considerably more than 50 per cent, and in Measured Transport as a whole it is 63 per cent after taking account of the inter-sectoral capital 'quality' shift change. The expectation would therefore be that ΔATOKE would correlate significantly in a positive sense with ΔP_{LI}, labour productivity movement; and because there is a high degree of correlation between ΔY, output change, and ΔP_{LI} then by deduction ΔY will correlate significantly with ΔATOKE. This expectation is realised and we find that for the whole period (1954 to 1963 in this analysis) the coefficient of correlation for output (ΔY) and ΔATOKE is 0.93, (0.86 for 1954–58 and 0.88 for

---

[1] This result shows that a relationship found to exist in manufacturing industry holds good for a service industry. It may be compared with a finding by N. Kaldor for the transport and communication industries as a whole across nine countries. In his Inaugural Lecture, 'Causes of the Slow Rate of Economic Growth of the United Kingdom', he finds no positive correlation between output and labour productivity, his R^2 is 0.102 for the nine countries over the period 1955 to 1964.

[2] See Chapter 1, page 32 n.

[3] See Chapter 4, section B, page 114, 'A Digression on the Residual', and Table 6.12.

1958–63). For labour productivity (ΔP_{LI}) and ΔATOKE it is even higher at 0.99 for 1954–63, (0.93 for 1954–58 and 0.97 for 1958–63). The 'residual factors', which include scale economies but which cannot be separately identified, are clearly important elements in labour productivity gain (and loss) in the sectors of the Measured Transport industry and in the industry as a whole. It has been shown (Chapter 5, page 136) that ΔATOKE represents the shift in the production function, particular efforts having been made in this research to eliminate any distortion of the shift which is due to other causes, such as labour 'quality' shift changes.

It was also shown in the interpretative analysis that the contribution of movement in capital intensity to labour productivity gain was relatively small in all sectors except sea transport. The relation of movements in capital intensity to movements in labour productivity, shown as product moment coefficients of correlation in Table 6.13, is not significant in any of the periods examined, nor is there significance in the correlation in any period examined between movements in capital intensity and in ΔATOKE, which represents total factor productivity as well as applied technical and organisational knowledge. It seems therefore that increased capital per unit of the labour force is not a major factor in the Measured Transport industry as a whole in explaining labour productivity gain, and this conclusion supports that derived from the interpretative analysis made in Chapter 5. Nor does it appear that technical knowledge is applied via increases in capital per head, but this does not prove that capital formation as such is not a vehicle for applied technical knowledge.

The final hypothesis, D, states 'that movement in capital stock input (ΔK) and in technical change (ΔATOKE) correlate significantly in a positive sense'. Technical knowledge, including economies of scale, may be applied by incorporation in new capital equipment as such without reference to changes in the input of labour services. From Table 6.13 it may be seen that for the whole period·the coefficient of correlation of ΔK and ΔATOKE is 0.81. This is right on the boundary between significance and non-significance, and for the two sub-periods examined the coefficients are non-significant. But the most that can be drawn from this result is that there must be some vehicle for technical change *besides* capital. What does this conclusion imply? First it must mean that applied technical and organisational knowledge and external factors, ΔATOKE, which as we have seen correlates significantly with movements in labour productivity and in output, exercises some of its influence in ways which do not involve the addition of new capital equipment. If this tentative negative conclusion is accepted, then there are basically three additional ways in which the influence of technical change (ΔATOKE) may possibly be exerted upon movement in labour productivity. The first of these is the application of ATOKE by the medium of improved labour skills. The second is the application of organisational knowledge (a part of ATOKE) via changes, in either direction, of managerial and administrative techniques. Included here will be not only the application of these techniques to the process of production of the services concerned, but also the application of managerial skills to labour relations (the avoidance or minimisation of strikes). The third and last way is the influence of external factors, such as statutory instruments preventing the free adjustment of capacity under dynamic situations involving changes in output, in either direction. Substantial and sustained output movements themselves should also be regarded as external factors which will have an influence upon productivity movements through economies and diseconomies of scale.

On the first possibility no completely definite answer can be given because we have found no satisfactory method by which labour skills as a whole may be measured. Some aspects of labour 'quality', reflecting skill, have been estimated in quantitative terms (see Chapter 3, Table 3.4) and movement in their contribution to movements in crude labour productivity (output per person employed per year) is shown in Table 6.14.

Table 6.14.   Movements in Labour 'Quality' in Relation to Movements in Crude Labour Productivity in the Measured Transport Industry, 1952–62

(Exponential rates of change per annum)

Labour 'Quality', ΔLQ.

(a)	(b)	
Intra-Sectoral 'Quality' Shift Change, ΔLQ$_s$	Inter-Sectoral 'Quality' Shift Change, ΔLQ$_i$	Crude Labour Productivity, ΔP$_L$ (output per person employed per year)
0.04	0.12	2.59

These labour 'quality' shift changes have been excluded from ΔATOKE. This was done because we wanted to make ΔATOKE as representative as possible of technical change and as little influenced as possible by such factors as changes in the age and sex structure of the sectoral labour force and changes in the sectoral distribution of labour of different skills.

It may be seen from the above table that these qualitative changes in labour input explain only a very small proportion of crude labour productivity movements. However, not all movements in labour skills are measured by these estimates. A deficiency occurs in the measure of intra-sectoral labour 'quality'. Account is taken above only of changes in the age and sex structure of the work force. Other changes in skills *within* sectors, which are included in ΔATOKE for sectors, are not measured, although changes in skills which arise from changes in the allocation of labour *between* sectors are reflected in the measure used in the table. We cannot, therefore, be definite on this point, and labour may or may not be a vehicle for technical change, although there is no conclusive evidence for the proposition that it is such a vehicle in the correlation analysis (Table 6.13), nor in the ranking of sectors (Table 6.12).[4]

The conclusion which is implied by the results of the foregoing analysis is that a part of the contribution to labour productivity gain which is seen to stem from the input of 'applied technical and organisational knowledge and external factors'

(ATOKE), and which the interpretative analysis (Chapter 5) showed as accounting for a large proportion of total labour productivity gain, is made in the form of organisational knowledge; in other words it is a question of the input of managerial and administrative skills. But this picture is incomplete because it takes no account of the externalities and constraints which inevitably set the context within which managements have to operate. There are two main types of external factor. They have been referred to in section A of the present chapter. They are the legal constraints which have applied for most of the longest period covered by our analysis (1952–65), and have hampered changes in supply and capacity in response to changes in demand. The second type of external influence is the substantial and sustained changes in demand for transport services which have occurred. It has been shown (by the test of hypothesis A) that output and labour productivity movements correlate closely. Economies of scale are likely to be involved in transport operations and these will add to 'applied organisational knowledge' when output rises consistently, but will subtract from it when output falls over a lengthy period and economies of scale are lost. The analysis of the productivity of capacity and of total capacity (section A of this chapter), brought out the lag of capacity movement on output movement as a large factor in productivity change, when such change is measured in physical terms. The railways and public road passenger transport, both declining sectors, have encountered loss of economies of scale and, furthermore, they have suffered from legal restraints upon the reduction of services. The railways have a still further problem in that by the nature of their assets, which are both relatively indivisible and of long life, they cannot adjust their capacity and therefore their potential capacity at all well.

So, in sum, the ratio of demand to potential output[1] which in expanding industries is typically unity, will inevitably be less than unity in declining industries due to loss of economies of scale and the indivisibility and specificity of assets. After some lapse of time, lasting several years, a cut down in potential output is brought about and this ratio is restored to unity but, during the period of the lag, productivity (whether measured by output per unit of total factor input or by output per unit of total physical and labour capacity) inevitably falls.

Summary

This chapter is divided into two parts. The first is concerned with capacity utilisation as an alternative physical measure of productivity level and movement, and as an explanatory exercise in relation to more conventional measures of productivity. The second part deals with the application of methods used by others, notably Salter, Reddaway and Kendrick,[2] to examine the degree of intercorrelation of the variables of output, labour productivity, net price and labour input. The application of these methods has been extended in this Paper

---

1 See page 156 for a description of this concept.

2 References are given in Chapter 1, page 17 n.

186

o include, in a single matrix (Table 6.13), product moment coefficients which are
ndicative of the degree of intercorrelation of the variables of capital stock,
apital intensity and total factor productivity (technical change and external
actors), and of their intercorrelation with movements of output, labour productivity,
et price and labour input.

An alternative measure of productive efficiency

Capacity utilisation levels

Very wide differences between the levels of carrying capacity utilisation were
ound to exist in road and rail *freight* transport (the only modes of freight
ransport included in this part of our analysis). In 1952, 1958 and 1962 the
on mileage performed per capacity ton available for service in the railways was
,523, 1,194 and 1,169 and in road haulage contracting 9,988, 13,126 and 14,417
espectively. Non-contractual road freight transport was found to have capacity
tilisation levels, in the same three individual years, of 6,961, 6,247 and 7,219
on miles per capacity ton. In 1962 the utilisation of carrying capacity was 12.3
imes greater in road haulage contracting than it was in rail freight transport.

n terms of value of gross output per capacity ton in service (fully maintained to
fficial standards, including vehicles undergoing normal maintenance) the
isparity between levels of capacity utilisation is even more striking. In 1958
he figure for the railways was £17, road haulage contracting £301 and
on-contractual road freight transport £279. Approximately 80 per cent of total
oad/rail carrying capacity was employed by British railways in 1962 to gain
only 16.8 per cent of the total freight market for transport services in value terms.

n rail and public road *passenger* transport the carrying capacity utilisation ratios
re much closer together than are the corresponding ratios for freight transport.
n 1952, 1958 and 1962 the levels in the railways were respectively 8,230,
,076 and 9,480, and in public road passenger transport 13,360, 11,730 and 11,158
assenger miles per capacity seating unit available for service; and in terms of
ross output values in 1958 at current prices, railways £56.4, public road
assenger transport £80.5 per capacity seating unit.

Capacity utilisation movements

Movement in the productivity of total capacity is measured as an alternative to
otal factor productivity movement. The former measure is obtained by adjusting
movement in capacity utilisation in accordance with the productive effect of
concurrent movement in the labour intensity of capacity; that is, the contribution
o capacity utilisation movement which arises from movement in labour input per
nit of capacity.

Physical capacity is measured by carrying capacity and seating capacity in road
ransport and by an average of movements in carrying capacity and track miles,
and seating capacity and track miles, in rail transport. This variable is employed
as an alternative to the financial measure of capital stock. The physical measure

has some advantages over the financial measure, which is founded on an average life of assets principle, when output is declining relatively fast.

A summary of movements in output, capacity, capacity utilisation and the productivity of total capacity in road and rail, freight and passenger transport is given in Table 6.15.

Table 6.15. Output, Capacity, Capacity Utilisation and the Productivity of Total Capacity in Road and Rail, Freight and Passenger Transport, 1952–62

Movement in:	Freight		Passenger	
	Road (Haulage Contracting)	Rail (British Railways)	Road (Buses and Coaches)	Rail (British Railways)
1. Output,[a] ΔY	7.23	−3.30	−1.67	−0.40
2. Capacity,[b] ΔC	3.56	−0.60	0.13	−1.18
3. Capacity Utilisation, ΔCU (Row 1 − Row 2)	3.67	−2.70	−1.80	0.78
4. Productivity of total capacity, ΔPTC	5.17	−1.80	−0.82	1.23

a As measured in physical terms of unweighted ton miles and passenger miles.

b As measured by carrying capacity and seating capacity in road transport and by an average of carrying capacity and track miles, and seating capacity and track miles in rail transport.

In freight transport the difference between movements in capacity utilisation in road and rail is particularly striking. Due to institutional constraints and to the indivisibility, long life and specificity of physical capital stock in the railways, capacity in this mode has been reduced at a much slower rate than output in the 1952–62 period; and this has occurred despite the fact that the average speed of freight trains has increased by 1.33 per cent per annum over this period. This means that *potential* capacity has *risen* in the face of a substantial *fall* in demand and output. Licensing constraints on the expansion of capacity in road haulage contracting have no doubt helped to induce higher capacity utilisation and productivity.

In passenger transport the road and rail movements in capacity utilisation differ rather less than they do in freight transport by the same modes. In road passenger transport, capacity actually increased in the face of a quite substantial and persistent decline in output (see Figure 11). This brings capacity utilisation down faster than output. There were during this period institutional constraints on cutting back bus services in some areas, but there was less of a problem in terms of the indivisibility and specificity of physical capacity in this mode than in the railways. Rail passenger output fell less rapidly than road passenger output and much less rapidly than rail freight output. As rail passenger capacity declined faster than output, capacity utilisation increased, but by only 0.78 per cent per annum. The average speed of passenger trains increased by 2.27 per cent per annum in this period (1952–62), so the utilisation of potential capacity declined.

In both road freight and passenger transport, changes in average speed are not calculable. It is known only that speed limits for both freight and public road passenger vehicles have been successively raised during the 1952–65 period. Although this factor has clearly worked to increase inter-urban average speeds, it is equally clear that intra-urban average speeds have declined due to increasing traffic congestion.

After Lord Beeching became chairman of British railways, physical capacity, as measured in the terms used here, was cut back much more drastically from 1962 to 1965 than it had been in earlier periods. The carrying capacity/track mileage average declined by 7.1 and the seating capacity/track mileage by 7.6 per cent per annum. As output did not fall anything like as fast as this, capacity utilisation improved by 5.6 and 5.8 per cent per annum in rail freight and passenger transport respectively.

By these means the lag of negative capacity movement on negative output movement, which had occurred in British railways in the 1952–62 period, was eliminated; but not before a heavy surplus of physical capacity and financial capital had been built up in relation to output. This surplus was accompanied by a surplus of overhead labour, part of which was employed to look after the under-used and even idle capacity. All this was much to the detriment of the rail productivity ratios of various kinds which are examined in this chapter.

The road passenger transport sector did not recover in the later 1962–65 period. Capacity was not reduced at all and output fell considerably faster than previously. The results for capacity utilisation and all productivity ratios for this sector were in negative terms and of a substantial magnitude.

Only provisional figures are available for road haulage contracting in the 1962–65 period. They indicate a rather slower rate of increase of capacity utilisation, compared with what occurred in the 1952–62 period; and the productivity of total capacity also increased more slowly due to labour requirements per unit of capacity falling much more slowly than they had done earlier (Table 6.5).

Movements in total factor productivity and in the productivity of total physical capacity compared

A comparison of movements in these alternative measures of 'combined input' productivity shows that they give broadly similar results for all periods (see Table 6.10).

These results, and the allied analyses, are first useful as a check, by use of physical capacity measures, upon the earlier results of estimating total factor productivity by methods which involve a financial measure of capital stock.

Second, they emphasise the importance of the degree of utilisation of capacity in productivity movement in transport.

Third, they show the great influence upon productivity movement (both measures of it) of declining output movement in circumstances where capacity cannot, for the several reasons which have been given, readily be adjusted to match a lower level of demand.

Fourth, increased average speeds in rail freight and passenger transport mean that *some* applied technical knowledge had a positive effect upon productivity movement in the 1952–62 period; it would have been surprising had it been otherwise. But the analysis indicates also that the effect upon capacity utilisation (and labour productivity) movement of movement in 'other factors' is very large and much larger in rail freight than in rail passenger transport (Table 6.11). By a process of elimination these 'other factors' are likely to include movement in applied organisational knowledge, institutional constraints and loss of economies of scale. Although average speed changes cannot be measured in road transport, the same type of conclusion may be drawn for road passenger transport and road haulage contracting. In the latter case, where output and productivity increased, the scale economies were likely to have been positive.

The Test of Hypotheses

Four hypotheses have been designed to throw light upon factors which underlie productivity movements and which are associated with such movements. The hypotheses, and the results of testing them, are considered in pairs.

Output, productivity and net price movements

The first pair of hypotheses tested are as follows.

A.   That movements in output and labour productivity correlate significantly[1] (across sectors of the Measured Transport industry)[2] in a positive sense.

B.   That movements in labour productivity and net price correlate significantly in a negative sense.

In terms of ranking order of movements the results of testing these hypotheses are shown in Table 6.12.

---

1   When the coefficient of correlation is greater than 0.81 the correlation in these exercises is significant at the 5 per cent level.

2   The correlations are of this nature throughout this chapter.

On hypothesis A the ranking orders are unexceptional in respect of movements of output and of both measures of productivity (labour and total factor). The relationship is a direct one.

On hypothesis B the ranking orders are also unexceptional in respect of movements in both productivity measures and of net price movements. The relationship is an inverse one in this case.

The relationships, indicated by the unexceptional rankings of movements in these variables, are confirmed and hypotheses A and B are validated by a calculation of product moment coefficients of correlation in respect of the movements concerned. The coefficient of correlation in respect of hypothesis A is 0.95 and that in respect of hypothesis B is −0.97. These coefficients are calculated from data for the 1954−63 period. In Table 6.13 may be found coefficients of correlation for other, related variables and also those for the variables concerned in these hypotheses in respect of sub-periods of the 1954−63 period.

These relationships have been found by others[1] to be valid for goods industries, but no clear conclusion has been reached for service industries and no doubt this is in part due to problems of measuring the output of service industries. Our findings may be compared with one by Kaldor[2] for total transport and communication across nine countries in respect of the relation between output and labour productivity, largely for the period 1955−64 but data for three countries were for different periods.

The following explanation of the relationships is offered.

As output rises more opportunities become available both to realise economies of scale and to apply the latest techniques, whether such techniques involve new capital equipment in application or only the scope for improved managerial and organisational skills. As output increases, the economies of scale and the application of improved techniques of both general types make possible increases in productivity. The productivity gains lead in turn to lower relative prices and thence, given an elastic demand for particular types and modes of transport service (a reasonable assumption in a market as competitive as are many sections of the market for transport services), to a feedback effect of higher output at a second round. The process is reversible for an initial decline in output.

Given a significant, *positive* correlation between movements in output and in two measures of productivity, we would expect to find a significant *negative* correlation between movements in output and net price. This corroborative evidence is found (see Tables 6.12 and 6.13).

---

1 Verdoorn, Salter, Kendrick op. cit.

2 N. Kaldor 'Causes of the slow rate of growth of the United Kingdom' Inaugural Lecture, 1966, p. 38. Cambridge University Press.

Output, technical change and capital input movements

The second pair of hypotheses tested are as follows.

C.   That movement in output and technical change (applied technical and organisational knowledge and external factors) correlate significantly in a positive sense.

D.   That movement in capital stock input and technical change (as defined under C) correlate significantly in a positive sense.

Hypothesis C is validated. The coefficient of correlation is 0.93 for the 1954–63 period (ΔATOKE represents total factor productivity movement). In respect of this industry of Measured Transport, this result extends Verdoorn's thesis of a significant positive correlation between movements in output and labour productivity to a significant positive correlation between movements in output and total factor productivity.

It was shown in the results of the interpretative analysis that movements in applied technical and organisational knowledge and external factors (ATOKE) have a very considerable amount of influence upon the amount of gain (or loss) in labour productivity. It was found that, with the exception of sea transport, ΔATOKE accounted for more than 50 per cent, and in some cases much more than 50 per cent of the gain (or loss) in output per unit of labour input in each sector of the Measured Transport industry and in postal services and telecommunications in the period 1952–62 (see Chapter 5, Table 5.4).

Since hypotheses A and C are both validated, it would be expected that movements in labour productivity and in total factor productivity would correlate significantly in a positive sense. This is confirmed by a direct test. The product moment coefficient of correlation for the 1954–63 period is 0.99. Movement in ATOKE is therefore likely to be an important factor in labour productivity gain (or loss), as already shown by the interpretative analysis.

The corollary is that capital intensity movement is of relatively slight importance in interpreting and explaining labour productivity movement and, in confirmation, the product moment coefficient of correlation is not significant in any period in this case (see Table 6.13).

To return to movement in ATOKE, the question remains: Which is the more important explanatory factor in labour productivity movement, technical knowledge applied via embodiment in capital equipment or via managerial, organisational and labour skills? Hypothesis D was designed to aid the search for an answer to this question.

For the whole period 1954–63, the product moment coefficient of correlation in respect of movements in capital stock input (ΔK) and in applied technical and organisational knowledge and external factors (ΔATOKE) was 0.81. This is on the boundary between significance and non-significance. For the two sub-periods, 1954–58 and 1958–63, the coefficients are non-significant, being 0.53 and 0.64 respectively. It is not admissable to conclude more from this than the observation that factors other than increased technical knowledge embodied in additional capital equipment have contributed to output and labour productivity movement.

An alternative method of presenting the results of the test of hypotheses C and D is in terms of a comparison of ranking orders of movements of the variables concerned. These are shown in Table 6.12.

The ranking orders of movements in labour productivity and technical change are unexceptional. The ranking orders of movements in technical change, capital intensity and capital stock input lack complete correspondence. This result neither validates nor invalidates hypothesis D.

Because movements in ATOKE correlate significantly with movements in labour productivity, and because neither additional capital nor additional capital per head are the *only* ways in which technical knowledge has been applied to the production process, the corollary is that ∆ATOKE has, in addition, been influential in other ways.

There are basically three other ways in which ∆ATOKE could have influenced output and labour productivity movements.

1.   Via improved labour skills.

2.   By the application of organisational knowledge (a part of ATOKE) via changes, in either direction, in managerial and administrative techniques of all kinds, including the managerial skills involved in labour relations (including strike avoidance or minimisation).

3.   Via the influence of external factors, such as institutional constraints (statutory instruments preventing the free adjustment of capacity, in either direction, under dynamic conditions involving output movement). Substantial and sustained output movements in themselves reflect the influence of external factors which influence labour productivity through economies and diseconomies of scale.

No completely definitive conclusion can be reached on the first of these three possibilities. Such 'qualitative' aspects of labour input as have been measured are very small in relation to labour productivity change (see Table 6.14). Other possible changes in labour skill, particularly those which occur within sectors (rather than between sectors) are not measurable. Labour skills, therefore, may or may not be a means for the application of technical change, but there is no conclusive evidence from the correlation analysis (Table 6.13) for the proposition that labour skills do provide such a means.

By a process of elimination, the second and third possible routes for ∆ATOKE now assume importance. The conclusion that movement in 'applied organisational knowledge' is a major element in the explanation of labour productivity movement must be qualified by pointing out the institutional constraints which have acted, particularly in the 1954–63 period, to limit the application of managerial skills in matching capacity to output under dynamic conditions in the railways, public road passenger transport, and road haulage contracting. Furthermore, other externalities have been involved through substantial and sustained upward downward movements in output. Economies of scale have been induced by these external factors. In the declining sectors, rail and public road passenger transport, there has been a considerable lag in capacity movement upon output movement, involving loss of scale economies. This has occurred at the same time as these two sectors were suffering from the institutional constraints which have already been noticed. On top of this the railways have had a still further difficulty; by the nature of their assets, which are relatively indivisible, specific and of long life, they could not adjust their capacity, nor their potential capacity, at all well, and this factor has worsened their productivity performance by whichever method it is measured.

7   Summary of Main Results

The results and conclusions of the work described in this Paper are quite fully summarised at the end of each chapter. This chapter sets out the main results and also provides a guide to the concepts, assumptions, qualifications and methods of working which are described in the other chapters.

A.   Scope of Study

The general object of this Paper is to measure employment, capital, output, labour productivity and technical change (total factor productivity) in the public, marketed transport industry in the United Kingdom (Chapters 2, 3 and 4). The results of these measurements are interpreted by fitting a production function to them (Chapter 5), and more fundamental explanations are attempted in Chapter 6.

The transport services provided by private cars and by privately owned 'C' licenced road freight vehicles were excluded from the study on the ground that the available statistics on inputs and outputs were insufficiently accurate to allow meaningful productivity measurement. Miscellaneous Transport Services and Storage was excluded for the same reason. The six sectors included in the major part of the analysis have been termed Measured Transport (Chapter 1, Table 1.1). Postal Services and Telecommunications has been included in the analysis as a separate sector outside the Measured Transport industry.

The assumptions underlying the methods of measuring and adjusting outputs and inputs, the method of combining factor inputs and of measuring productivity by alternative, physical means are explained in Chapter 1. The detailed methodology of measurement is described at the beginning of Chapter 2 (output measurement), Chapter 3, with methodological note, (factor inputs and factor 'quality'), and Chapter 4 (total, combined factor input and productivity). The method of fitting a production function to output and to factor inputs adjusted for various 'quality' shift changes is described in Chapter 5.

B.   Public Transport in Relation to the Rest of the Economy

The relationship of Measured Transport to the rest of the economy was examined in terms of input and output (but not productivity) movements. Output movements in Measured Transport and in gross domestic product were found to move together strongly over the period 1952–65 (Chapter 4, p. 119 and Figure 6). In the period

1952–62 output in Measured Transport grew at the rate of 1.65 per cent a year while gross domestic product increased over the same period at an annual rate of just over 3 per cent. In the last four years of this period, the annual rate of growth of output in Measured Transport was higher than in the earlier period, 2.04 as against 1.39 per cent, and in the period 1962–65 the provisional figures for Measured Transport indicate a continuation of this trend with an annual rate of growth of output of 3.08 per cent compared with a rate of growth of gross domestic product of 3.17 per cent (1958–62) and 3.90 per cent (1962–65) (Chapter 2, Table 2.15). In 1958 net output in Measured Transport was 5.8 per cent and postal services and telecommunications 1.9 per cent of gross domestic product.

The Measured Transport industry as a whole reduced its demand for labour at an annual rate of 0.94 per cent in the period 1952–62 (Chapter 3, Table 3.1). In the same period, manpower in all civilian service industries, excluding Measured Transport, increased at the rate of 1.46 per cent per annum while the total in civil employment rose at the rate of 0.90 per cent.

On the other hand, the Measured Transport industry was found to be a highly capital intensive industry relative to other civilian service industries. In 1962, average capital per person employed in Measured Transport was estimated to be £8,006; in all civilian service industries it was estimated at £3,252 and in the industrial sector (manufacturing, construction, gas, electricity and water, mining and quarrying) plus agriculture it was £2,791 per person employed.

In terms of total combined factor input the Measured Transport industry, on a fully adjusted basis, increased its use of factors by only 0.19 per cent per annum in the 1952–62 period. This was the net, weighted result of a 1.91 per cent per annum increase in net capital input and a 0.69 per cent per annum decline in labour input adjusted for hours and 'quality'.

C.   Output in Sectors of Measured Transport

Movements in output in the six sectors of Measured Transport together with postal services and telecommunications, private road passenger travel, and non-contractual road haulage, are shown in Table 2.9 for the whole period 1952–62 and for the sub-periods 1952–58 and 1958–62. Table 2.15 gives the provisional figures for 1962–65 together with net output levels in 1958.

The results of weighting output in three sectors of Measured Transport (Chapter 2, pp. 47, 53, 56) by a series of price relative weights, were that in railways and road passenger transport, little difference was found in the weighted and unweighted output index. In road haulage contracting, however, the unweighted index overstated the increase in output in the period 1958–62 by 1.7 per cent or 0.32 per cent a year. Using a weighted index, output in road haulage contracting increased at an exponential rate of 6.67 per cent a year between 1958 and 1962; the unweighted index gives a rate of growth of 6.99 per cent a year.

D. Results of Productivity Measurement

Productivity was measured both in terms of total factor productivity and of labour productivity (Chapter 4). In Measured Transport as a whole, there was an exponential rate of increase in labour productivity (adjusted) of 2.34 per cent each year, or an increase of 26.4 per cent over the period 1952–62. Measured in terms of total factor productivity (output per unit of combined factor input), the annual rate of increase was 1.46 per cent, 15.7 per cent over the period 1952–62, indicating that capital input was rising relatively to labour. This compares favourably with annual increases in total factor productivity estimated by R.C.O. Matthews[1] of 0.7 per cent in services and distribution together, and 1.7 per cent in manufacturing in the period 1948–1962.

The increase in capital input relative to labour input is a factor which is evident in each of the six sectors of Measured Transport. That is, total factor productivity movement, which takes account of movements of capital as well as labour input, is lower than labour productivity movement in each sector when measured over the period 1952–62.

In terms of total factor productivity, the highest rate of growth in the period 1952–62 was in air transport (5.47 per cent per annum) followed by road haulage contracting (4.46 per cent per annum) with smaller, but positive increases in port and inland water transport and sea transport. Labour productivity in these sectors increased much faster (8.02 per cent per annum in air transport and 5.87 per cent per annum in road haulage contracting), with the exception of port and inland water transport where movement in capital input over the period as a whole was nearly as negative as labour input (Chapter 3, Table 3.9), and therefore the difference between total factor productivity and labour productivity was very small (3.79 per cent per annum and 3.92 per cent per annum respectively).

Total factor productivity declined over the period 1952–62 by a total of −6.2 per cent in railways and −11.8 per cent in road passenger transport. In the same period labour productivity declined more slowly in the railways (−1.6 per cent between 1952 and 1962). In road passenger transport, as both labour and capital input movements were negative (Table 3.9, p. 104), there was little difference in the movements of total factor productivity and labour productivity.

Examination of movements over the period (1952–1962) does, however, obscure changes which were taking place within the period. These changes were particularly important in the case of the railways where the decline in total factor productivity slackened considerably in 1958–1962, and in road passenger transport there was a small increase of one half of one per cent. (Chapter 4, Table 4.7). In road haulage contracting, the rate of growth of total factor productivity in the last four years of the period was one half of what it had been in the first six years, while port and inland water transport and sea transport showed considerable gains in productivity in the period 1958–62.

In addition to *movements* in productivity, an estimate was made of the *level* of

---

[1] Op.cit.

productivity in each sector of Measured Transport in the year 1958. Full discussion of the way in which capital and labour inputs were converted to a common combined unit is in Chapter 1, p. 30. The levels of productivity after adjustment for labour 'quality' were found to be not widely different for four out of the six sectors of the Measured Transport industry. In terms of pence per standardised labour unit hour equivalent, sea, air, road haulage contracting and road passenger transport fell within the range of 70.6 to 86.2 pence in 1958; port and inland water transport fell some way below at 58.6 pence, and the railways quite a long way behind at 36.5 pence. Postal services and telecommunications, at 71.5 pence, rank at the lower end of the group of four.

The difference between the highest and lowest productivity levels in the six sectors, road haulage contracting and railways respectively, is a wide one. It began to narrow only in 1962 when the railways sharply increased the rate at which they reduced their underutilised factors, which had been building up to excess proportions for several years while output declined considerably and persistently (Table 4.2).

E.   Explanations and Interpretations

The pattern of demand for public freight and passenger transport services has shifted greatly over the period 1952–1965. The changes, in terms of output movements, are shown in Figure 1 (Chapter 2).

In respect of goods industries it has been established by others[1] that there is a close correlation between movements in output and labour productivity. A similar relationship is found to be valid for the service industry of transport. The product moment coefficient of correlation of movements in these two variables across sectors of the measured transport industry was 0.95[2] for the period 1954–1963 (Table 6.13, Chapter 6). This thesis may be extended, in respect of Measured Transport, to include the relationship between output and total factor productivity, where the coefficient of correlation was 0.93 in the same period. Furthermore, a significant *negative* correlation, –0.97, was found to exist between movements in labour productivity and net price.

These results suggest a circular process by which, given an elastic demand, increases in output lead to economies of scale, falling *relative* costs and prices and to increased demand and output at a second round; the process being reversible for the case of declining demand. It should be added that the relative net price movements appear to conform to this thesis; road freight net prices fell relatively to net prices of *all* rail services.

Relative price *levels* are estimated for a range of commodities transported by rail and contractual road freight transport (Chapter 2). Where, as occurs in six cases

---

1 Verdoorn, Kendrick, Salter op.cit.

2 Significant at 0.81 at the 5 per cent level.

(Table 2.11, p. 62), average hauls were similar, the price differential in 1966 was in every case in favour of rail. In other instances average haul was longer by road but price per ton mile was higher than by rail (p. 62). This suggests that the preference for road over rail freight transport services is at least in part due to the qualitative aspects of the service offered.

We have examined in some detail and in several ways the processes by which productivity has changed in the various sectors. By substituting a physical capacity measure for the more usual financial measure of capital an alternative view of productivity movement was obtained. The results show very clearly the importance in productivity movement of changes in the degree of utilisation of capacity, after allowance had been made for changes in the average amount of labour associated with each unit of capacity. The resultant measure is one of the productivity of total capacity, and it moves with total factor productivity in those sectors (rail freight, rail passenger, road haulage, contracting and road passenger transport) in which capacity can be measured (Table 6.10).

The productivity of total capacity is in part explained in some sectors by the existence of institutional constraints on the expansion or contraction of the transport services produced. That is, the licensing constraint on the expansion of road haulage contracting and the statutory obligations (current within the period examined) upon operators to provide rail and public road passenger transport services regardless of declining demand and consequent underutilisation.

Another factor which is explanatory of declining productivity performance, as measured in either financial or physical terms, lies in the nature of the assets involved. It has been noticed that transport sectors are relatively capital intensive. When output declines, capacity represented by physical assets cannot readily be adjusted downwards, at least not in the short run. Productivity must also decline as a result of this inflexibility. In the railways, one of the two declining sectors in Measured Transport, this difficulty is compounded; not only are many of the assets of exceptional longevity, they are also very specific to their designed uses. If they cannot be disposed of they are kept and labour is needed to maintain them. Management have the particularly difficult task in such circumstances of deciding when a decline in demand and output is a temporary or a longer term and permanent trend. In the railways this type of decision was long delayed.

Segregation and attribution of labour productivity movement

A production function is fitted to output and factor input data in order first to combine labour and capital inputs and to reach a measure of total factor productivity, which is also representative of 'applied technical and organisational knowledge and external factors'. This residual group of factors may be so identified because care is taken prior to fitting the production function to remove from labour input the aggregation bias which is due to intra- and inter-sectoral 'quality' shift changes. These changes are relatively small. Labour is also adjusted for changes in weekly hours of work and public and annual holidays allowed (Chapter 3, Table 3.4). Capital cannot be adjusted for intra-sectoral 'quality' shift changes because no vintage model of capital stock is available, but adjustments are made for the inter-sectoral capital 'quality' shift change which is relatively large (Chapter 3, Table 3.5).

The second reason for fitting a production function to the data is to segregate movements in labour productivity as being due separately to movement in capital per head and to technical change (movement in 'applied organisational knowledge and external factors'). In more theoretical terms this process shows the extent to which labour productivity changes are due to (a) movement along the production function (the K/L effect) and (b) a shift in the function itself.

The results show that with one exception the effect of increasing capital per man accounted for less than half, and in some cases much less than half the labour productivity gain in the period 1952–62 (Chapter 5, Tables 5.4 and 5.5). The exception is sea transport, where increased capital intensity accounted for 51 per cent of total labour productivity gain in this period.

The railways and road passenger transport registered labour productivity losses in the 1952–62 period. In both sectors in this period the contribution from increased capital per head was positive; i.e. the production function *sloped upwards*, but the contribution from 'applied technical and organisational knowledge and external factors' was negative; i.e. the production function *shifted downwards*. This is shown in Figure 9 where production functions are plotted for each sector incorporating the techniques of 1952 and, separately, those of 1962. There is a wide diversity among these sectoral production functions, and it may be concluded that there is not a typical transport production function.

The importance of applied technical and organisational knowledge and external factors (ATOKE)

The interpretative analysis (Chapter 5) shows the relative major importance of this group of factors as contributors to labour productivity gain. Furthermore, as would be expected, the product moment coefficient of correlation between these two variables in the 1954–63 period is very high at 0.99 (Table 6.13). The corollary is that capital intensity movement is of less importance as a contributor to labour productivity gain, and this is confirmed by the results of the correlation analysis (Table 6.13).

A correlation of movements in ATOKE and capital stock input, K, indicates that although this may be one route by which ATOKE influences labour productivity gain there are undoubtedly other routes.

The other routes are basically three in number, as follows:

1. Improved labour skills.

2. Changes in applied organisational knowledge. This includes managerial and administrative skills and the ability to handle labour relations (including the avoidance or minimisation of strikes).

3. External factors, such as institutional constraints, and substantial and sustained output movements (in either direction) which influence labour productivity through economies and loss of economies of scale.

No completely definitive conclusion can be reached on the first of these three routes. Such 'qualitative' aspects of labour input as were measured were very small in relation to labour productivity change (Table 6.14). There is no conclusive evidence from the correlation analysis for the proposition that labour skills do provide a means by which ATOKE exercises its influence.

If labour skills are not a major route for the application of knowledge then the second and third possibilities assume importance. The conclusion that movement in 'applied organisational knowledge' is a major element in the explanation of labour productivity movement must be qualified by pointing out the institutional restraints which have acted, particularly in the 1954–63 period, to limit the application of managerial skills in matching capacity to output under dynamic conditions in the railways, public road passenger transport, and road haulage contracting.

Sustained upward, or downward, changes in demand and output have occurred, particularly in air transport and road haulage contracting (upward movements), and in railways and road passenger transport (downward movements). These external factors tend to induce economies (or loss of economies) of scale and provide more (or fewer) opportunities to apply the latest techniques.

In the two sectors where output has declined throughout (railways and road passenger transport) this externality has caused a considerable lag of capacity movement upon output movement to occur, involving loss of scale economies. This happened during a period (1952–62) when the two sectors were suffering from the institutional restraints which have been noticed. On top of this the railways had a still further difficulty, which was a good deal less important in road passenger transport, in that their assets were relatively indivisible, specific to their design uses and of long life. Therefore they could not adjust their capacity, nor their potential capacity, at all well, and this factor is in part explanatory of the railway's labour, and total factor productivity movements.

O

Statistical Appendix

The purpose of this appendix is twofold.

1. To provide the data which have been used, but not explicitly quoted, in the analysis, analytical tables and graphs presented in the main text.

2. To explain the technical aspects of the basic statistics, the methods of calculating certain derived statistics and coefficients, and the procedures for making estimates. The main description of the economic philosophy applied in this Paper, and of the methods used in the analytical processes, is set out in Chapter 1.

United Kingdom SIC 1958

1958 = 100

Table A.1. Index of Output at 1958 Prices

	Railways	Road Passenger Transport	Road Haulage Contracting	Sea Transport	Port and Inland Water Transport	Air Transport	TOTAL MEASURED TRANSPORT	Postal Services & Tele-communications
1952	110.4	118.5	64.1	93.0	88.7	48.5	92.0	87.0
1953	111.6	117.4	68.7	93.2	92.7	57.3	94.1	89.6
1954	109.5	115.9	74.9	95.2	94.2	62.7	95.6	93.3
1955	106.4	115.3	81.4	97.1	96.1	75.9	97.5	97.4
1956	107.8	112.2	88.2	100.1	97.6	86.6	100.2	99.0
1957	108.3	106.7	95.0	101.2	98.4	95.4	101.7	99.0
1958	100.0	100.0	100.0	100.0	100.0	100.0	100.0	100.0
1959	98.5	100.7	109.8	101.2	104.3	113.4	103.0	104.5
1960	101.0	99.1	117.4	105.6	108.1	142.1	107.4	110.6
1961	97.2	96.9	125.5	105.4	108.5	163.6	108.5	115.3
1962	90.8	94.4	132.2	105.5	111.1	173.4	108.5	118.6
1963	90.5	92.3	137.8 p.	106.9	113.6	195.4	110.6 p.	124.9
1964	94.2	88.8	155.1 p.	107.5	115.4	239.7	116.4 p.	133.5
1965	90.3	84.4	162.6 p.	110.3	117.7	285.8	119.0 p.	143.2
1966	87.9	79.5	184.0 p.	103.2	116.3	337.6	122.1 p.	152.7

Notes: The output indexes for the period 1952–58 are 1954 weighted, and those for the period 1958–66 are 1958 weighted. Details of weights and indicators used in 1958 are given in the appendix note to Chapter 1.

The concept of output is gross value added (sales minus all bought-in materials and services. Depreciation is included; subsidies and subsidy equivalents are excluded).

p. Provisional.

205

Table A.2   Results of the D.A.E. Survey of Road Haulage Contractors

Commodity	Number of vehicles in fleet			All fleet sizes[a]
	21 and over	6 to 20	1 to 5	
FOODSTUFFS				
Cereals	5.30	4.86	4.49	4.93
Fresh fruit, vegetables, nuts and flowers	4.77	4.13	5.50	4.82
Meat and poultry	10.21	12.48	–	11.13
Fish	10.79	5.72	–	8.73
Live animals	9.56	10.57	–	9.97
Dairy produce, eggs	6.11	6.35	8.00	6.76
Beverages	6.34	8.39	6.80	7.06
Flour	4.59	4.97	9.80	6.31
Animal feeding stuffs	5.56	5.67	6.22	5.80
Oilseeds, etc. oil and fats	5.13	6.42	6.55	5.93
Other foods, tobacco	5.30	9.89	9.02	7.74
METALS, METALWORK AND HARDWARE				
Iron ore and scrap iron	5.95	6.91	4.72	5.84
Non-ferrous metal ores	6.42	4.53	3.70	5.05
Iron and steel finished and semi-finished products	4.80	4.72	3.99	4.53
Non-ferrous metals	5.37	4.53	–	5.03
Metal manufactures	7.21	6.14	–	6.78
BUILDING AND CONSTRUCTION MATERIALS				
Cement	3.34	4.44	5.22	4.23
Crude minerals other than ore	4.78	5.13	4.93	4.92
Building materials	5.20	5.03	4.90	5.06
COAL, COKE AND PATENT FUELS	5.66	5.61	5.62	5.63
PETROLEUM AND PETROLEUM PRODUCTS	6.04	2.70	5.95	5.08
CHEMICALS				
Lime	6.02	6.60	7.08	6.51
Crude and manufactured fertilisers	4.27	4.64	5.25	4.68
Other chemicals and plastics	4.85	5.58	–	5.15
Tars from coal and natural gas	6.48	–	–	6.48
ALL OTHER GOODS				
Wood, timber and cork	6.11	7.12	4.38	5.86
Textile fibre and waste	6.74	14.66	5.90	8.70
Other crude materials	11.39	6.73	–	9.50
Electrical & non-electrical machinery; transport equipment	5.48	7.02	–	6.10
Other manufactured articles	6.62	10.51	10.40	8.88
Mixed loads[b]	5.88	7.11	4.60	5.83

a See note 2 following for weights used.

b Including parcels

Technical Note to Table A.2

1. The prices shown in each of the size groups are weighted averages of individual prices given by respondents to the D.A.E. survey. The number of vehicles operated by the respondents was used as the weight. The total number of vehicles operated by the respondents in each of the size and commodity groups is as follows:

Commodity	Number of vehicles in fleet			All fleet sizes
	21 and over	6 to 20	1 to 5	
Cereals	921	140	16	1,077
Fresh fruit etc.	1,309	64	5	1,378
Meat & poultry	843	15	–	858
Fish	252	41	–	293
Live animals	96	42	–	138
Dairy produce, eggs	1,213	53	1	1,267
Beverages	1,344	30	2	1,376
Flour	900	63	5	968
Animal feeding stuffs	1,685	260	19	1,964
Oilseeds, etc.	1,309	107	13	1,429
Other foods, tobacco	1,203	149	5	1,357
Iron ore and scrap iron	1,440	138	15	1,593
Non-ferrous metal ores	218	75	10	303
Iron and steel finished and semi-finished	1,689	167	12	1,868
Non-ferrous metals	1,260	49	–	1,309
Metal manufactures	1,333	69	–	1,402
Cement	729	103	12	844
Crude minerals other than ore	1,305	176	37	1,518
Building materials	1,659	372	24	2,055
Coal, coke and patent fuels	1,304	171	38	1,513
Petroleum products	1,251	12	6	1,269
Lime	460	127	5	592
Crude and manufactured fertilisers	1,564	224	17	1,805
Other chemicals and plastics	1,927	118	–	2,045
Tars from coal and natural gas	771	–	–	771
Wood, timber and cork	1,537	83	9	1,629
Textile fibres and waste	522	25	5	552
Other crude materials	775	25	–	800
Electrical and non-electrical machinery; transport equipment	1,522	100	–	1,622
Other manufactured articles	1,585	184	4	1,773
Mixed loads	914	130	10	1,054

2. The weights used to combine the prices obtained in each of the size groups to give a single price for each commodity were based on the number of vehicles in each size group in Great Britain (including British Road Services) and on the average capacity load of the vehicles of operators who responded to the survey.

	Number of vehicles (as at 31.1.1963)	Average capacity load (tons)	Weight (per cent)
21 vehicles and over	76,800	10.41	41
6–20 vehicles	59,700	9.20	28
1–5 vehicles	69,100	8.75	31

3. British Road Services vehicles were excluded from the sampling frame in the first instance and separate information on tonnage carried and total receipts for carrying different types of commodities was supplied by British Road Services. Unfortunately, with the exception of parcels carriage it was not possible to calculate average prices per ton mile for commodities carried by British Road Services. It was assumed in the calculation of a combined price for all size groups that British Road Services pricing pattern would be similar to that of other road hauliers operating 21 vehicles and over and British Road Services vehicles were therefore included in this group.

4. British Road Services were able to supply more detailed information on the carriage of parcels and a separate price per ton mile was calculated for parcels. In the Ministry of Transport 1962 Road Goods Transport Survey, parcels were included under mixed loads and in the calculation of a combined price for the group account was taken of parcels carriage as a separate item.

5. Estimated tonnage equivalents of commodities measured in other ways.

Commodity	Measurement	Tonnage equivalents
Sheep	per head	.036
Calf	per head	.013
Pig	per head	.25
Other animals	per head	.5
Milk	per 200 gallons	1.0
Eggs	per box or crate (1,450 dozen eggs)	1.0
Fish	per cran	.33
Bricks	per 1,000	3.6
Sand	per cubic yard	1.0
Cement	per cubic yard	1.25
Wood	per standard	2.95

Source: Ministry of Transport estimates; *The Economist* conversion tables of 'Weights and Measures'.

Table A.3 Average Length of Haul
Road Haulage Contracting

Commodity	National Average Length of Haul[a]	Average length of haul from D.A.E. Survey			Weighted average[b] of D.A.E. survey results
		Number of vehicles in fleet			
		21 and over	6 to 20	1 to 5	
		miles			
Foodstuffs					
Cereals	40	81	69	78	77
Fresh fruit, vegetables, nuts and flowers	60	129	133	55	107
Meat and poultry	45	149	90	7	88
Fish	35	120	246	9	121
Live animals	30	76	56	–	68
Dairy produce, eggs	40	150	72	10	85
Beverages	45	93	49	65	72
Flour	40	110	95	40	84
Animal feeding stuffs	40	82	63	55	68
Oil seeds, etc.	50	114	109	53	94
Other foods, tobacco	80	131	101	59	100
Metals, metalwork and hardware					
Iron ore and scrap iron	30	101	56	60	76
Non-ferrous metal ores	50	77	104	120	98
Iron and steel finished and semi-finished products	60	143	125	126	133
Non-ferrous metals	50	130	141	–	134
Metal manufactures	50	112	119	25	87
Building and construction materials					
Cement	45	114	78	31	78
Crude minerals other than ore	15	40	36	23	34
Building materials	35	73	59	22	53
Coal, coke and patent fuels	20	74	58	34	57
Petroleum and petroleum products	45	93	138	68	98
Chemicals					
Lime	30	46	44	75	54
Crude and manufactured fertilisers	35	127	83	45	89
All other chemicals and plastic materials	70	146	122	90	122
Tars from coal and natural gas	25	69	–	–	69
Other goods					
Wood, timber and cork	40	85	65	83	79
Textile fibres and waste	50	91	106	–	97
Other crude materials	30	109	48	–	85
Electrical and non-electrical machinery; transport equipment	65	141	93	60	102
Other manufactured articles	55	108	86	30	78
Mixed loads	25	111	86	25	77

a The national average was obtained from data on tons carried and ton mileage in each licence category (but not by size of haulier) published in the Ministry of Transport Road Goods Survey, Commodity Analysis. It is therefore an unweighted average.

b The weighted average has been obtained by using the same weights (based on number of vehicles operated and average capacity of vehicles) as used to obtain weighted average prices. These weights are as follows:

21 vehicles and over	–	41 per cent
6–20 vehicles	–	28 per cent
1–5 vehicles	–	31 per cent

Table A.4.   Public Passenger Transport by Road

		Passenger Receipts (£ million)	Passenger Journeys (million)	Estimated average stage (miles)	Estimated passenger miles (000 million)	Estimated average receipts per passenger mile (pence)
1. Urban Stage Bus						
a. London	1957/59 a	48.4	2,642	2.13	5.63	2.063
	1962	51.1	2,515	2.12	4.70	2.609
	1964	52.9	2,004	2.12	4.25	2.987
b. Other main urban areas	1958	88.9	5,846	2.13	12.45	1.714
	1962	97.0	5,344	2.12	11.33	2.055
	1964	104.0	5,073	2.12	10.75	2.322
2. Express bus	1958	10.4	64 ⎫		1.73	1.443
	1962	14.3	78 ⎬	27.09 d	2.11	1.627
	1964	15.8	77 ⎭		2.09	1.818
3. Excursions/Tours	1958	7.9	35 ⎫		1.08	1.756
	1962	8.7	35 ⎬	30.94 d	1.08	1.933
	1964	9.3	34 ⎭		1.05	2.122
4. Contract	1958	24.0	268 ⎫		1.83	3.148
	1962	28.0	311 ⎬	6.81 d	2.12	2.170
	1964	29.7	320 ⎭		2.18	3.271
5. Non-Urban Stage Bus	1958 b	126.7	5,438 ⎫		22.10	1.376
	1962	142.0	5,046 ⎬	4.20 d	21.10	1.615
	1964	152.7	4,759 ⎭		19.98	1.834
6. Total Public c Services	1958	306.4	14,293	3.13	44.80	1.641
	1962	341.0	13,030	3.25	42.40	1.930
	1964	364.4	12,266	3.29	40.30	2.170

a   An average of figures for 1957/59 is taken in order to avoid the statistical effect of the London bus strike of 1958.

b   Includes statistics for the non-urban operations of London Transport on an average 1957/59 basis.

c   Columns do not in all cases add to total due to rounding.

d   Estimate for 1964.

Sources: National Travel Survey 1964, London Transport Annual Reports, Passenger Transport in Great Britain, 1963 & 1966.

(Thousands)

United Kingdom SIC 1958

	Railways	Road Passenger Transport	Road Haulage Contracting	Sea Transport	Port and Inland Water Transport	Air Transport	Total Measured Transport	Miscellaneous Transport Services and Storage	Total Transport	Postal Services & Tele-communications[a]	Total Transport & Communication[b]
1952	530	334	207	166	166	29	1,432	48	1,480	361	1,842
1953	524	324	201	163	156	29	1,397	53	1,450	358	1,808
1954	519	311	200	168	158	29	1,385	54	1,439	359	1,799
1955	498	307	203	169	166	30	1,373	56	1,429	363	1,792
1956	497	307	204	171	164	33	1,376	60	1,436	372	1,808
1957	498	304	201	173	163	35	1,374	59	1,433	369	1,802
1958	489	303	203	167	158	36	1,356	59	1,415	370	1,785
1959	466	296	206	158	155	38	1,319	67	1,386	371	1,755
1960	449	287	212	158	154	41	1,301	73	1,374	376	1,749
1961	449	290	218	159	151	46	1,313	77	1,390	389	1,778
1962	440	293	222	156	146	47	1,303	79	1,382	404	1,787
1963	413	294	225	141	143	47	1,263	87	1,350	408	1,756
1964	392	286	232	136	140	48	1,234	91	1,325	413	1,739
1965	362	287	239	128	139	54	1,209	95	1,304	424	1,730

a See note following this table.

b Sector totals do not in all cases add to these totals due to rounding.
  The above table includes self-employed as follows:

  Road Passenger Transport 1952 to 1960 16,000, 1961 to 1965 17,000.
  Road Haulage Contracting 1952 to 1960 22,000, 1961 to 1965 23,000.
  Sea Transport 1952 to 1965 1,000.
  Port and Inland Water Transport 1952 to 1965 1,000.
  Miscellaneous Transport Services and Storage 1952 to 1960, 3,000, 1961 to 1965 4,000.

211

Technical Notes to Table B.1

1. *Sources.* The dates of the statistics of employees registered for work in each year are end of May for 1952 to 1961; 'at June' from 1962 onwards. The figures for the wholly unemployed are 'at June' from 1952 to 1965. Data taken from Annual Abstracts of Statistics, 1960 to 1966 inclusive.

2. The figures for Manpower Employed given in Table B.1 are made up as follows:

    (a) *Total employees at work.* These statistics are derived from the published figures of employees registered for work less the registered unemployed. The figure for employees at work derived in this way will therefore include workers who are temporarily stopped at the date of the statistics, but who have not registered as unemployed. The published figures for employees at work include directors and managers insured under the ordinary class of the national insurance scheme.

    (b) *The self-employed.* The statistics of self-employed in the Transport and Communication industry and in a number of the constituent sectors were provided, on an unofficial basis, by the Ministry of Labour. There are no self-employed in Railways or in Postal Services and Telecommunications and the number in Air Transport is negligible. The basis for the estimates of the number of self-employed in the other sectors of Transport and Communication are the Censuses of Population in 1951 and 1961. The 1951 figures for self-employed are assumed unchanged over the period 1952 to 1960, and the 1961 figures are assumed unchanged over the period 1961 to 1965. The basis for this assumption is the stability of the sectoral figures of self-employed between 1951 and 1961.

3. The series for registered employees in Postal Services and Telecommunication was revised by the Ministry of Labour in 1964. Details are given in the Ministry of Labour Gazette for February, 1965 p.59. Previous mid-year estimates of registered employees classified under this heading and derived from the sources given under note 1 above, have accordingly been revised by making the following *additions:*

Number of Employees at mid-year

1963	77,000
1962	68,000
1961	64,000
1960	62,000
1959	58,000
1958	56,000
1957	56,000
1956	57,000
1955	57,000
1954	58,000
1953	54,000
1952	56,000

The source for the figures for 1954 to 1963 inclusive is the Ministry of Labour Gazette under the reference given above. The figures for 1952 and 1953 were supplied to us direct by the Ministry of Labour.

4. The statistics of employees registered for work have been converted for the years 1952 to 1958 (inclusive) from an SIC 1948 basis to an SIC 1958 basis by applying the following conversion coefficients which have been derived from the two sets of employment statistics which are given for the year 1959, one on SIC 1948 and one on SIC 1958, in the Annual Abstract of Statistics, 1961.

	Conversion Coefficients[a]
Railways	0.967
Road Passenger Transport	1.004
Road Haulage Contracting	1.011
Sea Transport	1.006
Port and Inland Water Transport	1.006
Air Transport	1.000
Postal Services and Telecommunications	1.000
Miscellaneous Transport Services and Storage	0.985

a   Coefficients calculated by dividing figures of employees registered for work on SIC 1958 by figures of employees registered for work on SIC 1948.

The statistics of unemployment have not been converted to take account of differences in the coverage of the 1948 and the 1958 SIC. As the figures used are rounded to the nearest thousand the difference between the coverage of the two SIC definitions would be negligible in the case of the unemployed.

5. In 1964 the method adopted by the Ministry of Labour of collecting and counting insurance cards (the basis for the figures of registered employees) was changed. The 'old' and 'new' methods are described in the Ministry of Labour Gazette for March, 1966, pp. 110–112. The figures given on Table B.1 are the 'old' basis for the whole period, 1952 to 1965. Ministry of Labour figures are available on the 'old' basis for the period 1952 to 1964 inclusive. The figures on Table B.1 for 1965 are derived by applying the percentage increase between the 'new' series for 1964 and 1965 (Annual Abstract of Statistics, 1966, Table 133) to the 'old' series figures for 1964. The differences between the 'old' and 'new' series for 1965 is nil for Road Haulage Contracting, Port and Inland Water Transport, Air Transport, Postal Services and Telecommunications, and Miscellaneous Transport Services and

Storage. For Railways and Road Passenger Transport it is one thousand in each case. For Sea Transport it is 31,000. The 'new' series for Sea Transport omits some merchant seamen who were away on long voyages. For productivity measures it is clearly necessary to include these employees and estimates of their numbers in 1965 and in earlier years are contained in the figures given in Table B.1.

(Thousands)

	Railways	Road Passenger Transport	Road Haulage Contracting	Sea Transport	Port and Inland Water Transport	Air Transport	Total Measured Transport	Miscellaneous Transport Services and Storage	Total Transport	Postal Services and Telecommunications	Total Transport & Communication
1952	503	327	199	158	161	25	1,373	42	1,415	319	1,734
1953	497	317	195	155	151	25	1,340	47	1,387	311	1,698
1954	492	304	193	160	153	25	1,327	48	1,375	317	1,692
1955	473	300	196	161	161	26	1,317	49	1,366	320	1,686
1956	472	300	197	162	160	29	1,320	53	1,373	328	1,701
1957	473	298	196	164	159	31	1,321	52	1,373	324	1,697
1958	468	297	196	159	154	32	1,306	52	1,358	332	1,690
1959	448	290	199	150	150	34	1,271	59	1,330	332	1,662
1960	432	281	205	150	149	35	1,252	63	1,315	328	1,643
1961	431	284	211	151	147	39	1,263	66	1,329	344	1,673
1962	421	287	214	148	143	42	1,255	68	1,323	356	1,679
1963	395	288	217	133	139	40	1,212	75	1,287	360	1,647
1964	376	280	225	128	137	41	1,187	78	1,265	365	1,630
1965	348	281	231	122	135	48	1,165	82	1,247	369	1,616

Technical Notes to Table B.2

1. *Sources.* The figures of average earnings which formed the basis of the conversion to standard labour units were taken from the following sources.

   (a) Ministry of Labour Gazette, 1952 to 1965. Reports on the enquiries into average hourly earnings conducted by the Ministry of Labour in April and October each year. All sectors of Transport and Communication were covered with the exception of Railways and Sea Transport. The average of the April and October figures was used in all cases.

   (b) Annual Reports of the British Transport Commission, 1952 to 1962 for data on average weekly earnings in Railways and Sea Transport (represented here by British Railways, shipping services only).

2. Coefficients were used to convert the simple total of people in work (man power in work) into Standardised Labour Units (SLU). The conversion coefficient F is the ratio of the average hourly earnings of all female workers in a sector, to the average hourly earnings of male adults in that sector. Similarly, the conversion coefficient YB is the ratio of average hourly earnings of youths and boys to the average hourly earnings of male adults. For Railways and Sea Transport average weekly earnings had to be used as a basis for the calculation of the coefficients in the absence of data of hourly earnings.

   Thus for any sector:

   $$\text{SLU} = L_m + L_f . F + L_{yb} . YB.$$

   where SLU is the number of standardised labour units.

   L_m is the number of adult male workers in employment.
   L_f is the number of females of all ages in employment.
   L_{yb} is the number of youths and boys in employment.
   F is average hourly earnings of female workers ÷
      average hourly earnings of adult male workers.
   YB is average hourly earnings of youths and boys ÷
      average hourly earnings of adult male workers.

3. At a number of points in the period studied, average earnings of all or some groups of employees were not available; in these cases conversion coefficients have been estimated as follows:

   Railways. From 1963 onwards estimates for F and YB were made by taking the average of the conversion coefficients for the three years 1960, 1961 and 1962.

   Sea Transport. Estimates for F and YB in 1952 were made by averaging the conversion coefficients for 1953 and 1954. In 1960 the average weekly earnings of youths and boys was greatly out of line with the other figures in the series for no apparent reason; an estimate of the YB conversion coefficient for 1960 was therefore made by averaging the 1959 and the 1961 figures of earnings. From 1963 onwards, estimates for F and YB were obtained by averaging the conversion coefficients for the three years 1960, 1961 and 1962.

Port and Inland Water Transport. The average earnings of females was not given for 1962; an estimate of the conversion coefficient for F in 1962 was obtained by averaging the figures for 1961 and 1963.

Air Transport. Prior to 1954, data on the earnings of Air Transport employees were included under Postal Services and Telecommunications. The average of the 1954 and 1955 conversion coefficients for females was taken as the estimated figure for both 1952 and 1953. The numbers of youths and boys employed in Air Transport during 1952 and 1953 were relatively small and were not taken into account. Estimates of the YB conversion coefficients for 1954 and 1955 were obtained by taking the average of the 1956 and 1957 figures.

Miscellaneous Transport Services and Storage. Estimates of the conversion coefficients for F and YB from 1960 onwards were made by taking the average of figures from 1952 to 1959 inclusive.

P

Table B.3.   Hours of Work, Holidays and Labour Input (Standardised Labour Unit Hours)

United Kingdom
SIC 1958

	Railways				Road Passenger Transport				Road Haulage Contracting				Sea Transport			
	Average Weekly Hours Worked[a]	Holiday Hours per Annum[b]	Average Manhours Worked per SLU per Annum[c]	LABOUR INPUT SLU HOURS[c] Mn.	Average Weekly Hours Worked	Holiday Hours per Annum	Average Manhours Worked per SLU per Annum	LABOUR INPUT SLU HOURS Mn.	Average Weekly Hours Worked	Holiday Hours per Annum	Average Manhours Worked per SLU per Annum	LABOUR INPUT SLU HOURS Mn.	Average Weekly Hours Worked	Holiday Hours per Annum	Average Manhours Worked per SLU per Annum	LABOUR INPUT SLU HOURS Mn.
1952	47.21e	146	2,309	1,161	48.06	154	2,345	767	50.87	168	2,477	493	59.73e	149	2,957	467
1953	47.45e	147	2,320	1,153	48.30	155	2,357	747	51.83	171	2,524	492	60.04e	150	2,972	461
1954	48.22e	149	2,358	1,160	49.38	158	2,410	733	52.52	173	2,558	494	61.01e	153	3,020	483
1955	49.04e	152	2,398	1,134	49.88	160	2,434	730	53.74	177	2,617	513	62.05e	155	3,072	495
1956	48.70e	151	2,381	1,124	49.46	158	2,414	724	53.66	177	2,613	515	61.62e	154	3,050	494
1957	48.41e	150	2,367	1,120	49.55	159	2,418	721	53.60	177	2,610	512	61.25e	153	3,032	497
1958	47.98e	149	2,346	1,098	48.78	156	2,381	707	53.81	178	2,620	514	60.71e	152	3,005	478
1959	48.56e	151	2,374	1,064	49.16	157	2,399	696	53.98	178	2,629	523	61.44e	154	3,041	456
1960	48.51e	150	2,373	1,025	49.49	158	2,415	679	54.63	180	2,661	546	61.38e	153	3,039	456
1961	47.98e	149	2,346	1,011	48.72	156	2,377	675	54.99	181	2,678	565	60.71e	152	3,005	454
1962	47.25e	146	2,311	973	48.28	154	2,357	676	54.33	179	2,646	566	59.79e	149	2,960	438
1963	47.78e	148	2,337	923	48.55	155	2,370	683	54.87	181	2,672	580	60.46e	151	2,993	398
1964	48.12e	149	2,353	885	48.91	157	2,386	668	55.49	183	2,702	608	60.89e	152	3,014	386
1965	48.22e	149	2,358	821	49.56	159	2,418	679	55.78	184	2,717	628	61.01e	214	2,959	361

a Averages compiled by weighting hours by Standard Labour Units (SLU).

b Public and annual holidays, equivalent in working hours per annum.

c See note 2 on method of calculation at the end of this table.

e Estimated figures. See note 3 on methods of estimation at the end of this table.

Table B.3. (Continued)   Hours of Work, Holidays and Labour Input (Standardised Labour Unit Hours)   United Kingdom   SIC 1958

	Port and Inland Water Transport				Air Transport				TOTAL MEASURED TRANSPORT				Miscellaneous Transport Services and Storage			
	Average Weekly Hours Worked[a]	Holiday Hours per Annum[b]	Average Manhours Worked per SLU per Annum[c]	LABOUR INPUT SLU HOURS[c]	Average Weekly Hours Worked	Holiday Hours per Annum	Average Manhours Worked per SLU per Annum	LABOUR INPUT SLU HOURS	Average Weekly Hours Worked	Holiday Hours per Annum	Average Manhours Worked per SLU per Annum	LABOUR INPUT SLU HOURS	Average Weekly Hours Worked	Holiday Hours per Annum	Average Manhours Worked per SLU per Annum	LABOUR INPUT SLU HOURS
				Mn.				Mn.				Mn.				Mn.
1952	49.43	153	2,417	389	38.94e	152	2,393	60	49.67e	152	2,431	3,337	46.77	145	2,287	96
1953	49.33	151	2,414	365	48.94e	152	2,393	60	49.98e	153	2,446	3,277	47.57	147	2,327	109
1954	49.43	153	2,417	370	48.46	150	2,370	59	50.81e	156	2,486	3,299	48.26	150	2,360	113
1955	50.55	157	2,472	398	49.22	153	2,406	63	51.71e	159	2,530	3,333	48.76	151	2,385	117
1956	50.04	155	2,447	392	45.90	142	2,245	65	51.29e	157	2,510	3,314	48.52	150	2,373	126
1957	49.68	154	2,429	386	45.19	140	2,210	69	51.11e	157	2,501	3,304	47.54	147	2,325	121
1958	49.11	152	2,402	370	45.00	140	2,200	70	50.63e	155	2,478	3,237	48.45	150	2,369	123
1959	49.29	153	2,410	362	45.13	140	2,207	75	51.06e	157	2,498	3,175	49.27	153	2,409	142
1960	48.97	152	2,394	357	44.44	138	2,173	76	51.21e	157	2,506	3,138	49.19e	152	2,406	152
1961	48.27	150	2,360	347	44.27	137	2,165	84	50.75e	156	2,483	3,136	49.42e	153	2,417	160
1962	47.12	146	2,304	329	45.97	143	2,247	94	50.11e	154	2,452	3,078	49.65e	154	2,428	165
1963	47.70	148	2,332	324	45.36	141	2,218	89	50.54e	156	2,472	2,996	49.88e	155	2,439	183
1964	47.24	146	2,310	316	46.09	143	2,254	92	50.90e	157	2,490	2,955	50.12e	155	2,451	191
1965	46.80	145	2,289	309	44.36	138	2,169	104	51.06e	164	2,491	2,902	50.35e	156	2,462	202

a Averages compiled by weighting hours by Standard Labour Units (SLU).

b Public and annual holidays, equivalent in working hours per annum.

c See note 2 on method of calculation at the end of this table.

e Estimated figures. See note 3 on methods of estimation at the end of this table.

	Postal Services and Telecommunications				TOTAL TRANSPORT AND TELECOMMUNICATION			
	Average Weekly Hours Worked[a]	Holiday Hours per Annum[b]	Average Manhours Worked per SLU per Annum[c]	LABOUR INPUT SLU HOURS[c]	Average Weekly Hours Worked	Holiday Hours per Annum	Average Manhours Worked per SLU per Annum	LABOUR INPUT SLU HOURS
				Mn.				Mn.
1952	46.44	158	2,257	720	49.00e	153	2,395	4,153
1953	47.38	161	2,303	716	49.44e	155	2,416	4,103
1954	46.77	173	2,259	716	49.98e	159	2,440	4,128
1955	47.90	177	2,314	740	50.90e	162	2,485	4,190
1956	47.45	176	2,291	751	50.48e	161	2,464	4,191
1957	46.95	174	2,267	735	50.21e	160	2,451	4,159
1958	45.69	187	2,189	727	49.60e	161	2,418	4,087
1959	46.88	192	2,246	746	50.17e	164	2,445	4,063
1960	46.92	192	2,248	737	50.29e	164	2,451	4,027
1961	46.40	190	2,223	765	49.81e	163	2,427	4,061
1962	45.41	186	2,175	774	49.10e	161	2,392	4,017
1963	46.21	189	2,214	797	49.56e	163	2,414	3,976
1964	47.02	193	2,252	822	50.00e	165	2,435	3,969
1965	46.53	191	2,229	823	50.00e	170	2,430	3,926

a Averages compiled by weighting hours by Standard Labour Units (SLU).

b Public and annual holidays, equivalent in working hours per annum.

c See note 2 on method of calculation at the end of this table.

e Estimated figures. See note 3 on methods of estimation at the end of this table.

Technical Notes to Table B.3

1. *Sources.*   The main source of information on hours worked was the Ministry of Labour Gazette, 1952 to 1965, which publishes the reports on the half-yearly enquiries held in April and October each year on average hours worked and average weekly earnings. The average of April and October figures was used in all cases.

Where the average hours worked were not available from the Ministry of Labour enquiries or where adjustments had to be made, the methods of estimating the figures are shown in note 3 below.

Up to October 1959, the Ministry of Labour earnings and hours enquiry was compiled on the basis of the 1948 SIC; from 1960 onwards the 1958 SIC.

was used. The effect of this change on the figures for average hours worked in the Transport and Communication industry was negligible.

2. Method of Calculating Labour Input

(Column titles as in Table B.3)

	(1) Average Weekly Hours Worked	(2) Holiday Hours per Annum	(3) Average Man-Hours Worked per SLU per Annum	(4) LABOUR INPUT SLU HOURS
Individual Sectors Railways, Road Passenger Transport, Road Haulage Contracting, Sea Transport, Port and Inland Water Transport, Air Transport (comprising Measured Transport); Miscellaneous Transport Services and Storage, Postal Services and Telecommunications	Average Weekly Hours Worked (weighted by the number of Standard Labour Units derived from the number of adult male workers, female workers and male workers under 21)	See note 4 on Holiday En-titlement in the Transport Industry	Column (1) × 52 − Column (2)	Column (3) × Number of SLU in Sector
TOTAL MEASURED TRANSPORT	Column (2) + Column (3) ÷ 52	Equivalent hours holiday per annum for all SLU in Measured Transport divided by the number of SLU therein	Column (4) for Measured Transport divided by the total number of SLU therein	Sub-total: the sum of sectors comprising Measured Transport
TOTAL TRANSPORT AND TELECOMMUNI-CATION	Column (2) + Column (3) ÷ 52	Equivalent hours holiday per annum for all SLU in the industry divided by the total number of SLU in the industry	Column (4) for the industry divided by the total number of SLU in the industry	Grand Total: sum of Measured Transport, plus Miscellaneous Transport Services and Storage and Postal Services and Telecommunications

3. *Coverage of Statistics of Average Weekly hours worked and Methods of Estimation.* Official statistics of average weekly hours worked by employees in Railways and Sea Transport (represented here by British Railways' shipping services only) are available for 1964 and 1965. Approximations for average hours worked by employees in these two sectors were made by linking the average of the 1964 and 1965 figures to an index of the average weekly hours worked by all workers (weighted by SLU) in Total Transport and Telecommunications.

The returns of average weekly hours worked in Air Transport in 1952 and 1953 were included with those for Postal Services and Telecommunications in the statistics given in the Ministry of Labour Gazette. Estimates of average weekly hours worked in 1952 and 1953 in Air Transport were made by taking an average, separately in respect of males and females, of hours worked in 1954 and 1955. The estimates of average weekly hours worked in Postal Services and Telecommunications were not adjusted for the years 1952 and 1953; the total number of employees in Air Transport represented by the returns in these years was small (7.7 per cent) in relation to the labour force in Postal Services and Telecommunications.

From 1960 onwards returns of average weekly hours worked in Storage were included with those for Postal Services and Telecommunications. The total number of storage workers represented by these returns was probably not large in relation to the labour force in Postal Services and Telecommunications. No separate figures are available after 1958 for employees in Storage. From 1952 to 1958 Storage employees numbered on average 16,500, and changed very little from year to year. Over this period they represented less than five per cent of the combined total labour force in Postal Services and Telecommunications and Storage. No adjustment was therefore made to the average hours worked in this sector from 1960 onwards.

The statistics given under Miscellaneous Transport Services and Storage for the years 1952 to 1959 inclusive relate to returns for storage employees only. From 1960 onwards this category of employee was included with Postal Services and Telecommunications in the Ministry of Labour Gazette. Estimates of the average weekly hours worked (weighted by SLU) in this sector for the years 1960 to 1965 were obtained by projecting the trend for the period 1952 to 1959 by the method of least squares: line equation $Y = 48.1425 + 0.2321\,t$.

4. *Holiday Entitlement of Employees in each Sector of the Transport and Communication Industry.* The data on the length of holidays with pay, including public holidays were obtained from the Ministry of Labour direct. The equivalent number of weeks holiday entitlement per annum was based on a 5½ day week throughout the period 1952 to 1965, for all grades of employees.

Public and Annual Holidays Allowed (Weeks to one decimal place)

	1952	'53	'54	'55	'56	'57	'58	'59	'60	'61	'62	'63	'64	'65
Railways	3.1	3.1	3.1	3.1	3.1	3.1	3.1	3.1	3.1	3.1	3.1	3.1	3.1	3.1
Road Passenger Transport	3.2	3.2	3.2	3.2	3.2	3.2	3.2	3.2	3.2	3.2	3.2	3.2	3.2	3.2
Road Haulage Contracting	3.3	3.3	3.3	3.3	3.3	3.3	3.3	3.3	3.3	3.3	3.3	3.3	3.3	3.3
Sea Transport	2.5	2.5	2.5	2.5	2.5	2.5	2.5	2.5	2.5	2.5	2.5	2.5	2.5	3.5
Port and Inland Water Transport	3.1	3.1	3.1	3.1	3.1	3.1	3.1	3.1	3.1	3.1	3.1	3.1	3.1	3.1
Air Transport	3.1	3.1	3.1	3.1	3.1	3.1	3.1	3.1	3.1	3.1	3.1	3.1	3.1	3.1
Postal Services and Telecommunications	3.4	3.4	3.7	3.7	3.7	3.7	4.1	4.1	4.1	4.1	4.1	4.1	4.1	4.1
Miscellaneous Transport Services and Storage	3.1	3.1	3.1	3.1	3.1	3.1	3.1	3.1	3.1	3.1	3.1	3.1	3.1	3.1

Table C.1. Capital Stock and Capital Intensity in Transport and Communication, 1952–1965 [a]

United Kingdom
SIC 1958

	Railways			Road Passenger Transport			Road Haulage Contracting			Sea Transport		
	Capital Stock	Manpower in Work	Capital Intensity per Man	Capital Stock	Manpower in Work	Capital Intensity per Man	Capital Stock	Manpower in Work	Capital Intensity per Man	Capital Stock	Manpower in Work	Capital Intensity per Man
	£'s Mn.	000's	£'s	£'s Mn.	000's	£'s	£'s Mn.	000's	£'s	£'s Mn.	000's	£'s
1952	5,455	530	10,292	430	334	1,287	272	207	1,314	2,200	166	13,253
1953	5,420	524	10,344	450	324	1,389	276	201	1,373	2,210	163	13,558
1954	5,380	519	10,366	465	311	1,495	284	200	1,420	2,250	168	13,393
1955	5,340	498	10,722	475	307	1,547	297	203	1,463	2,295	169	13,580
1956	5,310	497	10,684	485	307	1,580	313	204	1,534	2,325	171	13,596
1957	5,305	498	10,652	485	304	1,595	326	201	1,622	2,365	173	13,671
1958	5,330	489	10,900	470	303	1,551	339	203	1,670	2,405	167	14,401
1959	5,375	466	11,534	445	296	1,503	361	206	1,752	2,450	158	15,506
1960	5,425	449	12,082	420	287	1,463	391	212	1,844	2,510	158	15,886
1961	5,465	449	12,171	405	290	1,397	425	218	1,950	2,560	159	16,101
1962	5,485	440	12,466	405	293	1,382	457	222	2,059	2,570	156	16,474
1963	5,485	413	13,281	415	294	1,412	486	225	2,160	2,540	141	18,014
1964	5,465	392	13,941	420	286	1,469	513 [b]	232	2,211 [b]	2,525	136	18,566
1965	5,430	362	15,000	430	287	1,498	537 [b]	239	2,247 [b]	2,525	128	19,727

a Capital Stock is valued gross, as if new, at 1958 replacement cost. The figures for each year are averages of the stock in place at the beginning and end of the year.

b Estimated figures. See technical note following this table.

Table C.1. Continued Capital Stock and Capital Intensity in Transport and Communication, 1952–1965[a] United Kingdom. SIC 1958

	Port and Inland Water Transport			Air Transport			TOTAL MEASURED TRANSPORT			Postal Services and Telecommunications		
	Capital Stock	Manpower in Work	Capital Intensity per Man	Capital Stock	Manpower in Work	Capital Intensity per Man	Capital Stock	Manpower in Work	Capital Intensity per Man	Capital Stock	Manpower in Work	Capital Intensity per Man
	£'s Mn.	000's	£'s	£'s Mn.	000's	£'s	£'s Mn.	000's	£'s	£'s Mn.	000's	£'s
1952	1,120	166	6,747	155	29	5,345	9,632	1,432	6,726	1,370	361	3,795
1953	1,100	156	7,051	170	29	5,862	9,626	1,397	6,890	1,435	358	4,008
1954	1,085	158	6,867	190	29	6,552	9,654	1,385	6,970	1,500	359	4,178
1955	1,070	166	6,446	215	30	7,167	9,692	1,373	7,059	1,565	363	4,311
1956	1,050	164	6,402	245	33	7,424	9,728	1,376	7,070	1,610	372	4,328
1957	1,040	163	6,380	290	35	8,286	9,811	1,374	7,140	1,655	369	4,485
1958	1,040	158	6,582	345	36	9,583	9,929	1,356	7,322	1,720	370	4,649
1959	1,040	155	6,710	385	38	10,132	10,056	1,319	7,624	1,800	371	4,852
1960	1,040	154	6,753	420	41	10,244	10,206	1,301	7,845	1,895	376	5,040
1961	1,040	151	6,887	455	46	9,891	10,350	1,313	7,883	1,980	389	5,090
1962	1,040	146	7,123	475	47	10,106	10,432	1,303	8,006	2,065	404	5,111
1963	1,040	143	7,273	490	47	10,426	10,456	1,263	8,279	2,155	408	5,282
1964	1,040	140	7,429	515	48	10,729	10,478	1,234	8,491	2,245	413	5,436
1965	1,040	139	7,482	545	54	10,093	10,507	1,209	8,691	2,340	424	5,519

[a] Capital Stock is valued gross, as if new, at 1958 replacement cost. The figures for each year are averages of the stock in place at the beginning and end of the year.

225

Technical Note to Table C.1

The concept involved in the measurement of capital stock is gross, valued as if new, at constant 1958 prices. The assumption is made that replacements are by similar assets and therefore no allowance is made for technological change. The stock figures are gross in the sense that capital consumption has not been deducted.

Estimates, or assumptions, are made officially (by the Central Statistical Office) about the average length of life of each class of asset. The official method is then for gross fixed capital formation to be estimated for each class of asset for L years prior to Y, where L is the average life of the class of the asset in question and Y is the year for which gross capital stock figures are required. Price indexes are applied to these estimates to convert them to constant prices. They are then aggregated for L years to obtain an estimate of gross capital stock. Average lives are intended to take into account accidental damage by fire or other causes.

In the case of shipping in the measured transport sector, Sea Transport, the gross stock has been estimated officially by valuing tonnage statistics of the fleet.

The source of data on gross capital stock new at 1958 replacement cost in all but one sector of Measured Transport and Communication is the National Income and Expenditure 'Blue Book' for 1968, Table 66. The CSO supplied to us sectoral figures of capital stock to the nearest £10 million. (They are given only to the nearest £100 million in the 'Blue Book').

In Road Haulage Contracting estimates, using similar methods, were made for the purposes of this research. Statistics of gross fixed asset formation were made available to us by the CSO for specifically transport establishments. The data were for vehicles, plant and buildings separately. Average lives of 8, 10 and 20 years respectively were assumed. The series were deflated by the price indexes which are implicit in the statistics of gross fixed asset formation in 'other road vehicles', plant and machinery and buildings (cf., for example, the National Income and Expenditure 'Blue Book' for 1968) at both current and 1958 prices. The annual series for gross capital stock was then reached by the method which is used for the official series and which is outlined above. The series for gross fixed asset formation ceased in 1963. The annual series for gross capital stock (at 1958 replacement cost) was extended to 1964 and 1965 by extrapolation on the basis of changes in total tonnage carrying capacity in service.

In all cases, and it is particularly important where capital stock is changing rapidly in either direction, the annual capital stock figure is an average of the stock at the beginning and end of each year.

Table D.1. Factor Input and Productivity Movements in Measured Transport and Postal Services and Telecommunications, 1952–1965

United Kingdom
1958 SIC

	Railways				Road Passenger Transport				Road Haulage Contracting			
	(K/L) effect[a]	LI[b]	TFI (1) × (2)[c]	(Y/TFI) ≡ ATOKE[d]	(K/L) effect[a]	LI[b]	TFI (1) × (2)[c]	(Y/TFI) ≡ ATOKE[d]	(K/L) effect[a]	LI[b]	TFI (1) × (2)[c]	(Y/TFI) ≡ ATOKE[d]
1952	100.0	100.0	100.0	100.0	100.0	100.0	100.0	100.0	100.0	100.0	100.0	100.0
1953	100.1	99.3	99.4	101.7	102.3	97.4	99.7	99.4	101.5	99.9	101.3	105.8
1954	100.2	99.9	100.1	99.1	104.6	95.5	99.9	97.9	102.7	100.2	102.8	113.6
1955	100.9	97.7	98.6	97.8	105.7	95.2	100.6	96.7	103.7	104.1	107.9	117.7
1956	100.8	96.7	97.5	100.1	106.4	94.4	100.4	94.3	105.4	104.4	110.1	125.0
1957	100.8	96.4	97.1	101.0	106.6	94.0	100.2	89.8	107.2	103.8	111.2	133.3
1958	101.3	94.5	95.8	94.6	105.8	92.2	97.6	86.5	108.1	104.2	112.6	138.5
1959	102.7	91.6	94.1	94.9	104.8	90.7	95.1	89.3	109.7	106.1	116.4	147.2
1960	103.9	88.3	91.7	99.8	104.0	88.5	92.1	90.8	111.4	110.7	123.2	148.6
1961	104.1	87.1	90.6	97.2	102.7	88.0	90.4	90.5	113.2	114.6	129.7	150.9
1962	104.7	83.8	87.7	93.8	102.4	88.2	90.3	88.2	115.0	114.9	132.1	156.1
1963	106.2	79.5	84.4	97.1	103.0	89.0	91.7	85.0	116.6	117.6	137.2	156.7
1964	107.5	76.2	81.9	104.2	104.1	87.1	90.7	82.6	117.4	123.3	144.8	167.1
1965	109.3	70.7	77.3	105.9	104.7	88.6	92.8	76.8	117.9	127.3	150.2	168.9

Note: For a fuller explanation of the basis of these indices see the technical notes at the end.
The column headings refer to indices (base 1952 = 100) of the following variables:

a the effect of changes in capital per man (K/L) on total factor input

b labour input (LI) in standardised labour unit (SLU) hours

c total factor input (TFI), equal to col (1) × col (2)

d output per unit of total factor input (Y/TFI); also, an index of the change in output attributed to changes in applied technical and organisational knowledge and external factors (ATOKE).

227

Table D.1. (continued) Factor Input and Productivity Movements in Measured Transport and Postal Services and Telecommunications, 1952–1965

United Kingdom 1958 SIC

	Sea Transport				Port and Inland Water Transport				Air Transport			
	(K/L) effect [a]	LI [b]	TFI (1) × (2) [c]	(Y/TFI) ≡ ATOKE [d]	(K/L) effect [a]	LI [b]	TFI (1) × (2) [c]	(Y/TFI) ≡ ATOKE [d]	(K/L) effect [a]	LI [b]	TFI (1) × (2) [c]	(Y/TFI) ≡ ATOKE [d]
1952	100.0	100.0	100.0	100.0	100.0	100.0	100.0	100.0	100.0	100.0	100.0	100.0
1953	101.1	98.6	99.7	100.5	100.8	93.7	94.4	110.7	103.9	100.0	103.9	113.7
1954	100.5	103.4	104.0	98.5	100.3	95.0	95.3	111.4	108.9	99.0	107.8	119.9
1955	101.2	105.9	107.2	97.4	99.2	102.3	101.4	106.8	113.0	104.6	118.2	132.5
1956	101.3	105.8	107.1	100.5	99.0	100.6	99.6	110.4	114.7	108.8	124.8	143.1
1957	101.5	106.4	108.1	100.7	99.0	99.3	98.2	112.9	120.3	114.5	137.8	142.8
1958	103.9	102.3	106.3	101.2	99.5	95.1	94.6	119.1	128.2	117.7	150.8	136.7
1959	107.4	97.6	104.9	103.7	99.9	92.9	92.8	126.7	131.3	125.4	164.7	141.9
1960	108.5	97.6	105.9	107.3	100.0	91.7	91.7	133.0	132.0	127.1	167.8	174.6
1961	109.2	97.1	106.0	106.9	100.4	89.2	89.5	136.6	129.7	141.1	183.1	184.2
1962	110.3	93.8	103.5	109.7	101.2	84.7	85.7	146.2	131.1	157.8	206.8	172.9
1963	115.0	85.2	97.9	117.4	101.7	83.3	84.7	151.2	133.1	148.3	197.4	204.1
1964	116.6	82.6	96.2	120.1	102.2	81.3	83.1	156.5	135.0	154.5	208.5	237.1
1965	119.9	77.3	92.6	128.1	102.4	79.4	81.3	163.2	131.0	174.0	228.0	258.4

Note: For a fuller explanation of the basis of these indices see the technical notes at the end. The column headings refer to indices (base 1952 = 100) of the following variables:

a the effect of changes in capital per man (K/L) on total factor input

b labour input (LI) in standardised labour unit (SLU) hours

c total factor input (TFI), equal to col (1) × col (2)

d output per unit of total factor input (Y/TFI); also, an index of the change in output attributed to changes in applied technical and organisational knowledge and external factors (ATOKE)

228

Table D.1. (continued) Factor Input and Productivity Movements in Measured Transport and Postal Services and Telecommunications, 1952–1965

United Kingdom
1958 SIC

| | MEASURED TRANSPORT | | | | | | | | Postal Services and Telecommunications | | | |
| | Unadjusted* | | | | Adjusted* | | | | | | | |
	(K/L) effect[a]	LI[b]	TFI (1)×(2)[c]	(Y/TFI) ≡ATOKE[d]	(K/L) effect[a]	LI[b]	TFI (1)×(2)[c]	(Y/TFI) ≡ATOKE[d]	(K/L) effect[a]	LI[b]	TFI (1)×(2)[c]	(Y/TFI) ≡ATOKE[d]
1952	100.0	100.0	100.0	100.0	100.0	100.0	100.0	100.0	100.0	100.0	100.0	100.0
1953	100.8	98.2	99.0	103.4	101.2	98.2	99.4	102.9	101.1	99.5	100.6	102.4
1954	101.1	98.8	100.0	103.9	102.1	98.9	101.0	102.9	101.9	99.5	101.4	105.8
1955	101.5	99.9	101.4	104.5	103.1	100.2	103.4	102.5	102.6	102.9	105.5	106.1
1956	101.6	99.3	100.9	107.9	103.8	99.7	103.5	105.3	102.7	104.4	107.2	106.2
1957	101.9	99.0	100.9	109.6	104.5	99.5	104.0	106.3	103.6	102.0	105.7	107.6
1958	102.7	97.0	99.6	109.1	105.5	97.5	102.9	105.7	104.6	100.9	105.6	108.9
1959	103.9	95.1	98.9	113.2	106.8	95.8	102.4	109.4	105.8	103.6	109.5	109.6
1960	104.8	94.0	98.6	118.4	107.8	94.8	102.2	114.2	106.8	102.4	109.4	116.2
1961	105.0	94.0	98.7	119.5	108.3	95.0	102.9	114.6	107.1	106.2	113.7	116.5
1962	105.5	92.2	97.3	121.2	109.2	93.4	101.9	115.7	107.2	107.5	115.3	118.2
1963	106.6	89.8	95.7	125.6	110.8	90.9	100.7	119.4	108.1	110.7	119.7	119.9
1964	107.4	88.6	95.1	133.0	112.1	89.7	100.5	125.9	108.9	114.2	124.4	123.4
1965	108.2	87.0	94.1	137.5	113.3	87.9	99.6	129.8	109.4	114.2	124.9	131.7

Note: For a fuller explanation of the basis of these indices see the technical notes at the end. The column headings are explained in the note to the preceding page, and in the technical note.

* In Measured Transport, the capital input and the labour input (LI) are either unadjusted or adjusted for certain 'quality' differences (the 'intersectoral quality shift') in factor inputs. For a description of this process see the methodological note in the main text Chapter 3, page 108.

The ratio of the adjusted to the unadjusted capital intensity (K/L) effect gives an index for the capital quality (KQ) change effect referred to in Table 5.1.

229

Technical Notes to Table D.1.

1. In the table the indices are given to one decimal place. This rounding was done after the calculations were made.

2. There are several methods which can be used to combine changes in capital and labour inputs to provide a series for total factor input. The method used here is based on the principle of weighting individual factor inputs by their share of net output, but total factor input (TFI) in this case is built up, not from capital inputs and labour inputs, but from series of capital intensity (capital per man, K/L), and labour input (LI) in standardised labour unit (SLU) hours.

The share of profits (remuneration of capital) in net output is denoted by α. (The values of α used are given in the following table D.2; 1954 values were used from 1952–56, 1958 values from 1956–60 and 1963 values from 1960–65).

The suffix n refers to years.
The change in total factor input is given by

$$\log_e\left(\frac{TFI_n}{TFI_{n-1}}\right) = \log_e\left(\frac{LI_n}{LI_{n-1}}\right) + \alpha_n \log_e\left(\frac{(K/L)_n}{(K/L)_{n-1}}\right)$$

Thus, in index number form,

$$TFI_n = LI_n \times ((K/L) \text{ effect})$$

where

$$(K/L) \text{ effect} = \exp\left(\sum_{i=1}^{n} \alpha_n \log_e\left(\frac{(K/L)_n}{(K/L)_{n-1}}\right)\right)$$

In the table, the (K/L) effect is given as an index in col(1), for each sector or industry. In col(2), the labour input in SLU hours is given (LI). Their product (TFI) is given in col(3). Col(4) is derived by dividing the index of output (Y) (rebased to 1952 = 100) by total factor input (from col(3)). This is also an index of the change in output attributed to applied technical and organisational knowledge and external factors (ATOKE), since, where (Y/LI) denotes output per SLU hour,

$$\log_e\left(\frac{ATOKE_n}{ATOKE_{n-1}}\right) = \log_e\left(\frac{(Y/LI)_n}{(Y/LI)_{n-1}}\right) - \alpha_n \log_e\left(\frac{(K/L)_n}{(K/L)_{n-1}}\right)$$

$$= \log_e\left(\frac{Y_n}{Y_{n-1}}\right) - \log_e\left(\frac{TFI_n}{TFI_{n-1}}\right)$$

230

Table D.2. Factor Shares in Transport and Communication   United Kingdom
           GROSS REMUNERATION OF CAPITAL AS A   1958 SIC
           FRACTION OF NET OUTPUT, (α)

SECTOR	VALUE OF α IN YEAR		
	1954	1958	1963
Railways [a]	0.22	0.24	0.24
Road Passenger Transport	0.30	0.29	0.28
Road Haulage Contracting	0.34	0.30	0.29
Sea Transport	0.50	0.45	0.46
Port and Inland Water Transport	0.19	0.18	0.23
Air Transport	0.42	0.44	0.48
MEASURED TRANSPORT	0.32	0.30	0.31
Postal Services and Telecommunications	0.20	0.26	0.26

a Net output is in terms of gross value added (total factor rewards) *plus*
subsidies and 'subsidy equivalents' in this sector.

Table E.1.   Labour Productivity Levels at Constant 1952 and 1962 Levels of Technical Change, with associated   United Kingdom
Capital Intensity, in the Sectors of Measured Transport and Communication, 1952–1965   SIC   1958

Col. 1.   q   Output per standard labour unit hour in pence at constant 1958 values.

Col. 2.   A   Index of technical change as measured by ATOKE (applied organisational knowledge and external factors), 1952 = 100.

Col. 3.   q/A 1952   Labour productivity levels at constant, 1952 level of technical change.

Col. 5.   k   Gross capital stock per person employed, £'s 000 at 1958 replacement cost.

	Railways					Road Passenger Transport					Road Haulage Contracting				
	q	A	q/A 1952	q/A 1962	k	q	A	q/A 1952	q/A 1962	k	q	A	q/A 1952	q/A 1962	k
1952	62.5	100.0	62.5	58.6	10.3	89.8	100.0	89.8	79.2	1.3	66.8	100.0	66.8	104.3	1.3
1953	63.7	101.7	62.6	58.7	10.3	91.3	99.4	91.8	81.0	1.4	71.7	105.8	67.8	105.8	1.4
1954	62.1	99.1	62.6	58.8	10.4	91.9	97.9	93.9	82.8	1.5	77.9	113.6	68.6	107.1	1.4
1955	61.7	97.8	63.1	59.2	10.7	91.7	96.7	94.8	83.6	1.5	81.5	117.7	69.3	108.1	1.5
1956	63.1	100.1	63.1	59.3	10.7	90.0	94.3	95.4	84.2	1.6	88.0	125.0	70.4	109.9	1.5
1957	63.6	101.0	63.0	59.1	10.7	86.0	89.8	95.8	84.5	1.6	95.4	133.3	71.6	111.7	1.6
1958	59.9	94.6	63.3	59.4	10.9	82.1	86.5	95.0	83.8	1.6	100.0	138.5	72.2	112.7	1.7
1959	60.9	94.9	64.2	60.2	11.5	84.1	89.3	94.1	83.0	1.5	107.8	147.2	73.2	114.3	1.8
1960	64.8	99.8	64.9	60.9	12.1	84.8	90.8	93.4	82.4	1.5	110.5	148.6	74.4	116.1	1.8
1961	63.2	97.2	65.0	61.0	12.2	83.4	90.5	92.1	81.2	1.4	114.1	150.9	75.6	118.0	2.0
1962	61.4	93.8	65.4	61.4	12.5	81.0	88.2	91.9	81.0	1.4	119.9	156.1	76.8	119.9	2.1
1963	64.5	97.1	66.4	62.3	13.3	78.5	85.0	92.4	81.5	1.4	122.1	156.7	77.9	121.6	2.2
1964	70.0	104.2	67.2	63.0	13.9	77.2	82.6	93.5	82.4	1.5	131.0	167.1	78.4	122.4	2.2
1965	72.4	105.9	68.3	64.1	15.0	72.1	76.8	93.9	82.9	1.5	133.1	168.9	78.8	123.0	2.2

Table E.1. Labour Productivity Levels at Constant 1952 and 1962 Levels of Technical Change, with
(continued) associated Capital Intensity, in the Sectors of Measured Transport and Communication, 1952–1965

United Kingdom
SIC 1958

Col. 1 q Output per standard labour unit hour in pence at constant 1958 values.

Col. 2 A Index of technical change as measured by ATOKE (applied organisational knowledge and external factors), 1952 = 100.

Col. 3 $\frac{q/A}{1952}$ Labour productivity levels at constant, 1952 level of technical change.

Col. 5 k Gross capital stock per person employed £'s 000 at 1958 replacement cost.

	Sea Transport					Port and Inland Water Transport				
	q	A	q/A 1952	q/A 1962	k	q	A	q/A 1952	q/A 1962	k
1952	117.1	100.0	117.1	128.4	13.3	72.8	100.0	72.8	106.4	6.7
1953	119.0	100.5	118.4	129.9	13.6	81.2	110.7	73.3	107.2	7.1
1954	115.9	98.5	117.6	129.0	13.4	81.3	111.4	73.0	106.7	6.9
1955	115.5	97.4	118.5	130.0	13.6	77.1	106.8	72.2	105.5	6.4
1956	119.1	100.5	118.5	130.0	13.6	79.6	110.4	72.1	105.4	6.4
1957	119.7	100.7	118.9	130.4	13.7	81.3	112.9	72.0	105.3	6.4
1958	123.1	101.2	121.6	133.4	14.4	86.3	119.1	72.5	105.9	6.6
1959	130.5	103.7	125.8	138.0	15.5	92.1	126.7	72.7	106.3	6.7
1960	136.2	107.3	127.0	139.3	15.9	96.7	133.0	72.7	106.3	6.8
1961	136.6	106.9	127.8	140.2	16.1	99.8	136.6	73.1	106.9	6.9
1962	141.6	109.7	129.1	141.6	16.5	107.6	146.2	73.6	107.6	7.1
1963	157.9	117.4	134.5	147.6	18.0	111.9	151.2	74.0	108.2	7.3
1964	163.9	120.1	136.4	149.7	18.6	116.4	156.5	74.4	108.7	7.4
1965	179.7	128.1	140.3	153.9	19.7	121.6	163.2	74.5	108.9	7.5

Table E.1. Labour Productivity Levels at Constant 1952 and 1962 Levels of Technical Change, with
(continued) associated Capital Intensity, in the Sectors of Measured Transport and Communication, 1952–1965

United Kingdom
SIC 1958

Col. 1 q   Output per standard labour unit hour in pence at constant 1958 values.

Col. 2 A   Index of technical change as measured by ATOKE (applied organisational knowledge and external factors), 1952 = 100.

Col. 3 q/A Labour productivity levels at constant, 1952 level of technical change.
        1952

Col. 5 k   Gross capital stock per person employed, £'s 000 at 1958 replacement cost.

	Air Transport					Postal Services and Telecommunications				
	q	A	q/A 1952	q/A 1962	k	q	A	q/A 1952	q/A 1962	k
1952	107.0	100.0	107.0	185.0	5.3	109.3	100.0	109.3	129.2	3.8
1953	126.4	113.7	111.2	192.3	5.9	113.2	102.4	110.5	130.7	4.0
1954	139.7	119.9	116.5	201.4	6.6	117.9	105.8	111.4	131.7	4.2
1955	160.2	132.5	120.9	209.0	7.2	119.0	106.1	112.2	132.6	4.3
1956	175.6	143.1	122.7	212.2	7.4	119.2	106.2	112.2	132.7	4.3
1957	183.8	142.8	128.7	222.6	8.3	122.0	107.6	113.3	134.0	4.5
1958	187.5	136.7	137.2	237.2	9.6	124.5	108.9	114.3	135.1	4.6
1959	199.5	141.9	140.6	243.1	10.1	126.8	109.6	115.7	136.8	4.9
1960	246.6	174.6	141.3	244.2	10.2	135.7	116.2	116.8	138.1	5.0
1961	255.8	184.2	138.9	240.1	9.9	136.4	116.5	117.1	138.4	5.1
1962	242.5	172.9	140.3	242.5	10.1	138.6	118.2	117.3	138.6	5.1
1963	290.7	204.1	142.4	246.3	10.4	141.8	119.9	118.3	139.8	5.3
1964	342.4	237.1	144.4	249.7	10.7	147.0	123.4	119.1	140.8	5.4
1965	362.4	258.4	140.2	242.5	10.1	157.5	131.7	119.6	141.4	5.5

Table F.1. Vehicles, Capacity, Output, Capacity Utilisation and Average Haul

A. RAIL GOODS TRANSPORT

	Number of railway goods vehicles [a] at mid year	Carrying capacity of vehicles [a] at mid year	Tonnage forwarded [b]	Ton mileage performed [c]	Value of gross output at average (unweighted) 1958 prices [d]	Ton mileage of work performed per vehicle [c]	Ton mileage of work performed per capacity ton [c]	Average haul
	(000's)	(000tons)	(Mn. tons)	(000 mn)	(£'s Mn.)	(000)	(Ton miles)	(Miles)
1952	1,108	14,708	285	22.4	315	20.2	1,523	78.6
1953	1,106	14,851	289	22.8	321	20.6	1,535	78.9
1954	1,108	15,111	283	22.1	311	19.9	1,463	78.1
1955	1,110	15,410	274	21.4	301	19.3	1,389	78.1
1956	1,106	15,643	277	21.5	303	19.4	1,374	77.6
1957	1,096	15,788	274	20.9	294	19.1	1,324	76.3
1958	1,048	15,414	243	18.4	259	17.6	1,194	75.7
1959	975	14,623	234	17.7	249	18.2	1,210	75.6
1960	946	14,302	249	18.7	263	19.8	1,303	75.1
1961	945	14,343	238	17.6	248	18.6	1,227	73.9
1962	895	13,773	228	16.1	227	18.0	1,169	70.6
1963	786	12,273	235	15.4	217	19.6	1,255	65.5
1964	686	10,859	240	16.1	227	23.5	1,483	67.1
1965	631	10,094	229	15.4	217	24.4	1,526	67.2
1966	581	9,405	214	14.8	208	25.5	1,574	69.2
1967	509	8,378	201	13.6	192	26.7	1,623	67.7

a Excluding brake vans.

b All free-hauled traffic excluded.

c Before 1963 free-hauled traffic on revenue-earning freight trains is included; in 1963 and later years it is excluded.

d 3.38 pence per ton mile in 1958.

Table F.1. (continued)   B. ROAD HAULAGE CONTRACTING   Great Britain

	Number of vehicles at mid-year	Carrying capacity of vehicles at mid-year	Tonnage forwarded	Ton mileage performed	Value of gross output at average (unweighted) 1958 prices[a]	Ton mileage of work performed per vehicle	Ton mileage of work performed per capacity ton	Average haul
	(000's)	(000 tons)	(Mn. tons)	(000 Mn.)	(£ Million)	(000's)	(Ton miles)	(Miles)
1952	162	841	341	8.4	193	51.9	9,988	24.6
1953	159	827	...	...	...	...	...	...
1954	158	843	...	...	...	...	...	...
1955	159	863	...	...	...	...	...	...
1956	166	911	...	...	...	...	...	...
1957	171	959	...	...	...	...	...	...
1958	173	998	448	13.1	300	75.7	13,126	29.2
1959	175	1,004	...	...	...	...	...	...
1960	180	1,043	...	...	...	...	...	...
1961	184	1,135	...	...	...	...	...	...
1962	190	1,200	510	17.3	396	91.1	14,417	33.9
1963	196	...	530	18.0	413	91.8	...	34.0
1964	205	...	578	20.3	465	99.0	...	35.1
1965	215	...	586	21.3	488	99.1	...	36.3
1966	226	...	664	24.1	552	106.6	...	36.3
1967	235	...	687	25.0	573	106.4	...	36.4

a   5.50 pence per ton mile in 1958

TABLE 7.1. (continued) C. NON-CONTRACTUAL ROAD MILEAGE

	Number of vehicles at mid-year	Carrying capacity of vehicles at mid-year	Tonnage forwarded [b]	Ton mileage performed [b]	Value of gross output at average (unweighted) 1958 prices [a]	Ton mileage of work performed per vehicle	Ton mileage of work performed per capacity ton	Average haul
	(000's)	(000 tons)	(Mn. tons)	(000 Mn.)	(£ million)	(000's)	(Ton miles)	(Miles)
1952	755	1,494	506	10.4	464	13.8	6,961	20.6
1953	789	1,550	...	...	...	...	...	...
1954	825	1,611	...	...	...	...	...	...
1955	891	1,730	...	...	...	...	...	...
1956	951	1,827	...	...	...	...	...	...
1957	991	1,859	...	...	...	...	...	...
1958	1,036	1,937	613	12.1	540	11.7	6,247	19.7
1959	1,090	2,020	...	...	...	...	...	...
1960	1,151	2,107	...	...	...	...	...	...
1961	1,204	2,183	...	...	...	...	...	...
1962	1,224	2,258	738	16.3	727	13.3	7,219	22.1
1963	1,275	...	770	17.0	759	13.3	...	22.1
1964	1,303	...	832	18.7	834	14.4	...	22.5
1965	1,297	...	844	19.7	879	15.2	...	23.3
1966	1,264	...	786	17.4	776	13.8	...	22.1
1967	1,275	...	813	18.0	803	14.1	...	22.1

a 10.71 pence per ton mile in 1958

b Estimates have been made by the Ministry of Transport of tonnage carried and ton mileage performed in total road goods transport (but not broken down into contractual and non-contractual) by interpolating on the basis of road traffic counts between census years. The figures for tonnage and ton mileage for the years not given above are as follows:

	1953	1954	1955	1956	1957	1959	1960	1961
Tonnage forwarded. Mn. Tons	875	925	997	993	969	1,146	1,192	1,240
Ton mileage performed. 000 Mn.	19.7	21.1	23.0	23.2	22.9	28.1	30.1	32.3

237

Table F.2. Vehicles, Capacity, Output, Capacity Utilisation and Average Stage   Great Britain
A. RAIL PASSENGER TRANSPORT

	Number of vehicles (Passenger carriages) at mid year	Seating capacity of vehicles at mid year	Passenger journeys	Passenger miles	Value of gross output at average (unweighted) 1958 prices [a]	Passenger journeys per capacity seating unit	Passenger miles per vehicle	Average length of passenger journey (average stage)
	(000's)	(000's)	(millions)	(000 Mn.)	(£'s Mn.)		(000's)	(Miles)
1952	41,984	2,491	1,017	20.5	127.3	408	488	20.2
1953	41,822	2,475	1,015	20.6	127.9	410	493	20.3
1954	41,840	2,474	1,020	20.7	128.5	412	495	20.3
1955	41,816	2,470	994	20.3	126.0	402	485	20.4
1956	41,619	2,449	1,029	21.1	131.0	420	507	20.5
1957	41,675	2,442	1,101	22.6	140.3	451	542	20.5
1958	41,915	2,446	1,090	22.2	138.0	446	530	20.4
1959	41,270	2,403	1,069	22.3	138.4	445	540	20.9
1960	40,314	2,346	1,037	21.6	134.1	442	536	20.8
1961	38,970	2,267	1,025	21.1	131.0	452	541	20.6
1962	35,728	2,078	965	19.7	122.3	464	551	20.4
1963	32,710	1,884	938	19.2	119.2	498	587	20.5
1964	29,138	1,678	928	19.9	123.5	553	683	21.4
1965	25,443	1,479	865	18.7	116.1	585	735	21.6
1966	23,350	1,367	835	18.5	114.9	611	792	22.1

a 1.49 pence per passenger mile in 1958

Table F.2. (continued)   B. PUBLIC ROAD PASSENGER TRANSPORT

Great Britain

	Number of vehicles at mid year	Seating capacity of vehicles at mid year	Passenger journeys	Passenger miles	Value of gross output at average (unweighted) 1958 prices[a]	Passenger journeys per capacity seating unit	Passenger miles per vehicle	Average length of passenger journey (average stage)
		(000's)	(millions)	(000 Mn.)	(£'s Mn.)		(000's)	(Miles)
1952	82,815	3,750	16,336	50.1	344.4	4,356	605	3.07
1953	82,221	3,750	16,083	50.7	348.6	4,289	617	3.15
1954	81,025	3,700	15,968	50.0	343.8	4,316	617	3.13
1955	80,537	3,750	15,929	49.8	342.4	4,248	618	3.13
1956	80,169	3,800	15,510	48.6	341.3	4,082	606	3.13
1957	79,483	3,750	14,736	45.9	315.6	3,930	577	3.11
1958	78,491	3,700	13,840	43.4	297.8	3,741	553	3.14
1959	77,508	3,700	13,937	44.1	303.2	3,767	569	3.16
1960	77,209	3,750	13,680	43.9	301.8	3,648	569	3.21
1961	77,551	3,800	13,403	43.1	296.3	3,527	556	3.22
1962	77,930	3,800	13,030	42.4	291.5	3,429	544	3.25
1963	77,838	3,800	12,732	41.5	285.3	3,351	533	3.26
1964	77,276	3,800	12,266	40.3	277.1	3,228	522	3.29
1965	76,623	3,800	11,652	37.6	258.5	3,066	491	3.23
1966	75,804	3,800	11,028	36.3	249.6	2,902	479	3.29

a 1.65 pence per passenger mile in 1958.

Sources: See Technical Notes at the end for sources and methods for output and capacity measures and estimates.

Table F.3.   ROAD GOODS TRANSPORT, 1952–62
Number of Vehicles and Carrying Capacity at Mid-year

Category of Road Goods Vehicles:-	'A' Licence		Contract 'A' Licence		'B' Licence		British Road Services		British Rail		Total Contractual		Non-contractual ('C' licence)		Total Road Goods Vehicles	
	Number of Vehicles	Carrying Capacity	Number of Vehicles	Carrying Capacity	Number of Vehicles	Carrying Capacity	Number of Vehicles	Carrying Capacity	Number of Vehicles	Carrying Capacity	Number of Vehicles	Carrying Capacity	Number of Vehicles	Carrying Capacity	Number of Vehicles	Carrying Capacity
	000's	000 tons	000's	000 tons	000's	000 tons	000's	000 tons	000's	000 tons	000's	000 tons	000's	000 tons	000's	000 tons
1952	39	200	10	55	59	247	39	285	15	54	162	841	755	1,494	917	2,335
1953	38	191	10	57	59	247	37	275	16	57	159	827	789	1,550	948	2,377
1954	43	235	10	60	59	249	30	239	17	60	158	843	825	1,611	983	2,454
1955	49	286	13	83	60	258	19	175	17	61	159	863	891	1,730	1,050	2,593
1956	56	338	16	107	62	268	15	137	17	61	166	911	951	1,827	1,117	2,738
1957	58	363	19	126	63	275	15	133	17	62	171	959	991	1,859	1,162	2,818
1958	59	381	20	139	65	285	14	132	16	61	173	998	1,036	1,937	1,209	2,935
1959	57	368	22	150	66	293	14	131	17	62	175	1,004	1,090	2,020	1,265	3,024
1960	57	369	25	175	68	305	14	132	17	62	180	1,043	1,151	2,107	1,331	3,150
1961	88	588	27	204	70	343	a	a	a	a	184	1,135	1,204	2,183	1,388	3,318
1962	90	603	28	222	73	375	a	a	a	a	190	1,200	1,224	2,258	1,414	3,458

a   From 1961 onwards road goods vehicles of B.R.S. and British Rail have been included under the appropriate licence category.

Where detailed data of Contractual Vehicles do not add up to the total for Contractual Vehicles, differences are due to rounding to the nearest thousand.

Technical Notes to Section F (Tables F 1, 2 and 3)

Sources and Methods for capacity and gross value of output measures and estimates

A.   Freight Transport

1. *Vehicles*

Rail.   British Transport Commission Annual Report and Accounts. Volume II. Financial and Statistical Accounts, 1962 and 1961. Section XI. Freight Vehicles (excluding brake vans). At December 31st. British Railways only. Converted to mid-year statistics by averaging the stock figures at the beginning and end of each year. This conversion has been carried out on all stock figures of vehicles and capacities in Tables F.1, 2 and 3.

Road.   Numbers of vehicles, analysed by carriers' licence and unladen weight, for the period 1951 to 1962 were obtained from the Annual Abstracts of Statistics. This has been termed the 'Old Series' of data; all the vehicles in this series have carriers' licences, they do not necessarily have current road fund licences as well.

The size of British Road Services and British Railways fleets of goods vehicles in 1951 and 1952 were obtained from the Annual Reports of the British Transport Commission for those particular years. From 1953 until 1960 B.T.C. vehicles were shown by unladen weight in the Annual Abstracts under the following headings; Total B.T.C. vehicles (including service vehicles); British Road Services vehicles; British Railways vehicles. The actual numbers of B.T.C. service vehicles were obtained by deduction and were included with the 'C' licence category of vehicles. No breakdown of the number of B.T.C. service vehicles was obtainable from the 1951 and 1952 B.T.C. Annual Reports, but as the number of vehicles in this category remained fairly constant in subsequent years, an average of the 1953 and 1954 figures, broken down by unladen weight, was taken as an estimate for both the years 1951 and 1952. After 1960 the B.T.C. vehicles were not shown separately in the Annual Abstracts, but were included with either the contractual carriers' figures, or, in the case of the service vehicles under the 'C' licence category.

The 'New Series' of data on vehicles were obtained from the Ministry of Transport's Survey of Road Goods Transport, 1962. Final Results. Part I. Table 2. Vehicles in use during the September quarter. 'A', Special 'A', Contract 'A' and 'B' licence vehicles (and in 1952 only, B.T.C. vehicles not subject to carriers' licences before 1953) have been classified to Contractual Road Goods Transport. 'C' licence vehicles are classified to Non-Contractual Road Goods Transport. The 'New Series' excludes the vehicles with carriers' licences but no current road fund licences.

2. *Carrying Capacity*

Rail. B.T.C. Annual Reports 1962 and 1961. Section XI . Tonnage capacity of freight vehicles (excluding brake vans). At December 31st. British Railways only.

Road. Data of unladen weight/carrying capacity for each unladen weight group and licence category are given for 1952 in K.F. Glover, 'Outlines of the Road Goods Transport Industry', Journal of the Royal Statistical Society, Series A, 1954, (p. 301), and for 1958 in 'The Transport of Goods by Road, 1959'. Ministry of Transport, H.M.S.O., 1960. Data for 1962 by licence group have been obtained from records supplied direct from the Ministry of Transport in which the numbers of goods vehicles analysed by unladen weight and carrying capacity were given in respect of four separate weeks in the year. The mid-point of the range in carrying capacity was taken as the average carrying capacity per vehicle in each group. In the case of the final group, covering vehicles of 16 tons and over, an average of 20 tons was taken on the advice of the Ministry of Transport.

In 1952 there were in use a number of B.T.C. vehicles which were not subject to carriers' licences. Conversion ratios of unladen weight/ carrying capacity specific to these vehicles are given in the sources already cited.

Tables covering the period 1951 to 1962 were constructed, showing the average carrying capacity per vehicle related to unladen weight. These tables for 'A', Contract 'A', 'B' and 'C' licence, British Road Services and British Railways vehicles were based on the data for 1952, 1958 and 1962 referred to above.

The average carrying capacity for vehicles in each unladen weight group for the years between 1952, 1958 and 1962 were arrived at by interpolation.

The following example shows the process of conversion from unladen weight to carrying capacity.

Unladen Weight and Carrying Capacity, at end 1958
(The statistics in this example relate to 'A' and Special 'A' licence vehicles)

Unladen Weights		Number of Vehicles		Average Carrying Capacity per vehicle in Groups (Tons)	Total Carrying Capacity (Tons)
Sub-Groups	Groups	Sub-Groups	Groups		
	Less than 12 cwt.		58	0.30	17
	12 cwt. to 1 ton		767	0.45	345
1 ton to 1½ tons		652			
1½ to 2 tons		2,167			
	1 to 2 tons		2,819	1.90	5,356
	2 to 2½ tons		8,695	3.40	29,563
	2½ to 3 tons		23,167	5.15	119,310
3 to 4 tons		13,307			
4 to 5 tons		6,897			
	3 to 5 tons		20,204	7.55	152,540
5 to 6 tons		2,522			
6 to 7 tons		1,666			
7 to 8 tons		2,571			
8 to 9 tons		514			
9 to 10 tons		222			
Over 10 tons		127			
	5 tons and over		7,622	13.70	104,421
		Total Carrying Capacity at end 1958			411,552

The only exceptions to the above method of assessing the aggregate carrying capacity of road goods vehicles were those relating to B.T.C. vehicles in 1951 and 1952, where carrying capacities were given in the B.T.C. Annual Report.

The total tonnage capacities of British Road Services vehicles (excluding B.T.C. service vehicles) were quoted in the B.T.C. Annual Reports for 1951 and 1952, the carrying capacities of *additional* trailers have been excluded.

Having assessed the total carrying capacity of road goods vehicles, grouped by licence categories, on the 'old series' for the period 1951 to 1962 inclusive, these data were then converted to the 'new series' as follows: the ratios of the 'new series' to the 'old series' of numbers of road goods vehicles was calculated for each licence category for each year; these ratios were then used to convert the carrying capacity tonnages based on the 'old series' to carrying capacity tonnages based on the 'new series'.

Because no data of the numbers of vehicles in the 'new series' were available for 1951, the ratios used to convert 'old series' carrying capacity to 'new series' in 1952 were used to arrive at the 1951 'new series' carrying capacity tonnages and also the 'new series' numbers of vehicles in that year.

At this point the 'new series' carrying capacity tonnages show the position as at 30th September, mid-year figures have been arrived at in the following manner:

Total carrying capacity at mid-year (say 1954) = Total carrying capacity at September, 1953 + ¾ (carrying capacity at Sept. 1954 − carrying capacity at Sept. 1953).

The numbers of vehicles in the 'new series' as at 30th September were also converted to mid-year figures by a similar process. The average carrying capacity of contractual, non-contractual and total road goods vehicles were calculated from the 'new series' figures as at mid-year.

Table F.1 section B and C include statistics of contractual and non-contractual road goods vehicles in the 'new series' as at mid-year, covering the numbers of vehicles and total carrying capacities. Table F.3 gives the figures for total road goods vehicles in the 'new series' as at mid-year.

The following table gives detailed figures by licence categories, for 1958 only, of the number of vehicles and carrying capacities in the 'old' and 'new series'.

Table F.3. is the summary of a detailed working table, one year of which (1958) is shown.

3.   *Tonnage Forwarded and Ton Mileage Performed*

Rail.   B.T.C. Annual Reports 1962 and 1961. Section XI. Freight train revenue earning tonnage forwarded. Net ton miles by freight train, including free-hauled freight. British Railways only.

Road.   Ministry of Transport. 'Survey of Road Goods Transport. 1962. Final Results. Part I', Table (V) for 1952, 1958 and 1962 figures. Annual Abstract of Statistics, 1963, Table 234, for 1952 figures of ton mileage apportioned to public haulage transport and 'C' licence transport. The 1952 and 1958 figures are the grossed up results of sample surveys carried out during the weeks ended September 28th, 1952 and April 27th, 1958. In 1962 and 1963 the sample survey was carried out in four separate weeks (ended April 8, 1962, July 8, 1962, October 7, 1962 and January 13, 1963). Seasonal adjustments were made on the 1952, 1958 and 1962

244

The Process of Conversion from 'Old' to 'New' Series for Number of Vehicles and Carrying Capacity, 1958

Category of Road Goods Vehicles	Number of Vehicles			Conversion Factors $\frac{NS}{OS}$	Carrying Capacity		
	Old Series	New Series			Old Series	New Series	
		30 Sept.	Mid-year			30 Sept.	Mid-year
	000's	000's	000's		000 tons	000 tons	000 tons
'A' Licence	63	59	59	0.937	412	386	381
Contract 'A' Licence	25	20	20	0.800	178	142	139
'B' Licence	73	65	65	0.890	324	288	285
British Road Services	14	14	14	1.0	130	130	132
British Railways	16	16	16	1.0	60	60	61
Total Contractual	192	174	173		1,103	1,006	998
Non-contractual, 'C' Licence	1,098	1,048	1,036	0.954	2,057	1,962	1,937
Total Road Goods Vehicles	1,289	1,222	1,209		3,160	2,968	2,935

survey results by means of monthly traffic counts. In 1962, the 1958 survey results were adjusted to take account of certain unsampled cells in the 1958 survey which were sampled in 1962. In addition, the statistics for 1952 and 1958 were revised, in the grossing up process, to take account of the revisions made to the vehicle statistics (details and method given above) for each carriers' licence category.

4. *Gross Value of Output at* 1958 *User Cost*

Rail. B.T.C. Annual Report and Accounts. Volume II. Financial and Statistical Accounts. 1962. Section XI. Total freight train receipts. British Railways only.

Road. Total expenditure by users on road goods transport services in 1958 is given in 'Highway Statistics', 1965, H.M.S.O. 1966. Table 44. Ministry of Transport. The figure given for 1958 is £1,050 million. This includes consumer and business expenditure, taxes and estimated depreciation of vehicles; the purchase of new vehicles is excluded. The estimates in this table are based on the work of E. Rudd (J.R.S.S. Series A. 1953. 119(2)) for the years 1949 and 1950; and of R.F.F. Dawson (J.R.S.S. Series A. 1962. 125(3)) for 1960. Estimates for the other years are derived from interpolations and extrapolations. The methods used by Rudd and Dawson are to apply to estimates of vehicle miles by size of vehicle estimates of fixed and operating costs given in a continuing series appearing in the 'Commercial Motor'. The Ministry of Transport believe these estimates to be about 20 per cent too high. It is expected that lower and more accurate estimates will be made when the results of the 1966 M.O.T. 'Survey of Road Goods Operating Costs' have been fully analysed. The procedure adopted in this Paper is to reduce the 1958 figure of £1,050 million by 20 per cent. The estimate of the gross value of output at user cost of Contractual Road Goods Transport (that produced by 'A' and 'B' licence vehicles) in 1958 has been built up by taking the estimated receipts of the British Railways Executive for collection and delivery services (£12m.), the receipts of British Road Services (£48m.) and the estimate of £300m. for the receipts of 'other public road goods transport' given in the Report from the Select Committee on Nationalised Industries. British Railways, H.M.S.O. 1960. Annex to Appendix 8, p. 332. As this figure of £300m. is also derived from estimates of fixed and operating costs given in the 'Commercial Motor', it has also been reduced by 20 per cent. The estimates of gross value of output of contractual and non-contractual road goods transport in 1958 have therefore been made up as follows:

1. *Contractual Road Goods Transport*

	£s. m.
British Railways Executive (estimated receipts for collection and delivery services)	12
British Road Services, receipts	48
Other Public Road Goods Transport, estimated receipts	240
Total gross output in 1958	£300m

2. *Non-Contractual Road Goods Transport*

Total expenditure on all Road Goods Transport (as derived)	840
Less estimated receipts of Contractual Road Goods Transport Services	300
Total gross output in 1958	£540m.

At 1958 prices these estimates imply a cost to user of 5.50 pence per ton mile for contractual services and 10.71 for non-contractual road goods transport services. The comparable figure for rail goods transport services where the average haul is of course very much longer (75.7 miles in 1958 compared with 23.8 miles for all road goods transport services) is 3.38 pence per ton miles, although it should be noticed here that total net ton miles by British Railways used to reach this figure contain a small amount of free-hauled traffic.

In each transport mode these statistics of average cost to user per ton mile in 1958 have been applied to rail and road ton mileage to arrive at estimates of the gross value of output at constant 1958 user cost, for each year of the period 1952–1966 for which ton mileage figures were available.

246

B. Passenger Transport

1. *Vehicles*

Rail.   British Transport Commission. Annual Report and Accounts. Volume II. Financial and Statistical Accounts. 1962, 1961 and 1960. Section XI. Average of number of passenger carriages only (non-passenger stock excluded) at the beginning and end of each year. British Railways only.

Road.   'Passenger Transport in Great Britain, 1965'. Table 31. 1962. Table 25. Ministry of Transport. H.M.S.O. 1967 and 1963. 'Statistics of Public Road Passenger Transport in Great Britain 1957–58'. Table 1. Ministry of Transport and Civil Aviation. H.M.S.O. 1959. Figures are of total public service vehicles, including trains, trolley buses, buses and coaches with single and double decks. Average of number of vehicles at the beginning and end of each year.

2. *Seating Capacity*

Rail.   B.T.C. Annual Report and Accounts. Vol. II. Financial and Statistical Accounts, 1962, 1961 and 1960. Section XI. Average seating capacity of passenger carriages only at the beginning and end of each year. British Railways only.

Road.   'Passenger Transport in Great Britain'. 1965. Table 33. 1962. Table 27. Ministry of Transport H.M.S.O. 1967 and 1963. 'Public Road Passenger Transport in Great Britain Statistics for 1961–62'. Table D. Average seating capacity at the beginning and end of each year for all public service vehicles (see above under paragraph B.1 for coverage).

3. *Passenger Journeys and Passenger Miles*

Rail.   B.T.C. Annual Report and Accounts. Vol. II. Financial and Statistical Accounts, 1962 and 1961. Section XI. Passenger journeys, passenger miles (estimated). In 1952 and 1958 season ticket journeys have been calculated on the basis of 600 journeys per annum; in 1962 on the basis of 540 journeys per annum, reflecting a shorter average working week after this date.

Road.   'Passenger Transport in Great Britain' 1965. Table 5, Passenger Journeys, Table 1. Passenger Miles. 1962. Table 5. Passenger Journeys, Table 1. Passenger Miles. Ministry of Transport H.M.S.O., 1967 and 1963.

4. *Gross Value of Output at 1958 User Cost*

Rail.   B.T.C. Annual Report and Accounts. Vol. II. Financial and Statistical Accounts. 1962. Section XI. Passenger receipts. British Railways only.

Road.   'Passenger Transport in Great Britain, 1965'. Table 6. Ministry of Transport. H.M.S.O., 1967. In the case of both rail and road the average user cost per passenger has been calculated (rail 1.49 pence, road 1.65 pence) for 1958, and these figures have been applied to rail and road passenger mileage to arrive at estimates of the gross value of output for these years at constant 1958 user cost, for each year of the period 1952–1966.